The Enigma of V. S. Naipaul

Sources and Contexts

Helen Hayward

First published 2002 by
PALGRAVE MACMILLAN
Houndmills, Basingstoke, Hampshire RG21 6XS and
175 Fifth Avenue, New York, N.Y. 10010
Companies and representatives throughout the world

PALGRAVE MACMILLAN is the global academic imprint of the Palgrave Macmillan division of St. Martin's Press, LLC and of Palgrave Macmillan Ltd. Macmillan® is a registered trademark in the United States, United Kingdom and other countries. Palgrave is a registered trademark in the European Union and other countries.

ISBN 1–4039–0254–2 hardback
ISBN 1–4039–0293–3 paperback

This book is printed on paper suitable for recycling and made from fully managed and sustained forest sources.

A catalogue record for this book is available from the British Library.

A catalog record for this book is available from the Library of Congress.

10   9   8   7   6   5   4   3   2   1
11   10   09   08   07   06   05   04   03   02

Printed and bound in Malaysia

Acknowledgements

I wish to thank Karl Miller, whose searching readings proved of invaluable assistance in the preparation of this book. Thanks are also due to Warwick Gould, Richard Brown and Neil Rennie for their suggestions, and to the staff of the library of McFarlin Library at the University of Tulsa for their help. I am grateful to Rene Weis, Peter Swaab, Christopher Ricks and to Philip Horne, for advice offered over the years.

Abbreviations

AB	*Among the Believers*
AD	*An Area of Darkness*
AG	*The Adventures of Gurudeva*
AUI	*The Autobiography of an Unknown Indian*
BR	*A Bend in the River*
CD	*A Congo Diary*
EA	*The Enigma of Arrival*
F	*Fireflies*
FC	*Finding the Centre*
FI	*A Flag on the Island*
G	*Guerrillas*
HB	*A House for Mr Biswas*
HD	*Heart of Darkness*
IFS	*In a Free State*
IMMN	*India: A Million Mutinies Now*
IWC	*India: A Wounded Civilization*
JWM	*Journey Without Maps*
LED	*The Loss of El Dorado*
MM	*The Mimic Men*
MP	*Middle Passage*
MS	*Miguel Street*
MSKC	*Mr Stone and the Knights Companion*
Mystic	*The Mystic Masseur*
OB	*The Overcrowded Barracoon*
REP	*The Return of Eva Perón*
SE	*The Suffrage of Elvira*
TS	*A Turn in the South*
WW	*A Way in the World*

Chronology

1971   *In a Free State* published; Naipaul travels in India, Mauritius and Trinidad.

1972   *The Overcrowded Barracoon and Other Articles*, a collection of Naipaul's journalism.

1972–4   Naipaul begins to plan *Guerrillas*, while visiting Argentina and then Trinidad to report on the case of Michael X — material that was to be gathered in *The Return of Eva Perón*.

1975   Publication of *Guerrillas*. Naipaul goes to Zaire and revisits India.

1976   Publication of Seepersad Naipaul's *The Adventures of Gurudeva*, with an introduction by V. S. Naipaul.

1977   *India: A Wounded Civilisation.*

1978   Naipaul teaches at Wesleyan College, Connecticut.

1979   *A Bend in the River.* Naipaul travels in Islamic countries.

1980   *The Return of Eva Perón* and *A Congo Diary* are published.

1981   Publication of *Among the Believers*, based on his travels in a number of Islamic countries.

1982   Naipaul moves into the cottage near Salisbury in the English county of Wiltshire described in *The Enigma of Arrival*, and makes a journey to the Ivory Coast.

1984   *Finding the Centre*, which contains an autobiographical essay, is published.

1985   Death of Shiva Naipaul.

1987   Publication of *The Enigma of Arrival*, a semi-fictionalized account of his life in England.

1989   *A Turn in the South*, describing his travels in the American South, is published.

1990   *India: A Million Mutinies Now.*

1994   Publication of *A Way in the World*, which combines autobiography and historical fictions.

1996   Naipaul revisits the Islamic world, to collect material for *Beyond Belief*. Patricia dies, and Naipaul marries Nadira Khannum Alvi, a Pakistani journalist.

1998   *Beyond Belief.*

1999   *Letters Between a Father and Son.*

2000   *Reading and Writing* published.

2001   *Naipaul publishes "Half a Life" and receives the Nobel Prize for Literature.*

Contents

Introduction

The concern of this book is to examine the use Naipaul's work makes of its raw materials, and the process of their elaboration into art. These materials are found in autobiographical sources, in his reportage and earlier writings, and in the influence of other writers. The works selected for discussion are those which best exemplify this process: this book is interested in those texts which clearly concern Naipaul's personal past, or which rework earlier books, as this provides an insight into the stages of the evolution of the material.

Naipaul was born in Trinidad in 1932 to a family of East Indian descent. His ancestors migrated from India three generations previously on his mother's side, and four on his father's; his father's family came from Ayodhya, in Uttar Pradesh. At the time, Trinidad was a Crown Colony: it acquired its independence in 1962. Trinidad's Indians represent a large minority community (over a third of the population), whose presence on the island resulted from the importation of indentured labourers, between 1845 and 1917, with a view to providing cheap and easily controlled labour for the sugar plantations in the aftermath of the abolition of slavery. Predominantly rural and adhering to the traditions of their native land, the East Indian population remained largely distinct from the urban and creolized Afro-Caribbean majority, who resented them for depressing agricultural wages. Both groups tended to view the other's culture as uncivilized, and the build-up to independence exacerbated these divisions, with support for the principal political parties polarized according to racial lines.

Naipaul's father, Seepersad, worked as a journalist and wrote short stories; he married into the Capildeo family, one of the more important Hindu families of the island. During the early years of V. S. Naipaul's life, the family lived in a number of houses before moving to Port of Spain in 1938. Naipaul studied there at Queens Royal College, one of the principal schools of the island. He left Trinidad in 1950 to do a degree in English at Oxford, and has since made his home in England, despite extensive periods of travel abroad. After finishing his degree, he contemplated working in India, but instead moved to London, living in a variety of houses while contributing to the BBC's *Caribbean Voices* programme, for which his father had also written. His first book, *Miguel*

Street, was written at this time, although his first novel to be published was *The Mystic Masseur.*

Despite the fact that Naipaul has produced various accounts of his life, these are reticent about its detail. He expresses himself more freely on the subject of his life in interviews than in his non-fiction and fiction. His declarations in interviews show a tendency to dramatize himself in terms of an overstated pessimism, but they are broadly consistent with the sense of his life attainable from his writings. His discussions of and writing about his life tend to dwell on his feelings of non-alignment and alienation. He portrays his life as distinguished by "homelessness and drift and longing".[1] He describes himself as having been born into obscurity and poverty. His childhood, he states, was characterized by disorder. As a child, he says, he felt that he "was in the wrong place",[2] and that he was "a kind of helpless unit in this large family organisation".[3] He contends that, when he first came to England, he had "a great sense of being adrift".[4] He depicts his early experience of migration as a disappointment: "I had dreamed of coming to England. But my life in England had been savourless, and much of it mean" (*EA*, p. 95).

Once he received some measure of literary recognition his life is punctuated by a succession of travels, revisitings and publications. His travels he explains as a response to the lack of a "settled culture" such as other writers feed on,[5] to having "no society to write about".[6] He depicts his existence as beset by anxiety: "One has been slightly broken and damaged by one's disappointments".[7] The fulfilments of writing, he asserts, are only "momentary" (*EA*, p. 97). He cherishes solitude and detachment, and sees himself as comprehensively non-aligned: "I am never disturbed by national or international issues. I do not sign petitions. I do not vote. I do not march".[8] It is the contention of this book that, in spite of such assertions, Naipaul's sense of detachment can best be understood in the context of the conditions in which he grew up, as a member of a culturally displaced minority community, and in relation to the nature of colonial education, which encouraged an identification with the values of English civilization, and increased his sense of distance from the culture that surrounded him.

His output is almost equally divided between works of fiction and non-fiction. Some of his works blur the boundary between these categories, blending fact and fiction, and certain novels draw extensively on factual sources for their inspiration. He has stated: "I don't draw much distinction between my journalism and my imaginative work".[9] More recently he has described them as "all part of the same process of understanding".[10] At the risk of appearing to contradict himself, he has elsewhere affirmed, "I regard the novel writing as engaging the truer part of me. This doesn't mean that I don't take what I do in non-fiction seriously. I take it very seriously".[11] Discussion of his work inevitably involves some investigation of the relations between fact and fiction, life and art. Much of his writing, moreover, makes use of autobiographical material, to provide overlapping accounts of his life. Historical figures, travels and recent political events often furnish the subject-matter of his work; frequently, he treats material in a non-fictional form before going on to recast it as fiction. In the case of *A House for Mr Biswas*, the order is reversed, and the novel precedes "Prologue to an Autobiography". A tendency to revise and to revisit earlier works is a prominent feature of his output. This book is interested in the exploration of instances of self-reference, and of recurring preoccupations and motifs.

Naipaul's work invites meditation on the nature of individual identity, and on its relation to self-contradiction. His practice of self-reference combines consistency with divergence, variation with repetition. The frequency with which he returns to reinvent the narrative of his life, and to revise earlier works, affords a sense of the instability of his identity, of the provisionality of his conclusions, and of disjunction. "Every book is quite different from the other",[12] he has stated. This, however, is by no means an unqualified account, on Naipaul's part, of what he does. His work displays a notable ambiguity: it contains both centrifugal and centripetal tendencies, and blends formal fragmentation with thematic unity. This fragmentation is a response to what he perceives as the disparate nature of his experience, and to the disruption of his world, which he seeks to restore to a state of coherence. He defines as one aspect of his artistic project the aspiration "to reconstruct my disintegrated society, to impose order on the world, to seek patterns".[13] The fact that the various accounts of his life that he offers do not propose radically divergent interpretations of his experience, and that the views expressed in his books are more often in harmony than in conflict, ultimately fosters a perception of consistency in relation to his oeuvre. He has declared, "All my work is really one. I'm really writing one big book".[14]

This discussion attempts to locate Naipaul's work in relation to a social and literary context. An extensive debt to Conrad, and to the writings of Naipaul's father, is explored. His allusions are often ironic, serving to draw attention to a disparity between the literary forms he employs, and the societies he describes. Aspects of his writing can be seen to be shaped by the indirect influence exerted by the work of other post-colonial writers with whom he takes issue, and by those audience expectations he seeks to dispute: he writes as a scourge of liberal sentimentalities. This book attempts to contextualize the work of a writer who has styled himself, and has sometimes been read (notably by Paul Theroux[15]), as aloof from any background, solitary and adrift.

Part of the complexity of his work proceeds from its entertaining contradictory attitudes towards its material. There is an unresolved and important ambivalence in his attitude towards the history of empire: he conceives of colonial rule both as a system of base pillage and as a lost ideal of order, and he views the metropolitan centre at once as fulfilling and betraying an ideal. At times he seems to reconfirm imperialist assumptions, while at other times he offers to refute them. Another aspect of this ambivalence, and a recurring theme of this discussion, consists in the complex viewpoints he adopts in relation to his subjects. He moves between the stance of insider and that of outsider with regard to the societies he portrays, and blends, in an unsettling manner, sympathy with irony, cruelty with compassion, in the treatment of certain characters. These ambivalences are interpreted as the product of his situation of cultural dislocation.

The first three chapters establish a biographical context by considering his most directly autobiographical works. Chapter 1 examines Naipaul's early life and relation to his father's writing, while the second, Chapter 2, proceeds to discuss his account of his life in England in *The Enigma of Arrival*, and, in more general terms, the importance of autobiographical material to his output. Chapter 3 explores the political and historical context of his work, focusing on the interweaving of his personal history and the history of the West Indies in *A Way in the World*. Chapter 4 probes his complex relations to his Indian ancestry by means of a discussion of his Indian travel books. Subsequent chapters direct their attention to the interaction of documentary and literary sources, Naipaul's travels and earlier works, in the genesis of *Guerrillas* and *A Bend in the River*. A theme of all the chapters is his tendency to revisit the material of earlier works; this results in a certain amount of unavoidable overlap between the chapters.

There has been a shift of focus in recent years in post-colonial criticism away from treating literature as the vehicle of damaging stereotypes, and as a site for the elaboration of a rigidly polarized contrast between Europe and other parts of the world,[16] to an interest in discussing the hybrid, heterogeneous and disjunctive cultural identities — both individual and social — which have emerged as a consequence of empire, and in exploring the historical experience of imperialism and its aftermath as a matter of "overlapping domains".[17] This shift is exemplified, for instance, by the successive and contrasting approaches adopted by Edward Said in *Orientalism* and in *Culture and Imperialism*. This book undertakes to study one such displaced identity, and to examine the contradictions, and striving for consistency, that can be discovered in Naipaul's work.

Notes

1 *The Enigma of Arrival: A Novel in Five Sections* (Harmondsworth: Viking, 1987), p. 152.

2 Interviewed by Bernard Levin, "V. S. Naipaul: A Perpetual Voyager", *Listener*, 109 (June 23 1983), p. 16.

3 "The Novelist V. S. Naipaul Talks to Nigel Bingham about his Childhood in Trinidad", *Listener*, 88 (September 7 1972), p. 306.

4 Interviewed by Alex Hamilton, "Living Life on Approval", *Guardian* (October 4 1971), p. 8.

5 Interviewed by John Cunningham, "Floating up to a Point", *Guardian* (April 20 1984), p. 9.

6 Interviewed by Ian Hamilton, "Without a Place", *Critical Perspectives on V. S. Naipaul,* ed. by Robert D. Hamner (Washington: Three Continents Press, 1977), p. 42.

7 Interviewed by Linda Blandford, "Man in a Glass Box", *Sunday Telegraph Magazine* (September 23 1979), p. 90.

8 *The Overcrowded Barracoon and Other Articles* (London: André Deutsch), 1972, p. 16.

9 Interviewed by Raoul Pantin, "Portrait of an Artist", *Caribbean Contact*, 1 (May 1973), p. 19.

10 *Reading and Writing: A Personal Account* (New York: New York Review of Books, 2000), p. 36.

11 Interviewed by Charles Wheeler, "It's Every Man for Himself — V. S. Naipaul on India", *Listener*, 98 (October 27 1977), p. 537.

12 Interviewed by Raoul Pantin, p. 19.

13 Interviewed by Adrian Rowe-Evans, "An Interview with V. S. Naipaul", *Quest*, 78 (September–October 1972), p. 52.

14 Interviewed by Ronald Bryden, "The Novelist V. S. Naipaul Talks about his Work to Ronald Bryden", *Listener*, 89 (March 22 1973), p. 367.

15 *V. S. Naipaul: An Introduction to his Work* (London: Deutsch, 1972).

16 This, broadly, is the approach adopted by Rob Nixon, in *London Calling: V. S. Naipaul, Post-Colonial Mandarin* (New York: Oxford University Press, 1992).

17 Edward Said, *Culture and Imperialism* (London: Vintage, 1994), p. 313.

1 | Sons and brothers: family and textual relations in Naipaul's early Trinidadian fiction

> My father was extremely important in my childhood: nearly everything that I am I am because of this great link I felt with him, and a lot of my work — especially my early work — I meant to be dedicated to him.[1]

> The writing that has mattered most to me is that of my father, which has never been published. It taught me to look at things that had never been written about before, and seemed dull in life, yet when transformed to paper became very surprising. A great deal of my vision of Trinidad has come straight from my father.[2]

These assertions, dating from 1972 and 1963, give some indication of the extent of the debt of influence that Naipaul owes to his father, Seepersad. It is a debt he has acknowledged in "Prelude to an Autobiography", which investigates his own "literary beginnings"[3] by means of an exploration of his father's life. The autobiographical element forms a substantial component of Naipaul's output, appearing not only in explicitly autobiographical works, but also in fiction and travel books. *A House for Mr Biswas* follows the contours of Seepersad Naipaul's life. It stands at an interesting point of intertextual relations — using as a starting-point a story by Seepersad, incorporating his suggestions concerning subjects that his son might write about, and taking its cue from the tone of his stories and journalism. The book portrays the complex and troubled relations of a father and son, and is also an aspect of such relations. Naipaul points out that "the writing ambition bound us all together";[4] literary production appears to have served as an extension of family relations. The Naipaul family also produced another writer in Shiva, whose novel *Fireflies* covers similar ground to that of *A House for Mr Biswas*. There is a family resemblance which encompasses the preoccupations of the three writers: these include entrapment in a society of restricted opportunity, frustrated ambition and dreams of escape, and the rituals and customs of Hindu family life.

The present account of Seepersad's life is derived from Naipaul's "Prelude to an Autobiography" and foreword to his father's book, *The Adventures of Gurudeva*,[5] which provide an interpretation of his life that can be contrasted with the fictional treatment of the subject in *A House for Mr Biswas*. Seepersad Naipaul was born in 1906. His father, a pundit, died when he was young, and the family was left in poverty. Seepersad's older brother was sent to work in the canefields; Seepersad was saved for education. Attempts to make him a pundit failed. He did odd jobs, drawing on the patronage of wealthy family members among his own and his wife's families: he married Droapatie, a member of the wealthy Capildeo family. Naipaul writes that his father "dangled all his life in a half-dependence and half-esteem between these two powerful families" (*FC*, p. 34).

In 1929 Seepersad began to contribute articles to the *Trinidad Guardian*; and in 1932 he was made staff correspondent in Chaguanas, the town in central Trinidad where the Capildeo family lived. "It was through his journalism on MacGowan's *Guardian* that my father arrived at that vision of the countryside and its people which he later transferred to his stories".[6] He wrote about eccentric characters, "village feuds, family vendettas, murders, bitter election battles" (*FC*, p. 38). Naipaul quotes facetious headlines which indicate a bond of mischievous humour between Seepersad and his editor, Gault MacGowan. With a report on the "superstitious practices" (*FC*, p. 80) favoured in the Indian countryside, Seepersad incurred the wrath of Hindu traditionalists, who demanded that he make a sacrifice to Kali. Naipaul places great emphasis on this incident in the "Prelude to an Autobiography", identifying it as a significant element in his father's breakdown, when, in his mother's words, " 'he looked in the mirror one day and couldn't see himself. And he began to scream' " (*FC*, p. 82). He began to contribute less to the paper. MacGowan was replaced as its editor, and its ethos changed. Seepersad lost his job, and was "idle and dependent for four years"[7] (1934–8):

> It was the story of a great humiliation. It had occurred just when my father was winning through to a kind of independence, and had got started in his vocation. The independence was to go within months (*FC*, p. 74).

> The house where this terror befell him became unendurable to him. He left it. He became a wanderer, living in many different places, doing a variety of little jobs, dependent now on my mother's family, now on the family of his wealthy uncle by marriage. For thirteen years he had no house of his own (*FC*, p. 82).

Naipaul here presents his father's life as a tale of independence lost, which is in contrast to the way the story is told in *A House for Mr Biswas*.

Naipaul was born in 1932; he was preceded by an elder sister, Kamla, and was to have four younger sisters and a younger brother, Shiva, born in 1945. The family lived in the house of his mother's family, the Lion House in Chaguanas, where his father remained a vague and shadowy figure. The Capildeo family comprised landowners and pundits and was among the leading Indian families of the island: Rudranath Capildeo later became the leader of the Democratic Labour Party, Trinidad's principal opposition party at the time of independence. This family was a "totalitarian organisation" (*FC*, p. 76). Seepersad found himself at odds with it, partly as a consequence of his reporting activities, and partly due to his reformist principles, which set him in opposition to the family's Hindu orthodoxy.

In 1938 Seepersad resumed his work for the *Guardian*, and the family moved to the more cosmopolitan environment of Port of Spain, to another house belonging to his wife's family. Naipaul recalls that this was an idyllic time, in which he got to know his father and the life of the street. After two years the Capildeo family moved to a cocoa estate outside Port of Spain, the intention being to work the land communally: "After the quiet and order of our two years as a separate unit we were returned to the hubbub of the extended family and our scattered nonentity within it" (*FC*, p. 39). In 1942, the Naipaul family returned to some rooms in the house in Port of Spain. Three years later, Seepersad left the *Guardian* to work for the Department of Social Welfare; his tasks included the surveying of rural conditions. In 1946, the family moved to a "small, box-shaped, two-storeyed house on Nepaul Street",[8] the prototype of Biswas's Sikkim Street house. Seepersad returned to work for the *Guardian* again in 1948. Two years later, Naipaul left for England. Seepersad's circumstances deteriorated: he was in debt, and he suffered a heart attack. He died in 1953, at roughly the same age as Biswas. Seepersad wrote stories: in 1943 he published *Gurudeva and Other Indian Tales*, in a limited edition in Trinidad. "They Named Him Mohun", which contributed a founding element to *A House for Mr Biswas*, was read to a Port of Spain literary group, which included Edgar Mittelholzer and George Lamming. Around 1950, Seepersad began to write stories for the BBC's *Caribbean Voices* programme.

Biswas's life resembles Seepersad's in respect of the abortive apprenticeship as a pundit, the poverty of his origins, and his marriage into a rich, powerful, engulfing and conservative family. Both have nervous breakdowns, and work as journalists and civil servants. Both write stories, and transfer their ambitions to a talented son who leaves the island on a scholarship. Both live in a succession of houses, moving from their wife's family house in the country and then in Port of Spain to an old estate house and back, before finally acquiring a house of their own.

Seepersad Naipaul, however, began to work as a journalist at a much earlier period than Biswas: he already possessed a measure of independence in 1929, when he lived in the country. This change to the chronology of his father's life has the effect of rendering Biswas's acquisition of independence at once more of a struggle and more of a lasting achievement than Seepersad's: it is the culminating point towards which the narrative progresses, rather than something attained early on and interrupted by a backsliding into dependence. As Landeg White argues, the change is made in the interests of novelistic pattern, and allows the book to trace a move from humiliation in Hanuman House to independence at The Chase, then frustration and return, to a new independence in his own house at Green Vale; and from collapse there to Port of Spain and journalism, and eventually to Sikkim Street, the goal of the trajectory (White, p. 97).

Paradoxically, although *A House for Mr Biswas* sets out to pay homage to Seepersad's memory and writing, it portrays in his fictional counterpart a man incapable of his literary achievement, and tempers tenderness with mockery of its hero. Biswas's stories remain unfinished, unpublished and unread, except by Shama, and are confined to fantasies of romantic escape. They concern either a wish-fulfilment figure, or a character akin to Biswas.

> The hero, trapped into marriage, burdened with a family, his youth gone, meets a young girl. She is slim, almost thin, and dressed in white. She is fresh, tender, unkissed; and she is unable to bear children. Beyond the meeting the stories never went.[9]

This appears to be based on an early story by Seepersad called "Gopi".[10] The only other literary work that Biswas completes is a prose poem addressed to the memory of his mother. "He wrote of a journey he had made a long time before. He was tired; she made him rest. He was hungry; she gave him food. He had nowhere to go; she welcomed him" (*HB*, pp. 436–7). The clauses satisfyingly answer each other, in this representation of the fulfilment of essential needs. Naipaul echoes the Bible: "For I was hungered, and ye gave me meat: I was thirsty, and ye gave me drink: I was a stranger, and ye took me in" (Matthew, 25: 35).[11] Biswas reads his piece to a literary group, where his head rings "with the names of Lorca and Eliot and Auden" (*HB*, p. 432), and is also set spinning by the ready supply of whisky. Biswas embarrasses himself by breaking down in the course of the reading, and then retreats into an ill-humoured and awkward silence, with a comic bathos which deflates the solemnity of mood. "They Named Him Mohun" was read to a literary group. This episode refers to the occasion of the reading of the story which helped to inaugurate the novel, but associates Biswas's literary efforts with the danger of appearing ridiculous.

A less reverential attitude towards Seepersad perhaps underlies *The Mystic Masseur*. Ganesh can be seen as akin to Seepersad in his aspiration to be a writer; this is an aspect of his fraudulence, and he has difficulties in producing enough text to fill even a slim booklet. Much humour is extracted from the misplaced priorities of his reverential attitude towards the printed word: he is more interested in the physical qualities of books than in their content. Ganesh's aspiration to be a writer furnishes Naipaul with an opportunity to expose the absurdity of literary pretensions in the Trinidadian setting. The boy in the printing shop asks, " 'You ever hear of Trinidad people writing books?' "[12] It can appear that the characters in *The Mystic Masseur* are condemned to absurdity for the mere fact of being Trinidadian. The book highlights their marginality by invoking the existence of a world beyond, refracted through their whimsical perceptions: Ganesh has a plan to end the Second World War in two weeks, and discusses with Beharry whether Hitler is likely to bomb Trinidad.[13] Naipaul can give the impression that he seeks to vindicate his decision to leave Trinidad by proclaiming that to remain is to condemn oneself to absurdity and frustration — as, at times, he appears to think that Seepersad did. "A reading to a small group, publication in a magazine soon lost to view: writing in Trinidad was an amateur activity" (*AG*, p. 9). In the interview quoted at the beginning of this chapter, he stated in 1963 that Seepersad's stories had not been published, as if publication in Trinidad did not count.

The Mimic Men might likewise be interpreted as including an element of mockery of the father-figure. It contains autobiographical parallels in respect of Ralph's background and childhood, and emphasizes the embarrassment caused by Ralph's father. Some of the incidents described in *A House for Mr Biswas* are repeated in this novel: the occasion on which the father gives his son a ride on his bicycle,[14] for instance, or the family excursion by car (*MM*, pp. 145–8). Ralph's father is a parodic precursor, whose activities as a political and religious leader prefigure his son's career in politics, as Seepersad's career anticipated that of his son. The name he takes, Gurudeva (*MM*, p. 154), alludes to Seepersad's fictional creation.

Naipaul has openly avowed a feeling of ambivalence towards his father:

> Perhaps if my father lived, it might have damaged me.... .
> When he died I was free.... . Probably all my family relations

have an element of oddity: malice, reverence, all these things come together.[15]

A House for Mr Biswas would appear to combine contradictory impulses: it both acknowledges and seeks to conceal a literary debt to Seepersad. It could be argued that it manifests an Oedipal ambivalence in its treatment of the father figure. Occasionally there are hints of literary rivalry in Naipaul's references to his father. Ambivalence might in general be thought to inhere in the practice of allusion, which expresses the impulse to revise or reinterpret the predecessor's work, as well as to acknowledge its influence. A desire to be self-originating is suggested by Naipaul's statements: "I never had a model that I wanted to become".[16] "I am not aware of other styles of writing. I do my own. I write in my own way. I have no models".[17] In "Jasmine" (1964), Naipaul discusses the remoteness of the metropolitan literary culture in which his education has qualified him to participate, from his immediate environment in Trinidad, which he describes as "without shape and *embarrassing*" (*OB*, 25). He makes an exception for "some local short stories" (*OB*, p. 25), by which he may mean his father's work, but this, it appears, is not the place for the explicit acknowledgement of literary debts. On balance, he concludes, "my material had not been sufficiently hallowed by a tradition" (*OB*, p. 26). The publication of *The Adventures of Gurudeva and Other Stories* in England was a delayed act of homage; Naipaul records that before he died, Seepersad had collected together his stories and sent them to his son in order that he might effect their publication. "Publication for him, the real book, meant publication in London. But I did not think the stories publishable outside Trinidad, and I did nothing about them." (*AG*, pp. 18–19.) The existence of the book indicates that Naipaul has revised his opinion. "I no longer look in the stories for what isn't there; and I see them now as a valuable part of the literature of the region" (*OB*, p. 26). He has belatedly worked up to "a proper wonder at his achievement" (*FC*, p. 67).

It is possible that Biswas is confined to a literary achievement of negligible proportions in order to satisfy the logic of the novel's portrait of a "simple, colonial philistine" (*OB*, p. 9) society, where significant action is a virtual impossibility. Naipaul seeks to emphasize the difficulty of the circumstances against which Biswas, like Seepersad and himself, have battled, and to have Biswas rising above them would be to weaken the thesis of their crushing inexorability.[18] Such a story calls to mind the self-help literature of which Biswas is fond:

> Samuel Smiles was as romantic and satisfying as any novelist, and Mr Biswas saw himself in many Samuel Smiles heroes: he was young, he was poor, and he fancied he was struggling. But

there always came a point when resemblance ceased. The heroes had rigid ambitions and lived in countries where ambitions could be pursued and had a meaning. He had no ambition, and in this hot land, apart from opening a shop or buying a motorbus, what could he do? (*HB*, p. 71).

The portrait of a society where ambition is inevitably thwarted through lack of opportunity is familiar from the pages of Naipaul's earlier books: the narrator of *Miguel Street* ascribes his wild behaviour to such frustration: " 'Is not my fault really. Is just Trinidad. What else anybody can do here except drink?' "[19] It is also a feature of *The Mystic Masseur*, which depicts the dull dereliction of Fuente Grove, where the only amusements are rum-drinking and wife-beating, and whose inhabitants resemble the flies trapped in Ramlogan's dilapidated glass case. In such a society it is seemingly only the trickster who makes good.[20] It is everyone for himself; and admiration attaches to the sharp character who lives by his wits. Ganesh, a descendant of Seepersad's Gurudeva, is the first of many a successful fraudster in the pages of Naipaul's work, and the predecessor of such confidence-trickster revolutionaries as Abdul Malik, Miranda and Lebrun, in *A Way in the World*.

Whatever the satirical tendencies in Naipaul's portrayal of Seepersad's fictional counterparts, the majority of his references to his father are unambiguously respectful. Naipaul's excursion into his father's biography in the "Prologue to an Autobiography" testifies to the extent of his influence: "The ambition to be a writer was given to me by my father" (*FC*, p. 33). Naipaul's debt to his writing is directly felt in the fact that the starting-point of *A House for Mr Biswas* involved, in Naipaul's words, a "cannibalising" (*AG*, p. 19) of Seepersad's "They Named Him Mohun". Naipaul interprets the tale in the context of his father's family relations, as Seepersad's imaginative reconciliation with the father he could not forgive in reality:

> My father hated his father for his cruelty and meanness; yet when, in "They Named Him Mohun", he came to write about his father, he wrote a tale of pure romance, in which again old ritual, lovingly described, can only lead to reconciliation (*AG*, p. 16).

The beginning of the first chapter of *A House for Mr Biswas*, "Pastoral", rewrites the story, and Bruce MacDonald argues that there is in Naipaul's rendering of the story a satirical element absent from the original.[21] Seepersad's priest "was known to be a good man and a holy one" (*AG*, p. 126); Naipaul's pundit is "a small, thin man with a sharp, satirical face and a dismissing manner" (*HB*, p. 16). Naipaul's pundit is unconcerned about the child's ominous prospects: " 'Oh, well. It doesn't matter. There are always ways and means of getting over these unhappy things' ''(*HB*, p. 16). He is not, however, indifferent to the size of his payment. In contrast, Seepersad's pundit tells Soomin she "was not to worry on that score and that she had done well enough, according to her means" (*AG*, p. 128). The celebration of the birth of the child is a much more elaborate affair in Seepersad's tale than in the novel; it is described as a "carouse", a coming together of the village. In Seepersad's story the pundit is the agent of a reconciliation between husband and wife, which he effects by invoking the solemnity of the marriage bond. Seepersad's story ends on this note of forgiveness; Biswas's struggles have just begun.

There is a certain degree of ambivalence to Naipaul's presentation of the rituals of Indian village life, which mingles satire and lyricism. In places, he describes the rituals of his childhood as beautiful, acknowledging the "need of a deep belief in a spiritual link between oneself and the earth".[22] The beginning of *A House for Mr Biswas* is set before the time of his childhood, in "an antique, 'pastoral' time, and almost in a land of the imagination",[23] known to him mainly through his father's stories. "When I was of an age to observe, that culture had begun to weaken; and the time of wholeness had seemed to me as far away as India itself, and almost as dateless" ("Writing *HB*", p. 22). Naipaul suggests that an element of distance is necessary for the comprehension of individual experience: at the time he lived in Trinidad he was "too close to childhood to see the completeness and value of that experience" ("Writing *HB*", p. 22). This view is echoed in Naipaul's argument that his father only wrote lyrically about Hindu ritual once the family was breaking up and he lived in the city: "When he was a young man this Indian life was all he knew; it seemed stagnant and enduring; and he was critical" (*FC*, p. 79). The Proustian overtones of this attitude towards the past are also present in the passage from *A House for Mr Biswas* which imagines Anand, at a suitable temporal and spatial remove from the distresses of his childhood, recalling it with tenderness:

> In a northern land, in a time of new separations and yearnings, in a library grown suddenly dark, the hailstones beating against the windows, the marbled endpaper of a dusty leatherbound book would disturb: and it would be the hot noisy week before Christmas in the Tulsi store: the marbled patterns of oldfashioned balloons powdered with a rubbery dust in a shallow white box that was not to be touched. So later, and very slowly, in securer times of different stresses, when the memories had lost the power to hurt, with pain or joy, they would fall into place and give back the past (*HB*, pp. 523–4).

The book here anticipates the circumstances of its own composition, suggesting that, by means of the writing of it, Naipaul has recovered his past, and arrived at a truce with it. This is consistent with the fact that ''Prologue to an Autobiography'' — which reworks the material of the novel as non-fiction, and is coloured by the writing of the novel — refers to his childhood with less bitterness than had previously been evident in his treatment of it. The impulse behind these texts is akin to what Salman Rushdie describes when discussing the originating motive of *Midnight's Children*: ''I realized how much I wanted to restore the past to myself''.[24] He argues that it is a characteristic of writers in exile that they are ''haunted by some sense of loss, some urge to reclaim, to look back, even at the risk of being mutated into pillars of salt''.[25]

''Prologue to an Autobiography'' did not emerge directly from the writing of *A House for Mr Biswas*, but was preceded by an abandoned attempt, entitled ''A Visit to Valsayn Park'' (1972–3). ''Valsayn Park'' could be thought to form an endeavour on Naipaul's part to come to terms with the wound of his past and the ''servility of my own background''.[26] It is less concerned than ''Prologue to an Autobiography'' with the history of Naipaul's immediate family: its emphasis is on exploring that of the Trinidad Hindu community. Naipaul contrasts an outsider's and an insider's view of this community: ''There are two ways of looking at this story; both are right; but each by itself excludes one truth''.[27] The former view is represented by his uncle's bitterness: ''He was like a man who had just been granted the ability to see himself'' (*ibid*). Even though he was later successful, his sons shared ''this vision of their helplessness, their various solitudes, ... the outsider's vision of who and what they were'' (*ibid*). Naipaul attempts to recover the experience of the past as it was lived, and in contrast to the way it is recorded by historians. ''The records that remain'', he writes, falsify the past, and reduce ''people to units and a human history to statistics; and ... miss the other side of the truth: the truth as it was for my aunt'' (*ibid*). He describes a society governed by strict code of honour: ''The social organization, which must have seemed non-existent to outsiders, or at the most chaotic and violent, was complex, of a piece, to people who knew how to read the happenings''(*ibid*).

The lyricism with which Naipaul on occasion evokes Hindu ritual can be interpreted as mediated by filial piety: these rituals were communicated to him by his father's stories. The stories ''gave a beauty (which in a corner of my mind still endures, like a fantasy of home) to the Indian village life I had never known'' (*FC*, p. 42). This accounts for some of the unexpected tenderness of the description of the preparation of his fighting sticks by Mungroo, the local thug whom Biswas endeavours to defy.

Designs were cut into the bark of the *poui*, which was then roasted in a bonfire; the burnt bark was peeled off, leaving the design burnt into the white wood. There was no scent as pleasant as that of barely roasted *poui*: faint, yet so lasting it seemed to come from afar, from some immeasurable depth captive within the wood: as faint as the scent of the *pouis* Raghu roasted in the village like this, in a yard like this, in a bonfire like this: bringing sensations, not pictures, of an evening meal being cooked over a fire that shone on a mud wall and kept out the night, of cool, new, unused mornings, of rain muffled on a thatched roof and warmth below it: sensations as faint as the scent of the *poui* itself, but sadly evanescent, refusing to be seized or to be translated into a concrete memory (*HB*, pp. 156–7).

The preparation of the sticks is associated with the action of memory. The passage refers to the circumstances of its own composition. Raghu is Biswas's father: the book has Seepersad's fictional counterpart recalling his father with difficulty, in a passage in which Naipaul alludes to the stick-fighting antics of his father's creation, Gurudeva. The allusion is suffused with regret, as if to signal an anxiety about failing adequately to do justice to the elusive memory of the father. In Seepersad's story, there is more precise detail of the procedures involved in the preparation of the sticks, and less nostalgia and lyricism:

Out in the yard, he [Gurudeva] would make a blazing fire of dry leaves and bake the sticks in it and beat the barks off them on the ground. Then he would cut each stick into the desired length — from ground level to his lower ribs — and then with cutlass, with broken bottles with razor-sharp edges, and finally with sand paper, he would impart to each stick the smoothness and uniformity of a ruler. Then he would go to the giant bamboo clump near by and bring forth a length of bamboo, stout and ripe and roomy in its hollowness, and an inch or two longer than his stick; and he would punch out all the compartments but the last, and order Ratni to make enough oil from coconuts and fill the bamboo vessel with it to the very top (*AG*, pp. 36–7).

More often, however, Naipaul's depiction of ritual is satirical. It is the mechanical aspect of ritual, devoid of spiritual meaning, which is emphasized in Biswas's training as a pundit:

Mechanically he cleaned the images, the lines and indentations of which were black or cream, with sandalwood paste; it was

easier to clean the small smooth pebbles, whose significance
had not yet been explained to him (*HB*, p. 49).

Anand's experience repeats Biswas's: "Untutored in the prayers he
could only go through the motions of the ritual" (*HB*, p. 375). Comedy
ensues in *The Mystic Masseur* from Ganesh's taking his initiation
ceremony too seriously:

> "Cut out this nonsense, man. Stop behaving stupid. You think
> I have all day to run after you? You think you really going to
> Benares? That is in India, you know, and this is Trinidad"
> (*Mystic*, p. 17).

(Ironically, in *An Area of Darkness*, Naipaul mentions that this ritual no
longer seems to him to illustrate the anomaly of being a Hindu in
Trinidad, and now appears "touching and attractive".[28]) Ritual is
informed with an absurdity akin to that of the characters of *Miguel Street*
who do not work, but put up signs advertising the services they never
provide, or of the advertisements Ganesh invents to fill the empty pages
of his magazine. Ganesh also takes the kedgeree-eating ceremony more
seriously than is intended, turning the tables on Ramlogan, who has
hitherto had the upper hand, and eliciting from him a generous marriage
settlement, in his guise of clever trickster.

Naipaul traces his satirical tendencies to his father's influence:

> I was always very critical, liable to too easy a contempt. I think
> this is something my father gave me. My father was a defeated
> man: I think contempt was all that he could teach me, and I was
> contaminated by this.[29]

Biswas's use of satiric invective constitutes a fragile assertion of his tenuous
dignity in difficult circumstances, and a means of revenge on the Tulsis for
the power they have over him as a result of his position as their dependent.

> "And what about the two gods? It ever strike you that they
> look like two monkeys? So, you have one concrete monkey-
> god outside the house and two living ones inside. They could
> just call this place the monkey house and finish. Eh, monkey,
> bull, cow, hen. The place is like a blasted zoo, man."
> "And what about you? The barking puppy dog?"
> "Man's best friend." He flung up his legs and his thin slack
> calves shook. With a push of his finger he kept the calves
> swinging.
> "Stop doing that!"
> By now Shama's head was on his soft arm, and they were
> lying side by side (*HB*, p. 108).

Shama is right: Biswas is in no position to call people names. More than one thing is taking place in this passage: in addition it demonstrates the growth of intimacy in his relations with her. Biswas's satirical wit hits home, and the narrative makes use of his nicknames, to good comic effect, as, for instance, in the confrontation scene between Biswas, Seth, Mrs Tulsi and her sons (*HB*, p. 98).

The use of animal analogies represents a further dimension of Seepersad's legacy. He wrote to his son in England:

> As soon as you can, get working on a novel. Write of things as they are happening now, be realistic, humorous when this comes in pat, but don't make it deliberately so. If you are at a loss for a theme, take me for it. Begin: "He sat before the little table writing down the animal counterparts for all his wife's family. He was very analytical about it. He wanted to be correct; went to work like a scientist. He wrote, 'The She-Fox', then 'The Scorpion'; at the end of five minutes he produced a list which read as follows: ..." All this is just a jest, but you can really do it (*AG*, p. 17).

The animal satire alludes to Seepersad's stories: Seepersad includes a similar episode in "The Adventures of Gurudeva", which Naipaul says exerted a profound influence on his imagination as a child: "I was involved in the slow making of this story from the beginning to the end. . . . It was the greatest imaginative experience of my childhood. . . . It was my private epic" (*FC*, p. 43). Gurudeva sets to work exactly in the spirit Seepersad has described:

> He was careful not to let his prejudices interfere with his fitting the right animal to the right person. He went to work with the detachment of a scientist spotting his microbes without getting himself into a jitter. He was getting a great deal of fun out of the exercise. He went on writing and soon enough had produced the following list:
>
> *The Old She-Fox*
> *The Old Donkey*
> *The Scorpion*
> *The Thug*
> *The Human*
> *The Hippo*
> *The Donkey*
> *The Donkey*
> *The Donkey* (*AG*, pp. 109–10.)

Seepersad's later stories often satirize Hindu society, and show solidarity with characters who seek to defy the constraints of their circumstances. They paint a picture, in Landeg White's words, of

> a place where custom and ambition, opportunity and talent, ritual and imagination, are in direct conflict; a place where
> · ability is squandered for the sake of ancient prejudices, and where romance is finally accommodated in dreams of escape (White, p. 45).

"The Adventures of Gurudeva" mingles sympathy and irony in its attitude towards its hero, in a complex blend which anticipates Naipaul's writings. Seepersad is sympathetic towards Gurudeva in so far as the character is seen as trapped by his situation: a marriage is imposed on him as a young boy, in conformity with his father's orthodox notions, and he is thereby deprived of the opportunity for an education: " 'That is orright, Schoolmaster', he said. 'He know 'nough. He could read. He could write a letter. He could even write a receipt. What mo' he want?' " (*AG*, p. 27). Gurudeva is both victim and agent of the cruelty of his society:

> So, too, he beat Ratni; not from any overwhelming surge of anger, nor from any conscious wickedness, but because the privilege and prerogative of beating her was his, by virtue of his being her husband. He was not doing anything shameful. He was only beating his wife (*AG*, p. 30).

Gurudeva in this way conforms to his society's impoverished definition of what it is to be a man.

He is set apart from his surroundings by his ambition:

> From boyhood he was obsessed with a craving for fame. Had other things been equal he might at least have risen to the distinction of a legislator; he might have been a doctor or a lawyer or an electrical engineer; for his father was wealthy as well as indulgent (*AG*, p. 34).

His imagination is fired by stories "of the dare-devil exploits of dead and gone bad-Johns" (*AG*, p. 35), and he sets himself up as a stick-fighter. He is a fraud, but nevertheless earns a prison sentence for his exploits, which sets the seal on his attainment of manhood: his father proudly looks on while the police take him to prison, and Gurudeva asserts, " 'Is orright, Bap, I is a man' " (*AG*, p. 51). Gurudeva's desire for glory subsequently expresses itself in the sphere of religion; he seeks to transform himself into a holy man, upholder of the pieties. His holiness is based on empty imitation and rivalry, and he merely goes through the motions of ritual.

Gurudeva bathes, murmuring invocations to the deity, "just as he had seen Pundit Shivlochan do a long time ago" (*AG*, p. 66). The irony operates partly at his expense and partly at the expense of his society: "So Gurudeva remained a Hindu, and was proud of his being a Hindu, though he hardly knew what Hinduism meant" (*AG*, p. 56).

The character is a progenitor of Naipaul's Ganesh, who fraudulently sets himself up as a masseur and mystic, and later as the legislator Gurudeva could never aspire to be. Ganesh's tale corresponds to Gurudeva's in the way that the ritual of wife-beating establishes him in the state of manhood:

> It was their first beating, a formal affair done without anger on Ganesh's part or resentment on Leela's; and although it formed no part of the marriage ceremony itself, it meant much to both of them. It meant that they had grown up and become independent. Ganesh had become a man; Leela a wife as privileged as any other big woman. Now she too would have tales to tell of her husband's beatings; and when she went home she would be able to look sad and sullen as every woman should (*Mystic*, p. 55).

The novel is not untinged by sympathy for Ganesh, however, who is ridiculed as a country boy when he goes to school in Port of Spain, and is embarrassed by his origins. He is not entirely a fraud: he succeeds in curing the boy who is haunted by a black cloud, and his speeches are said to make people feel a little nobler. The dereliction against which he rebels — the treeless cracked earth of the ironically-named Fuente Grove — is all too real. There is sympathy for Ganesh when it looks as if he is to be ensnared by Ramlogan's wiles: but when Ganesh transforms himself from victim into triumphant trickster, he is likely to lose the author's sympathy.

Gurudeva, with his aspirations to be a "bad-John", is also a prototype of Bogart in *Miguel Street*, who models himself on the Hollywood tough guy in a bid for significant identity, and in a fantasy of escape. The society of the street is one in which the conception of manhood is severely attenuated: it is only when Popo's wife deserts him, and he abandons his project of making the thing without a name, and takes to drink, that Hat announces, " 'We was wrong about Popo. He is a man, like any of we' " (*MS*, p. 21). As in the case of Gurudeva, a prison sentence sets the seal on his accession to manhood. The majority of the characters do not work for a living. They assert their identity by a reduction of the self to some whimsical eccentricity: in Trinidad, "only a man's eccentricities can get him attention" (*OB*, pp. 9–10), Naipaul has written elsewhere. Here, the eccentricity verges on derangement in the case of Man-man, who has himself crucified. Edward's identity is defined by his enthusiasm for all things American. *Miguel Street* represents Naipaul's first exploration of the theme of the mimic man. Ironically, he sees his earlier self in similar terms: the idea of the writer which his father gave him is a "fantasy of nobility" (*FC*, p. 45), which he likens to Bogart's self-styling as the Hollywood hard man, as another dream of escape from limiting surroundings.

For all his reformist stance in relation to Hinduism, Seepersad's earlier fiction often confines itself to describing the detail of customs and ritual without passing judgement on them. Rituals are associated with the redemption of a disrupted social order. "They Named Him Mohun" culminates in a celebration of the birth of the child; the coming together of the community in singing and dancing is matched by a reconciliation between the estranged parents. "Panchayat", in which a village council adjudicates a marital dispute, works towards a similar outcome. Naipaul highlights the element of wish-fulfilment in Seepersad's approach by contrasting it with the events which inspired the story — it was based on Seepersad's sister's disastrous marriage: "In the story ritual blurs the pain and, fittingly, all ends well; in life the disaster continued" (*AG*, p. 16). The romance of Seepersad's stories also manifests itself in the manner in which they succeed in reconciling individual will with social necessity. "The Wedding Came" describes the contrivance by which a young man manages to marry the bride of his choice, all the while satisfying the demands of the matchmaker and an antipathetic, conservative father that the wedding be arranged in a proper orthodox fashion. "The Engagement" describes the arrangements for a marriage with a bride demure enough to meet the requirements of the bridegroom's orthodox father. She also wins over the initially reluctant bridegroom: " 'Yes, I like she', said Kanhaia, surprised at the vigour of his own voice" (*AG*, p. 184).

Seepersad's stories adopt contrasting tones and approaches: they blend satire and romance with documentary detail and a relish for the drama of everyday life. Naipaul contends that Seepersad begins as "a writer concerned with the rituals and manners and what he has seen as the romantic essence of this community" (*AG*, p. 8). He associates some of the freshness of Seepersad's approach with the influence of Gault MacGowan, editor of the *Trinidad Guardian*, who

> was new to Trinidad, discovering Trinidad, and he took nothing for granted. He saw stories everywhere; he could make stories out of nothing; his paper was like a daily celebration of the varied life of the island (*AG*, p. 14).

Seepersad's stories combine an insider's knowledge of the society with the perceptions of an outsider. An aspiration to see things afresh is expressed by the epigraph to the collection of his stories privately printed in Port of Spain. It is a quotation from Robert Burns:

> Oh, wad some Pow'r the giftie gie us,
> To see oursels as others see us![30]

Naipaul traces MacGowan's indirect influence on his own writing:

> It was through his journalism on MacGowan's *Guardian* that my father arrived at that vision of the countryside and its people which he later transferred to his stories. And the stories have something of the integrity of the journalism: they are written from within a community and seem to be addressed to that community: a Hindu community essentially, which, because the writer sees it as whole, he can at times make romantic and at other times satirize. There is reformist passion; but even when there is shock, as in "In the Village", there is nothing of the protest — common in early colonial writing — that implies an outside audience; the barbs are all turned inwards. This is part of the distinctiveness of the stories. I stress it because this way of looking, from being my father's, became mine: my father's early stories created my background for me (*AG*, p. 15).

A House for Mr Biswas is indebted to the quality of Seepersad's vision. It commemorates the father by paying him the tribute of literary emulation, as well as by replicating the details of his life in the novel:

> I was writing about things I didn't know; and the book that came out was very much my father's book. It was written out of his journalism and stories, out of his knowledge, knowledge he had got from the way of looking MacGowan had trained him in. It was written out of his writing (*FC*, p. 72).

In 1951 Seepersad wrote to his son:

> And as to a writer being hated or liked — I think it's the other way to what you think: a man is doing his work well when people begin *liking* him. I have never forgotten what Gault MacGowan told me years ago: "Write sympathetically"; and this, I suppose, in no way prevents us from writing truthfully (*FC*, p. 68).

Elsewhere Naipaul has suggested that not to make himself disliked is a dereliction of the writer's duty: "Unless one hears a little squeal of pain after one has done some writing, one has not really done much".[31] In Naipaul's first three books, ironies are more prominent than sympathy. But in the case of *A House for Mr Biswas*, Naipaul does write sympathetically, and he has been liked for it.

The essay "Jasmine", in which Naipaul expresses the view that his society was insufficiently hallowed by a literary tradition, cites as an exception "some local short stories", not published outside Trinidad, by which he probably refers to his father's writings. "Where I had seen a drab haphazardness they found order; where I would have attempted to romanticize, to render my subject equal with what I had read, they accepted" (*OB*, p. 25). It is to this quality of acceptance that *A House for Mr Biswas*, more than Naipaul's other works, is indebted. Acceptance is most clearly manifested in its treatment of its hero. Biswas is a complex character, whose weaknesses are not passed over, and whose ordinariness is combined with something of the heroic. His ambitions are limited, yet invested with symbolic depths which render them commensurate with the most significant of enterprises. His acquisition of independence is shot through with compromise and failure, but is nonetheless presented as wondrous.

Anthony Boxhill compares Wells's *History of Mr Polly* to Naipul's novel.[32] Wells's novel closely resembles *A House for Mr Biswas*, in both its subject and its tone. Naipaul has acknowledged his admiration for and delight in the "universality" of Wells's comedy.[33] *A History of Mr Polly* portrays with affectionate mockery the life of a statistically insignificant man. Wells writes with a feeling for Mr Polly's romanticism and for his disaffection from his dingy circumstances: he hungers for "bright and delightful experiences, for the gracious aspect of things, for beauty".[34] The novel's comedy operates in part at Mr Polly's expense: his dreams are not without absurdity. There are numerous parallels between the works: like Biswas, Mr Polly has a grotesque, whimsical verbal wit, and is made vividly present as a physical being. Like Biswas, he is sucked into marriage as if by an inexorable social logic. He is also a shopkeeper whose days disappear in an undifferentiated tedium. He only escapes the trap that is his shop by means of a fire; and he runs away from his marriage. Unlike Biswas, he does not go back to his wife — evasion, rather than accommodation, is seen by Wells as the solution to his hero's difficulties. There is some uncertainty as to whether Mr Polly or his circumstances are to blame for his unhappiness; while, at the beginning, his dreams and capacity for joy are seen as a positive feature, transcending the meanness of his environment, they are increasingly presented as a form of acquiescence.

A House for Mr Biswas neglects no opportunity to emphasize Biswas's physical vulnerability, and portrays his frailty with compassion:

> The malnutrition that had given him the sixth finger of
> misfortune pursued him now with eczema and sores that
> swelled and burst and scabbed and burst again, until they

stank; his ankles and knees and wrists and elbows were in particular afflicted, and the sores left marks like vaccination scars. Malnutrition gave him the shallowest of chests, the thinnest of limbs; it stunted his growth and gave him a soft rising belly. And yet, perceptibly, he grew (*HB*, p. 21).

The last sentence reads as a triumphant assertion of human resilience and tenacity against all the odds. In so doing, it may be thought to summarize the novel to which it belongs. The novel does not gloss over Biswas's more significant failings: he gives vent to his frustrations at the expense of Shama and his children — as his dependants, they are perhaps the only people over whom he has power. Nor does the novel ignore the absurdity of his position, when he finds himself in rebellion against the family which feeds him. On the other hand, it never loses sight of the circumstances which have caused his frustration. Biswas's smallness is in his situation, rather than an internal quality.

He didn't feel a small man, but the clothes which hung so despairingly from the nail on the mud wall were definitely the clothes of a small man, comic, make-believe clothes (*HB*, p. 141).

The overall impression created by Biswas is of a vulnerable figure, but not that of a victim of circumstance.

The novel conveys a need to accept certain necessary compromises, while simultaneously exalting Biswas's refusal to capitulate to his situation. The narrative includes, as an aspect of his achievement, an anatomy of the development of affection between Biswas and Shama:

Since they had moved to the house Shama had learned a new loyalty, to him and to their children; away from her mother and sisters, she was able to express this without shame, and to Mr Biswas this was a triumph almost as big as the acquiring of his own house (*HB*, pp. 7–8).

The novel records the growth of their intimacy by means of indirect hints: "So Mr Biswas moved to The Chase, to the shop. Shama was pregnant when they moved" (*HB*, p. 126). The development of their relationship, like Biswas's acquisition of independence, is not uninterrupted by regression and backslidings — Shama more than once deserts Biswas for the security of Hanuman House — but can ultimately be seen to belong to a narrative of progression.

A similar softening characterizes their attitude towards the houses they inhabit. The house at The Chase becomes bearable, at least, with time: "The grime, increasingly familiar, eventually became their own, and therefore supportable'' (*HB*, p. 132). The drawbacks of the house on Sikkim Street are painstakingly enumerated by the narrator: it is flawed, jerry-built, sagging, cracking. But this comes to cease to matter to the family. Varieties of accommodation — a quest for adequate accommodation, the hero's refusal to accommodate himself to the indignities of dependency and nonentity, a realistic accommodation to necessary compromises: the subject is at the heart of *A House for Mr Biswas*. Biswas's ambition to acquire a house is equivalent to a desire to leave his mark on a world that ''carried no witness to Mr Biswas's birth and early years'' (*HB*, p. 38).

> He had lived in many houses. And how easy it was to think of those houses without him! ... In none of these places he was being missed because in none of these places had he ever been more than a visitor, an upsetter of routine. Was Bipti thinking of him in the back trace? But she herself was a derelict. And, even more remote, that house of mud and grass in the swamplands: probably pulled down now and ploughed up. Beyond that, a void. There was nothing to speak of him (*HB*, pp. 118–9).

By the time he dies, there is plenty to speak of him. The battered furniture which Biswas gradually acquires in the course of his life is an index of his achievement. The narrative is at pains to familiarize us with these objects: ''I wanted to tell the story of the life as the story of the acquiring of those simple, precious pieces'' (*FC*, p. 72), Naipaul says, of his earliest attempts at writing the novel. The furniture is invested with human meaning and associations. It is first introduced when, at the very start of the novel, Biswas contemplates in amazement the wonder of what he has accomplished, the miracle of the house. ''He could not quite believe that he had made that world. He could not see why he should have a place in it''(*HB*, p. 12). People have a habit of being grouped together with things in the novel, which animates these things. It uses physical objects to represent the characters: the difficulty the family has in accommodating their furniture in the cramped space of the house in Port of Spain can appear to reproduce its human overcrowding. The furniture has been dispersed around the house in Port of Spain in the same way the family has been engulfed by the social organization of the Tulsis, but they are re-united as a unit in the house on Sikkim Street: ''the gatherings of a lifetime ... for so long scattered and even unnoticed, now all together on the tray of the lorry'' (*HB*, p. 519).

A House for Mr Biswas successfully fuses the general and the particular. The veracity of detail with which it presents the individual case is balanced by a recognition of its wider significances and symbolic overtones. The house is both a reality, and the metaphor at the centre of the book. It is given a depth of meaning which transcends the physical object, without effacing its solidity. Naipaul describes the book as "the story of a man's search for a house and all that the possession of one's own house implies" ("Writing *HB*", p. 22). The house is made to imply a great deal. Critics[35] have noted the allusion to *King Lear* in the weighty reflection that begins the book:

> How terrible it would have been, at this time, to be without it: to have died among the Tulsis, amid the squalor of that large, disintegrating and indifferent family; to have left Shama and the children among them, in one room; worse, to have lived without even attempting to lay claim to one's portion of the earth; to have lived and died as one had been born, unnecessary and unaccommodated (*HB*, pp. 12–13).

There are further echoes of the play in Biswas's arithmetic lesson — "*Ought oughts are ought*" (*HB*, p. 41) — which seems to condemn him to a perpetuity of non-achievement, with the inevitability of numerical logic; and in the storm which accompanies and symbolizes his breakdown, turmoil within echoing turmoil without. The disintegration of Biswas's house at Green Vale is simultaneous and intimate with his nervous breakdown; the house is an extension of the self and a symbol of individual identity: "The rain and the wind swept through the room with unnecessary strength and forced open the door to the drawingroom, wall-less, floorless, of the house Mr Biswas had built". (*HB*, p. 263.) Biswas thinks of a home of his own as a way to arrest his descent into the void. The void here momentarily engulfs Biswas.

Such a house is the prerequisite of an orderly life:

> Soon it seemed to the children that they had never lived anywhere but in the tall square house in Sikkim Street. From now their lives would be ordered, their memories coherent (*HB*, p. 523).

The Green Vale area abounds in symbols of compromised hopes and failed aspirations: in unfinished houses that began in "concrete and dressed wood and ended with mud walls and tree branches" (*HB*, p. 215). Such is the fate of Biswas's first attempt to build a house, which meets the inevitable doom of compromise, unfulfilled intentions and ultimate failure.

Biswas's condition of homelessness is presented as a state of solitude; Biswas is a metaphoric orphan.

> And so Mr Biswas came to leave the only house to which he had some right. For the next thirty-five years he was to be a

wanderer with no place he could call his own, with no family
except that which he was to attempt to create out of the
engulfing world of the Tulsis (*HB*, pp. 37–8).

Biswas's abandonment is echoed and symbolized by the figure of the boy
he glimpses from a passing bus: "a boy leaning against an earth house
that had no reason for being there, under the dark falling sky, a boy who
didn't know where the road, and that bus, went" (*HB*, p. 171). Later
Anand is compared to the boy — "standing and staring like that other
boy Mr Biswas had seen outside a low hut at dusk" (*HB*, p. 213) —
which is indicative of the way that Anand's story repeats, with significant
variations, Biswas's life. Michael Gorra observes that "the relation
between home and homelessness provides the central metaphor of all
Naipaul's work",[36] and adduces such figures as Ralph Singh, in *The
Mimic Men*, and Salim, the narrator of *A Bend in the River*. Ralph
describes the house as a "sacred symbol" (*MM*, p. 86); when his new
house is damaged, recalling the imagery of *A House for Mr Biswas*, he
invokes the tears of "children outside a hut at sunset, the fields growing
dark" (*MM*, p. 89). Biswas's state differs from that of Salim and Ralph in
that his placelessness is the consequence of dependency.

Biswas's experience of homelessness involves a making-do with shifts
and expedients. Of his time in a mud hut, Naipaul writes: "He was not
happy there and even after five years considered it a temporary
arrangement" (*HB*, p. 44). This is akin to the condition of the Indian
exiles, the old men who gather in the arcade of Hanuman House:

> They could not speak English and were not interested in the
> land where they lived; it was a place where they had come for a
> short time and stayed longer than they expected. They
> continually talked of going back to India, but when the
> opportunity came, many refused, afraid of the unknown, afraid
> to leave the familiar temporariness (*HB*, p. 174).

A story of repatriated Indians who, once they have reached India,
clamour to be taken back to Trinidad was reported on by Seepersad,[37]
and is referred to by his son (*FC*, p. 61), as symbolizing the placelessness
resulting from colonial experience. Biswas's situation is emblematic of
that of the uprooted colonial.

Biswas nurtures romantic dreams of exotic escape: he feels that "real
life was to begin for them soon, and elsewhere. The Chase was a pause, a
preparation" (*HB*, p. 132). He reads foreign magazines and novels:

> They introduced him to intoxicating worlds. Descriptions of
> landscape and weather in particular excited him; they made
> him despair of finding romance in his own dull green land

which the sun scorched every day; he never had much taste for westerns (*HB*, pp. 70–1).

Dreams of a wider world emphasize the narrowness of his circumstances:

> Though he never ceased to feel that some nobler purpose awaited him, even in this limiting society, he gave up reading Samuel Smiles. That author depressed him acutely. He turned to religion and philosophy.... But now, though his philosophical books gave him solace, he could never lose the feeling that they were irrelevant to his situation. The books had to be put down. The shop awaited; money problems awaited; the road outside was short, and went through flat fields of dull green to small, hot settlements (*HB*, p. 164).

European civilization is presented here as inappropriate to the colonial situation. Biswas registers a sense of global insignificance: he is in "a place that was nowhere, a dot on the map of the island, which was a dot on the map of the world" (*HB*, p. 213). Mr Blackwhite, in *A Flag on the Island*, shares this sense: " 'This place, I tell you, is nowhere. It doesn't exist. People are just born here. They all want to go away' ".[38]

Biswas's situation is analogous to that of his creator, as Naipaul portrays it: "I had a disturbed, disturbed childhood. One felt unsettled. One lived at the margin, the edge. The world was stopped, was not real, in fact, for me".[39] Trinidad, he asserts, seemed to him "achingly remote from places that seemed worthwhile and real because fully known" (*AD*, pp. 176–7). Echoing Biswas, he writes that he felt that Trinidad was "only a dot on the map of the world" (*AD*, p. 198). English literature "made me despairingly conscious of the poverty and haphazardness of my own society" (*OB*, pp. 24–5):

> To us, without a mythology, all literatures were foreign. Trinidad was small, remote and unimportant, and we knew we could not hope to read in books of the life we saw about us. Books came from afar; they could offer only fantasy (*OB*, p. 23).

At times, Naipaul treats Biswas's romanticism with irony, as deluded; it is rendered slightly absurd by issuing in fantasies of escape into a romance with a young woman. Biswas has an exaggerated sense of the value of the foreign. Nevertheless, the author is sympathetic to Biswas's sense of the constrictions of his surroundings, and the autobiographical parallels examined here are confirmation of this.

There are further similarities between the character and his author: Naipaul has described his situation at the time of writing the novel as akin to the hero's. He, too, lacked a place to call home; old furniture and homelessness defined his experience ("Writing *HB*", p. 22). He gives his own rebellious instincts to Biswas; Biswas's defiance of the Tulsis is reminiscent of an incident Naipaul relates in a letter, when he rose up against what he perceived as a "campaign of humiliation"[40] against him on the part of the Capildeos, with whom he stayed temporarily in England. Another respect in which Biswas resembles his creator is in their shared fear of being engulfed by a void of non-achievement. Naipaul contends that this fear formed part of his inheritance from his father.

> With the vocation, he so accurately transmitted to me — without saying anything about it — his hysteria from the time when I didn't know him: his fear of extinction. That was his subsidiary gift to me. That fear became mine as well. It was linked with the idea of the vocation: the fear could be combated only by the exercise of the vocation (*FC*, p. 84).

This fear is perceptible in the novel in the episode when Biswas looks in a mirror and fails to see his face. Stephen Casmier interprets the episode as a symbol of the colonial predicament — of being unrepresented and invisible in metropolitan culture.[41] *An Area of Darkness* propounds the paradox that experience is felt to be more real for being replicated in a fictional form: "No city or landscape is truly real unless it has been given the quality of myth by writer, painter or by its association with great events" (*AD*, p. 205).

In Green Vale, the tedium of Biswas's existence is set off by the newspapers that line his room, recording that *"Amazing scenes were witnessed yesterday when . . ."* (*HB*, p. 205), and taunting him with their jaunty reminder of what is lacking from his life. These references to the MacGowan school of journalism contain a premonition of the profession by means of which Biswas is to obtain his long-cherished independence, while also alluding to Seepersad's work. They reproduce his journalistic style — "Workmen Besiege a Road Board Meeting: Remarkable scenes were witnessed yesterday when . . ."[42] — and the words in which the disruption to Gurudeva's first lecture is reported: *"Amazing scenes were witnessed at a meeting of Hindus . . ."* (*AG*, p. 101.)

A sense of dereliction is a pronounced feature of the early story "This is Home", which contains the germ of the themes and settings of *A House for Mr Biswas*. The tale describes the arrival of a young husband and his pregnant wife at their new home; the man feels reluctant to assume the responsibilities of his new role as a husband. The story prefigures Biswas's arrival at The Chase, and the natural hostility of Green Vale, where he has his breakdown. The character's unease is transferred to the environment, which is invested with a meretricious treachery:

> On the dying trees yellowing leaves still hung meaninglessly
> — leaves that were yellow almost as soon as they were green.
> All around the grass grew high and free and wild, and smelled
> of dampness and sorrow. . . . The dead green lay like a weight
> on him. . . . There was something ominous about the croaking
> of the frogs.[43]

The author does not appear to treat these reflections with irony. Human society is seen as a necessary but fragile defence against solitude: "We can never live alone. We need protection. We created a mutual protection society and called it love: called it marriage and home".[44] In *A House for Mr Biswas,* Naipaul addresses similar themes with greater detachment.

The affirmative nature of the novel's conclusion — however qualified by a sense of compromise — is indicated by contrasting it with "Potatoes", another story written at the beginning of Naipaul's career, which touches on similar territory. It concerns the attempts of Mrs Gobin to set herself up in business. She proclaims, " 'It never does pay to be dependent on anybody. But mark my words, Ma, I am going to make myself independent' ".[45] The family house she inhabits is a prototype of Hanuman House: solid, and ornamented with elephant and monkey gods, and statues of lions. Mrs Gobin's business deals bring her into contact with a wider world, with which she feels ill-equipped to deal. Her unease is displaced onto the house of a carrier she employs — "The house seemed quietly insulting, stonily indifferent — like the carrier" ("Potatoes", p. 7) — which anticipates the way the physical environment is invested with animate life in the novel. Her venture ends in failure: she is consigned to poverty by the tale's terse conclusion. In this tale, the author seems unsure whether her attempts are ridiculous or admirable. It looks forward to the unsuccessful business enterprises of the Tulsi widows, which are portrayed as comic.

The affirmations expressed in *A House for Mr Biswas* in however guarded a fashion furnish a notable contrast with Shiva Naipaul's *Fireflies*, which contains an account of the same biographical territory, but recasts it as a tale of failure and independence lost. An examination of' the similarities and differences of these two novels provides a sense of what is particular to V. S. Naipaul's treatment of the material. *Fireflies* concerns the Lutchmans, who are located on the fringes of an extended family: the restless father dies young; his sons go abroad; the tenaciously optimistic mother soldiers on. The familiar themes of constricting circumstance and frustrated ambition are present, but the novel is more pessimistic than *A House for Mr Biswas* concerning the possibilities of reshaping one's destiny through an effort of the will: ambition seems to dissipate itself in *Fireflies*, consumed by its own restless energies.

Like *A House for Mr Biswas*, *Fireflies* portrays in Mr Lutchman a figure with certain resemblances to Seepersad Naipaul, but of lesser achievement. At times he seems superior to his environment; at other times he seems to participate in its limitations. His resemblances to Seepersad and Biswas include his restless disposition and rebellious tendencies, and his job as a civil servant. He ridicules his wife's family for their supposed business sense, their self-importance and their assumption of his inferiority. His vague ambitions express themselves in dissatisfaction:

> But Doon Town, after all, could only offer so much to a young man who had imbibed the geography and history of the British Isles and who could recite the capitals of so many countries. It was not enough.[46]

Shiva distances himself from the character, by mocking the narrow scope of Lutchman's achievements, though he would appear to agree that Doon Town is a limiting environment. His affair with Doreen resembles the scenario of one of Biswas's escape stories. Doreen offers the fulfilment of a dream of sophistication: " 'Come and have a drink.' Echoes of the elegance he had long dreamed of floated free in that statement ..." (*F*, p. 54). But this fantasy goes stale, establishing a pattern apparent in subsequent enthusiasms. Mr Lutchman's ambitions issue in actions of less consequence than Biswas's, whose journalistic career and literary aspirations coincide with his author's choice of profession. There is less sense than in *A House for Mr Biswas* that potential achievement is frustrated by lack of opportunity. Lutchman's life is not in any case the central focus of the novel: he dies half-way through it. The emphasis is rather on Mrs Lutchman and her sons.

The lives of the sons, Romesh and Bhaskar, also function as case studies in the futility of rebellion. Romesh is a distant descendent of the Gurudeva type: like Bogart in *Miguel Street*, he has a passion for cinema, and models himself on Hollywood's tough guys. He pursues notoriety rather than achievement, and his mimicry of film stars is a version of the escape fantasy. As with Gurudeva, his initiation into a limited conception of manhood involves a prison sentence.

Bhaskar follows the path of the scholarship boy. He conceives the desire to be a doctor, but appears not to possess the ability to pursue his ambitions. A sententious tale of successful self-help mentioned in the novel, concerning the boy who studies by the light of fireflies to become a doctor, is exposed as fantastical by Bhaskar's story. He manages to obtain a scholarship to study abroad through sheer force of determination, but the costs of ambition are high: he has a breakdown, and is forced into an ignominious return home. Bhaskar's story indicates the ''terrors of ambition'' (*F*, p. 347). The fireflies to which the novel owes its title could be interpreted as signifying the insignificance of the characters' lives.

Fireflies takes up the story of the family at the point where *A House for Mr Biswas* ends: Mr Lutchman buys a house at the beginning of the novel. After his death, Mrs Lutchman's thoughts are described, in a passage saturated with echoes of *A House for Mr Biswas*, which leave no doubt that the novel forms part of a fraternal dialogue:

> The house had become for Mrs Lutchman the most concrete symbol of her independence. If that were to go she would have nothing left. She had identified herself completely with it. The roses, the avocado tree, the camera and developing kit which she had secreted in the wardrobe, all of these things were more to her than merely physical objects. They represented her husband's frailties, that part of him on which, without his knowing it, she had lavished much of her tenderness and affection. . . . They embodied his struggles and his weaknesses. In a sense, she had, by making them symbols of his failure, animated them (*F*, pp. 226–7).

By the end of the book, Mrs Lutchman has indeed been forced to sell the house. In Bhaskar's words, '' 'We have to become serfs' '' (*F*, p. 386). The book portrays, not the difficult acquisition of a tenuous and unlikely independence, but its loss. Mrs Lutchman's life is marked by a series of disappointments. Her perennial optimism, exemplified by the desire to name her chicken farm ''Esperanza'', after a failed provision stall, comes to appear less an heroic defiance of the constraints imposed by reality than a form of delusion, a wilful blindness. She is said to have a ''capacity for seeing only what she chose to see'' (*F*, p. 400).

Fireflies could be read both as an admiring imitation and as a stand against the elder brother's novel — as a displacement of sibling rivalry onto the sphere of literary production, with Shiva's own bid for autonomy and independence passing into emulation and allusion, in keeping with the pessimism in the novel concerning the possibility of independence. Shiva, born in 1945, also studied at Oxford and wrote novels and travel books; he died in 1985. Shiva writes that he was brought up in the shadow of his absent brother. ''An intimidating burden of expectation weighed upon me''.[47] Naipaul represented the standards against which Shiva was judged: ''I suffered by comparison. No one ever quite lives up to the demands of an Absolute''.[48] He is eager to refute the charge that he merely imitates his brother, describing his work as a breaking loose from the "doppelgänger absolutism which had so marred and scarred my childhood".[49] At the beginning of his career, he was less confident. Diana Athill, Naipaul's editor, wrote to V. S. that Shiva "wonders whether he's writing as a younger-brother answer to the challenge of your achievement".[50]

Biswas focuses his feelings of entrapment on the Tulsi family, and his rebellion against fate is partly a rebellion against the world the Tulsis represent: the orthodox Hindu world where the future is preordained, and individuality submerged in caste identity and a predetermined succession of ritual attitudes. Biswas is caught up in marriage at an early age: "The world was too small, the Tulsi family too large. He felt trapped" (*HB*, p. 82). He ascribes his failure to get on in life to the family, and to the encumbrance imposed by his wife and children. At Green Vale he is wont to think: "He was 'trapped' in a 'hole'. 'Trap', she heard him say over and over. 'That's what you and your family do to me. Trap me in this hole' " (*HB*, p. 200). The phrase is drawn directly from biographical sources; Seepersad had written to his son, referring to the difficulties of writing a novel while working for the *Trinidad Guardian*, "I feel trapped".[51] The oppressive quality of the family is suggested by the description of Hanuman House, which is compared to an "alien white fortress" (*HB*, p. 73), its walls "bulky, impregnable and blank" (*HB*, p. 73). The novel portrays the cruelty of family life: "Affection between brother and sister was despised. No alliance was stable. Only enmities were lasting" (*HB*, p. 372). A passage from *India: A Million Mutinies Now* furnishes an autobiographical parallel:

> Cruelty, yes: it was in the nature of Indian family life. The clan that gave protection and identity, and saved people from the void, was itself a little state, and it could be a hard place, full of politics, full of hatreds and changing alliances and moral denunciations. It was the kind of family life I had known for much of my childhood.[52]

There is a tyranny to conform, indicated when Shama is compelled to destroy Savi's doll's house — a miniature version of the house which Biswas aspires to. Poorer family members have a status little distinguished from the servants. The family organization engulfs the identity of the individual: Biswas "was expected to become a Tulsi" (*HB*, p. 88). According to the ethos of traditional Hindu life, even emotion is somehow impersonal. Shama's aspiration is

> to be taken through every stage, to fulfil every function, to have her share of the established emotions: joy at a birth or marriage, distress during illness and hardship, grief at a death. Life, to be

full, had to be this established pattern of sensation (*HB*, p. 144).

The Tulsis, nevertheless, do not altogether account for Biswas's frustration. The novel manifests a certain ambivalence towards the extended family and the freedom that Biswas desires: the family is both constricting and supportive; freedom is both enviable and fraught with anxieties. The Tulsis provide security and a solid sanctuary: Hanuman House is "an organism that possessed a life, strength and power to comfort which was quite separate from the individuals who composed it" (*HB*, p. 272). One compares Naipaul's observations concerning his childhood: "I had felt swallowed up by our extended Hindu family, ... but that family had given me a very bright idea of who I was".[53]

The novel balances a sense of the value of independence against a recognition of the terrors of freedom. The pattern is set early on when Biswas is given a day off from the rum shop: "As fatigue overcame him he began to long for the day to end, to relieve him of his freedom" (*HB*, p. 58). His rebellion against the Tulsis is presented as initially exhilarating, but subsequently depressing. The independence he wins for himself at The Chase fails to provide the fulfilments he had hoped for:

> He wanted to comfort her. But he needed comfort himself. How lonely the shop was! And how frightening! He had never thought it would be like this when he found himself in an establishment of his own (*HB*, p. 58).

In a moment of subsequent disillusionment, Biswas feels trapped by the very impression he has been at pains to make on the world:

> Here, claimed by no one, he had reflected on the unreality of his life, and had wished to make a mark on the wall as proof of his existence. Now he needed no such proof. Relationships had been created where none existed; he stood at their centre. In that very unreality had lain freedom (*HB*, p. 479).

Landeg White discusses the novel's recognition of complexity and contradiction, pointing to the way it portrays achievement and failure as part of a single experience, writing as an escape as well as a means of coming to terms with life, and relationships both as a necessary extension of the self and as a trap (White, p. 98). Despite its acknowledgement of complexity, however, there can be no doubt that the novel thinks rebellion, independence and freedom preferable to capitulation and servitude.

Rebellion against the Tulsi family, moreover, has overtones of futility, in view of the fact that the old order is itself in the process of collapsing under its internal stresses. Biswas's story unfolds against a background of wider social change on the island — the passing away of the rural Hindu way of life which Seepersad's stories had recorded. The decay of the Tulsi clan is matched by the degeneration of the body of Mrs Tulsi, the matriarch who had held the family together.

The rate of family disintegration is intensified by the Shorthills interlude, which is invested with mythic overtones: the description of the laying waste to an old colonial estate is suggestive of the pillaging of the New World under imperialism, while also prefiguring a future post-colonial disorder. Naipaul describes the incident on which the episode is based — when the Capildeo family lived on a former cocoa estate outside Port of Spain — in terms which he has also applied to the disruptions which attend the colonial situation:

> Unsupported by that Chaguanas world, with no one outside to instruct us in our obligations, even to ourselves, our own internal reverences began to go; our Hindu system began to fail (*FC*, p. 40).

A House for Mr Biswas draws attention to the fecundity of the land, which, "though fruitful from a former cultivation, felt new" (*HB*, p. 359). The descent of the Tulsis on the estate, located on Christopher Columbus road, is described as an "invasion" (*HB*, p. 361). Its wanton devastation, as much through aimless stupidity as greed, is nightmarishly accelerated: within a few pages, the land reverts to bush, and the very soil itself is being sold off. The old ethos of communalism is replaced by new, individualistic imperatives: Biswas senses "it was now every man for himself" (*HB*, p. 368). The incident sets the seal on the fate of the Tulsi clan.

Critics have pointed to the political overtones of Biswas's story, suggestive of the struggles of emergent countries against the colonial order: the book was published the year before Trinidad attained its independence, in 1962. The novel's solidarity with his efforts can be interpreted as signalling a sympathy with the project of decolonization. Gordon Rohlehr sees analogies between the Tulsi order and a slave society.[54] The Shorthills episode, however, might be thought to express Naipaul's fears concerning the future of the island under self-government; it foresees the destruction of the remnants of a decaying order by a new regime of senseless pillage. The novel may thereby be thought to complicate its alignment with the hero's pursuit of freedom and independence. Such ambivalence is akin to the mingled nostalgia and satire which distinguish the novel's treatment of Hindu ritual. There is, of course, an element of paradox involved in the celebration of rebellion and independence in so allusive a literary mode: allusion may be associated with deference to the literary predecessor, as well as with the urge to revise his or her work.

Biswas's increasing intimacy with Shama is part of his achievement, but is less central to the book than the developing relation of Biswas to Anand: the work is concerned with patrilinear legacies and homages. There is scarcely a mention of Anand's relationship with his mother, which is paralleled by the paucity of references to his mother in Naipaul's interviews and non-fictional writings. "'I love her;'" he wrote to his sister, "but who has shaped my live [*sic*], my views, my tastes? Pa''.[55] The relations between a mother and son do, however, form the subject of Naipaul's early story "The Enemy" (1955): the boy considers "this woman, my mother, as the enemy" (*FI*, p. 62). The story incorporates elements of autobiographical material which is given a more extensive treatment in *A House for Mr Biswas*. Some of the awkwardness of the relations of Biswas and Anand is anticipated by the boy's attitude towards his mother, "someone from whom I was going to escape as soon as I grew big enough" (*FI*, p. 71), while the conclusion of the tale suggests that, secretly, the boy has longed for his mother's affection.

Realizing he will not fulfil his ambitions in his lifetime, Biswas transfers them to his son. He is pictured, towards the end of his life, with no other occupation than to "wait for Anand. Wait for Savi. Wait for the five years to come to an end. Wait. Wait" (*HB*, p. 528). Biswas's investment in his son is represented from Anand's point of view as faintly ridiculous, and as an embarrassment; his attentions are well-meaning but inept. Anand is partly a victim of his father's ambitions: his life is made a misery by the work expected of him: "Childhood, as a time of gaiety and irresponsibility, was for these exhibition pupils only one of the myths of English Composition" (*HB*, p. 345).

The novel's temporal scheme combines a cyclical structure with linear progression: Anand's life both repeats and transcends that of Biswas. Anand's physical frailty, too, is emphasized: "... the boy's narrow shoulder blades below the thin cotton shirt; the slender neck, the large head; the thin eczema-stained legs in small, loose trousers; the blackened soles" (*HB*, p. 211). Anand's ill-fitting and ungainly home-made clothes recall Biswas's unsightly floursack trousers:

> Mr Biswas was irritated by his shyness, but he was again touched by the boy's fragility and the carefully ragged "home clothes" which Anand, like the other children, wore the minute he came from school (*HB*, p. 213).

Anand's humiliation — he has been afraid to use the school toilets — echoes that of Biswas at pundit Jairam's. Anand almost drowns, as Biswas was feared to have done as a child. Anand may share the humiliation of enforced dependency on the Tulsis, but he is permitted the possibility of an escape denied to Biswas.

This is in keeping with the way the novel moves from the delineation of a closed world of ritual repetition, to a more open and uncertain world where ambition can be pursued.[56] It begins in a world of magic and predestination (the pundit may be satirized, but all his predictions come to pass), set in an "antique, 'pastoral' " Hindu community ("Writing *HB*", p. 22), which denies any latitude for the exercise of the individual will. It charts a movement to the city, and to a more open-ended form of narration, akin to the Victorian novel rather than Hindu fable, in which there is greater scope for the individual to mould his or her fate. Constraints are imposed on Biswas's capacity to shape his destiny: the prologue portrays Biswas reflecting back at the end of his life, and remains the predetermined conclusion towards which he struggles and the novel progresses. Naipaul furthermore frustrates the expectations of narrative progression which attach to the realistic mode, by means of frequent repetitions: Biswas's recurring frustrations and failures, his retreats from a fragile independence into dependence. For the most part, though, the novel registers a shift away from magic to realism.

Naipaul has described his relationship with his father as

> the big relationship in my life, and what is odd about it is that I always felt protective towards my father. I never felt that he was the man protecting me, I always felt quite the other way around: that it was up to me to look after him.[57]

Anand feels pain when others ridicule his father. There are times when Anand stands by his father — when he refuses to abandon him at Green Vale, for instance — and times when Anand is unnecessarily cruel to him. Biswas's relationship with Anand is characterized by a succession of advances and retreats. Anand shows considerable embarrassment at displays of emotion. Even when he stands by his father he does so petulantly: " 'Because — ' The word came out thin, explosive, charged with anger, at himself and his father. 'Because they was going to leave you alone' " (*HB*, p. 251). Anand's failure to return to assist the family in its distress, when Biswas has a heart attack and loses his job, is based on historical events. The book does not in any way seek to excuse Anand for his cruelty, or to mitigate the importance of its effect on Biswas. "Prologue to an Autobiography" and *A House for Mr Biswas* can be interpreted as seeking to make restitution for this absence. They look back belatedly to the father whom, like the narrator at the end of *Miguel Street*, Naipaul had ignored at the moment of his departure from Trinidad. "And it was with that sudden churlishness, a sudden access of my own hysteria, that I had left my father in 1950, not looking back. I wish I had" (*FC*, p. 47).

Notes

1 Interviewed by Nigel Bingham, p. 306.
2 Interviewed by David Bates, "Portrait Gallery", *Sunday Times Supplement* (May 26 1963), p. 13. Seepersad Naipaul's stories had, in fact, been published privately in Trinidad (1943–44), but were not published in England until 1976.
3 *Finding the Centre: Two Narratives* (London: André Deutsch, 1984), p. 9.
4 "My Brother's Tragic Sense", *Spectator*, 258 (January 24 1987), p. 22.
5 I am also indebted to Landeg White's chapter on *HB*, in *V. S. Naipaul: A Critical Introduction* (London: Macmillan, 1975), which explores the parallels between Seepersad Naipaul and Biswas.
6 *The Adventures of Gurudeva* (London: André Deutsch, 1976), p. 15.
7 *FC*, p. 72
8 Shiva Naipaul, *Beyond the Dragon's Mouth: Stories and Pieces* (London: Hamish Hamilton, 1984), p. 30.
9 *A House for Mr Biswas* (London: André Deutsch, 1961), p. 311.
10 As discussed by White, p. 36; the story is not collected in *AG*.
11 *Holy Bible: King James Version* (New York: Penguin, 1974), p. 27.
12 *The Mystic Masseur* (London: André Deutsch, 1957), p. 44.
13 This perhaps alludes to the character in Samuel Selvon's *A Brighter Sun* (1951) who flees to the hills for fear that Hitler is going to bomb Trinidad. Other similarities with Naipaul's work — the hero, Tiger, takes to speaking in dictionary definitions, like Ganesh — suggest that Naipaul knew of this book.
14 *The Mimic Men* (London: André Deutsch, 1967), p. 149.
15 Interviewed by Roy Plomley, *Desert Island Discs* (July 5 1980), BBC Radio 4, V. S. Naipaul Archive, IV, B: 4, Special Collections, McFarlin Library, University of Tulsa.
16 Interviewed by Curt Suplee, "Voyager with the Dark and Comic Vision", *Washington Post* (November 19 1981), p. C 17.
17 Interviewed by Jason Cowley, "The Long Road to Happiness", *Times* (May 11 1998), p. 17.
18 The case is argued by Andrew Gurr in *Writers in Exile: The Identity of Home in Modern Literature* (Brighton: Harvester, 1981), pp. 80–1.
19 *Miguel Street* (London: André Deutsch, 1959), p. 216.
20 See *The Middle Passage: The Caribbean Revisited. Impressions of Five Societies — British, French and Dutch — in the West Indies and South America* (London: André Deutsch, 1962), p. 72.
21 "The Birth of Mr Biswas", *Journal of Commonwealth Literature*, 11, 3 (April 1977), pp. 50–4.
22 Introduction to *East Indians in the Caribbean: Colonialism and the Struggle for Identity. Papers Presented to a Symposium on East Indians in the Caribbean, The University of the West Indies, June 1975* (Millwood, New York: Kraus International Publications, 1982), pp. 5–6.
23 "Writing *A House for Mr Biswas*", *New York Review of Books*, 30 (November 24 1983), p. 22.
24 *Imaginary Homelands: Essays and Criticism 1981–1991* (London: Granta, 1991), p. 9.
25 *Imaginary Homelands*, p. 10.
26 Interviewed by Andrew Salkey, *The Arts and Africa*, (December 16 1971), André Deutsch Archive, 96, *IFS* folder, Special Collections, McFarlin Library, University of Tulsa.

27   "A Visit to Valsayn Park", V. S. Naipaul Archive, I, 1:3.
28   *An Area of Darkness* (London: André Deutsch, 1972), p. 37.
29   Interviewed by Nigel Bingham, p. 306.
30   *The Adventures of Gurudeva* (Port of Spain, 1943–44), V. S. Naipaul Archive, I, 1:4.
31   Interviewed by Charles Wheeler, p. 537.
32   "Mr Biswas, Mr Polly and the Problem of V. S. Naipaul's Sources", *Ariel*, 8, 3 (July 1977), pp. 129–141.
33   The Masters, (April 10 1962), BBC Written Archives Centre, Caversham.
34   *The History of Mr Polly and the War in the Air* (London: The Literary Press, 1940), p. 90.
35   Bernard Krikler, "V. S. Naipaul's *A House for Mr Biswas*", *Listener*, 71 (February 13 1964), pp. 270–1; Gordon Rohlehr, "Predestination, Frustration and Symbolic Darkness in Naipaul's *HB*", *Caribbean Quarterly* 10, 1 (March 1964), pp. 3–11; and Boxhill, "Mr Biswas, Mr Polly, and the Problem of V. S. Naipaul's Sources".
36   *After Empire: Scott, Naipaul, Rushdie* (Chicago and London: University of Chicago Press, 1997), p. 64.
37   "Repatriated Indians' Bitter Homecoming in India", *Trinidad Guardian* (November 27 1933); "Colonial Outcasts in India", *Trinidad Guardian* (April 23 1933).
38   *A Flag on the Island* (London: André Deutsch, 1967), p. 164.
39   Interviewed by Scott Winokur, "The Unsparing Vision of V. S. Naipaul", *Image: The San Francisco Chronicle Magazine* (May 5 1991), p. 12.
40   *Letters Between a Father and Son* (London: Abacus, 2000), p. 203.
41   "Black Narcissus: Representation, Reproduction, Repetition and Seeing Yourself in V. S. Naipaul's *HB*, and *EA*", *Commonwealth: Essays and Studies*, 18, 1 (Autumn 1995), pp. 92–105.
42   *Trinidad Guardian* (August 19 1932), copied into a notebook by Naipaul (V. S. Naipaul Archive, I, 1:2).
43   "This is Home", *Caribbean Voices* (June 24 1951), p. 3, BBC Written Archives.
44   "This is Home", pp. 3–4.
45   "Potatoes", *Caribbean Voices* (April 27 1952), p. 4, BBC Written Archives.
46   *Fireflies* (London: André Deutsch, 1970), p. 10.
47   *Beyond the Dragon's Mouth*, p. 11.
48   *An Unfinished Journey* (London: Hamish Hamilton, 1986), p. 25.
49   *An Unfinished Journey*, p. 28.
50   Letter from Diana Athill to V. S. Naipaul (February 10 1969), André Deutsch Archive, 95, *LED* folder.
51   *Letters Between a Father and Son*, p. 120.
52   *India: A Million Mutinies Now* (London: Heinemann, 1990), p. 178.
53   "My Brother's Tragic Sense", p. 22.
54   "Character and Rebellion in *A House for Mr Biswas*", in Hamner, pp. 87–91.
55   *Letters Between a Father and Son*, p. 139.
56   This is noted by Homi Bhabha, who discusses the way the novel plays off contrasting narrative codes, in "Representation and the Colonial Text", *The Theory of Reading*, ed. by Frank Gloversmith, (Sussex: Harvester, 1984), pp. 93–122.
57   Interviewed by Nigel Bingham, p. 306.

2 | *The Enigma of Arrival:* autobiography and revision*

Much of Naipaul's writing — both his fiction and non-fiction — draws on autobiographical material, to furnish overlapping accounts of his life. These various accounts serve, in some measure, to revise each other. This process of revision affects both the relationship between Naipaul's works, and the structure of *The Enigma of Arrival.* It is possible to perceive analogies between the practice of revision and certain of the motives which produce an autobiography. To write an autobiography is, in a sense, to engage in an act of revision — an act which involves the reworking of a life, the editing out of unsuitable material, and a tidying-up of the confusions of experience according to some ordering principle. The writing of autobiography is shaped by an interplay between the desire to assert a connection between a past and present self — to establish a continuity over time which could be thought to define the very notion of identity — and an opposing sense of distance from the earlier self. The revision of a literary text similarly implies a dialogue between past and present selves, and a continuity of concerns — those of the earlier writer remain those of the later writer — which is balanced by the assumption that the older writer is better able to express what the younger writer has endeavoured to articulate, or that the emphases are now different. Revision need not involve a disowning of the writing of the earlier self; the work of the younger writer is not necessarily superseded by the efforts of the older. Both autobiography and revision invite meditations on the nature of identity within difference.

The Enigma of Arrival combines elements of fiction and of non-fiction, and blends autobiography with material not directly concerned with the personality of the author. It interweaves a description of Naipaul's development as a writer with a detailed narrative of rebirth in the Wiltshire countryside, in the course of which the lives of the local inhabitants are subjected to Naipaul's intense scrutiny. Attention is distributed equally between the consciousness which perceives and the object of its perceptions: the writer is "defined by his writing discoveries, his ways of seeing" (*EA*, p. 309). The Wiltshire sections have a fullness of detail which suggests that they derive from observation, but they also incorporate elements of invention, as Naipaul indicates:

> There are two kinds of truths: I couldn't take the real life I saw
> in Wiltshire and hang philosophical ideas about change on it.
> You can't do it, legally or imaginatively, so you create your
> own construct, which sums up the truth, to talk about flux and
> so on.[1]

The Enigma of Arrival expresses Naipaul's response to England, and
supplies images which both conform to and defy traditional conceptions
of it. It embodies a complex of conflicting attitudes towards England,
based partly on a distinction between past and present, town and country,
idea and reality. On the one hand, the work narrates the process of an
initial disillusionment with England. On the other hand, the preconceptions with which Naipaul emigrated are exposed as inadequate. As this
discussion of the Wiltshire sections of *The Enigma of Arrival* will argue,
he destroys idealized images of rural England by portraying the invading
pressures of modernity — gone are Goldsmith's and Gray's lowing herds
— but at the same time finds historical continuities: what he has read both
validates and is validated by what he sees. To judge by the work's use of
allusion, he appears to retain an affection for the idea of England which is
enshrined in its literary culture. His ambivalence might be interpreted as
arising from a ''colonial'' condition of cultural dislocation.

''The Journey'' moves back in time to offer an account of his first
impressions of England, when he arrived in 1950. He proclaims here a
distance from his younger self, who had harboured idealized notions of
metropolitan culture. The section is written from the point of view of the
writer Naipaul has become, and explores the process by means of which
he has arrived there.

> To be what I wanted to be, I had to cease to be or to grow out of
> what I was. To become a writer it was necessary to shed many of
> the early ideas that went with the ambition, and the concept my
> half-education had given me of the writer (*EA*, p. 221).

He discusses the arbitrary images which surrounded him as a child in
Trinidad — the advertisements for unobtainable products — and likens
them to the idea of metropolitan culture supplied by his schooling:

> So I was used to living in a world where the signs were without
> meaning, or without the meaning intended by their makers. It
> was of a piece with the abstract, arbitrary nature of my
> education, like my ability to ''study'' French or Russian
> cinema without seeing a film, an ability which was, as I have
> said, like a man trying to get to know a city from its street map
> alone (*EA*, pp. 120–1).

"The Journey" is shaped by a narrative of disillusionment, or at least of preconceptions overturned: "I had come to London as to a place I knew very well. I found a city that was strange and unknown" (*EA*, p. 123). *An Area of Darkness* also points to this disjunction between expectation and experience: "I came to London. It had become the centre of my world and I had worked hard to come to it. And I was lost. London was not the centre of my world" (*AD*, p. 45). He transfers his disappointment to the unnamed narrator of "Tell Me Who to Kill", in *In a Free State*: "I used to have a vision of a big city. It wasn't like this, not streets like this".[2] Naipaul locates the ideal at an earlier point in time rather than at a different point in space:

> So I grew to feel that the grandeur belonged to the past; that I had come to England at the wrong time; that I had come too late to find the England, the heart of empire, which (like a provincial, from a far corner of the empire) I had created in my fantasy.
> Such a big judgement about a city I had just arrived in!
> (*EA*, p. 120.)

The appended exclamation appears to indicate that Naipaul wishes to question the judgement, but *The Enigma of Arrival* proceeds to confirm the view that London is subject to decline, and the Wiltshire sections of the novel rehearse once more the process of the destruction of an illusory conception of England. Naipaul is ambivalent, disowning the preconceptions of his younger self which blinded him to the more interesting reality of the experience, while cherishing a lost imaginative capacity.

The manor furnishes the Wiltshire sections of *The Enigma of Arrival* with an equivocal symbol both of imperial decay and of power. Its architecture

> was part of the taste of the time for a special idea of the past, the assertion — with the wealth and power of an unbelievably extensive empire — of racial and historical and cultural virtue (*EA*, pp. 184–5).

There are obvious political overtones to his description of the manor's increasing ruin, and the disruption of its social organization: it is overrun by people who, "sensing an absence of authority, an organization in decay, seemed to be animated by an opposite instinct: to hasten decay, to loot, to reduce to junk" (*EA*, p. 292). The image of the imperial centre subjected to the vandalism of barbarian hordes is one which Naipaul also applies to the London he encountered when he first came to England:

> I see that lunch in the Earls Court boarding house as slightly less than it seemed to me even at the time. I see the participants

as servants, in a degraded setting, the gentlefolks whom the servants were meant to serve being gone, with the war, and leaving a looted house, full of foreigners now (*EA*, p. 128).

This statement signals a distance from his impressions at the time, but he writes that even then he thought of his fellow lodgers as — like the manor's inhabitants — campers in the ruins:

I felt the house was no longer being used as the builder or first owner had intended. I felt that at one time, perhaps before the war, it had been a private house; and (though knowing nothing about London houses) I felt it had come down in the world. . . . And I felt, as I saw more and more of my fellow lodgers . . . that we were all in a way campers in the big house (*EA*, p. 119).

Naipaul laments having failed to realize in 1950 that "the flotsam of Europe not long after the end of the terrible war" (*EA*, p. 130) could form suitable material for literary treatment. He has since made of displacement a subject entirely his own — it is hard to think of a work by him that does not deal with it. Naipaul draws on classical analogies to characterize these migrations:

In 1950 in London I was at the beginning of that great movement of peoples that was to take place in the second half of the twentieth century. . . . Cities like London were to change. They were to cease being more or less national cities; they were to become cities of the world, modern-day Romes, establishing the pattern of what great cities should be, in the eyes of islanders like myself and people even more remote in language and culture. They were to be cities visited for learning and elegant goods and manners and freedom by all the barbarian peoples of the globe, people of forest and desert, Arab, Africans, Malays (*EA*, p. 130).

Naipaul courts political controversy with the term "barbarian". The metropolis disappoints him by being invaded by migrants and having gone down in the world, but at least it still has learning and freedom to offer.

This portrait of London is akin to the view of England expounded by Naipaul's articles for *The Illustrated Weekly of India* in the 1960s. He describes a "feverish, colonial atmosphere of greed, extending from big man to 'little man' ".[3] He laments the destruction of Victorian houses, and wonders, "In this great behemoth of London, each home an identical, separate cell, how can the sense of community survive?"[4]

Everyone is adrift. ''We are all non-residents''.[5] People live in ''little red rat-traps''.[6] There is little to distinguish this view of England from his perception of post-colonial nations: ''There is something flavourless about the new town, a brightness which is *colonial*, in the suggestion which it holds of a people sundered from their roots''.[7]

> The classless state had in fact become the proletarian state, where old aspirations had been abandoned and old sanctions shown to be without value, and where, as in a colony just after independence, there was an atmosphere of holiday revenge, self-destruction.[8]

The image of the colony serves for Naipaul to denote England's deterioration.

A comparable complex of attitudes concerning the idea of the metropolis is manifested in other narratives of migration from the colonies or former colonies. Dan Jacobson's *Time of Arrival* also contains an ambivalent account of the first few months the South African novelist spent in England. Jacobson records his initial response: ''Anything in those days could be an occasion for wonder''.[9] The London he inhabits has, like Naipaul's Earls Court, gone down in the world, and, under a siege of ''rationing, austerity and gloom'' (Jacobson, p. 17), still bears the visible scars of the ravages of war.

> The public buildings were filthy, pitted with shrapnel-scars, running with pigeon dung from every coign and eave; eminent statesmen and dead kings of stone looked out upon the world with soot-blackened faces, like coons in a grotesque carnival; bus tickets and torn newspapers blew down the streets or lay in white heaps in the parks; cats bred in the bomb-sites, where people flung old shoes, tin cans, and yet more newspapers; whole suburbs of private houses were peeling, cracking, crazing, their windows unwashed, their steps unswept, their gardens untended (Jacobson, p. 17).

There is less of a sense in Jacobson's work that the dereliction is felt as a betrayal of expectation. Like Naipaul, he testifies to an oppressive consciousness of past lives and achievement, but weighs a sense of gains against losses.

> There was so much I did not know and never would know; there was so little I could ever do, in comparison with what had been done and done and done and done a hundred thousand times, and more. Yet better that burden, I was sure, than none at all (Jacobson, p. 23).

Jacobson explores the way his expectations shaped, and obscured, his perceptions of the place:

> It was impossible, in those first confused few weeks, really to look at the buildings. All I could do was to confirm that they were there, as the pictures and books had told me they would be. There was deep satisfaction in this confirmation: so deep I cannot easily describe it, for it was not just the reality of the buildings that was confirmed, but also, in an odd, unexpected way, my own reality too (Jacobson, p. 16).

This notion is reminiscent of Naipaul's depiction of colonial experience as seemingly emptied of reality — reality being the province of that which was read about in books. *Time of Arrival* is shaped, like *The Enigma of Arrival*, by a dialogue between the person Jacobson was and the writer he has become. Jacobson provides an account of metropolitan migration that balances unfulfilled expectations against unexpected compensations.

Other records of colonial migration tend more unambiguously to involve narratives of disenchantment. Jean Rhys is a writer who displays a sensibility akin to Naipaul's, and his identification of the themes of her work might well serve to mediate those of his own: she writes about "isolation, an absence of society or community, the sense of things falling apart, dependence, loss".[10] Rhys's fictional portrait of London in *After Leaving Mr Mackenzie* is closely analogous to the London sections of *The Mimic Men* and *The Enigma of Arrival*. Her emigration from the West Indies was, according to Naipaul, a "break in a life";[11] this journey was "from one void to another. There is no innocence in Jean Rhys's world; there has always been loss".[12] In Rhys's novels, passion is "an aspect of loss, of being adrift, of being without money; it is an aspect of dependence".[13] Ralph Singh's alienation and psychological wounds are similarly manifested in his sexual relations: his visits to prostitutes, his casual liaisons with foreign students, his sense that intimacy is a form of "violation and self-violation" (*MM*, p. 30). At the centre of Rhys's work, Naipaul writes, "there is always something like withdrawal".[14] This brings to mind similar tendencies in Naipaul's work: Ralph Singh's taste for seclusion, or Naipaul's own sense of kinship with his landlord's retreat to the manor.

In Jean Rhys's autobiography, *Smile Please*, she portrays her Dominican childhood in terms of a state of cultural dislocation. She describes losing herself in books, in "what I thought was the real world",[15] and nurturing dreams of a distant place. Life in Dominica may have been exciting, but "was not, of course, anything like as wonderful as England would be",[16] Rhys records, in the voice of her younger self.

The reality of England is presented as far from wonderful. At a certain point on the crossing, "quite suddenly it seemed, it began to grow cold";[17] the sun only shines again once she leaves England, feeling as if she "had got out of prison".[18] In the meantime she inhabits a series of dingy, over-priced bedsits, policed by disapproving landladies, her life resembling that of her fictional heroines — beset by a sense of exclusion, and consisting in a disconnected sequence of empty experiences, emotionlessly, curtly recounted:

> I would never be part of anything. I would never really belong anywhere, and I knew it, and all my life would be the same, trying to belong, and failing. Always something would go wrong. I am a stranger and I always will be, and after all I didn't really care. Perhaps it's my fault, I really can't think far enough for that. But I don't like these people, I thought.[19]

Her experiences in England are pervaded by a blank despair. Unfulfilled expectation makes her sour. "It was Jack, who is a writer, who told me that my hatred of England was thwarted love. I said disappointed love maybe".[20]

In a review of Samuel Selvon's *An Island is a World*, Naipaul defines a West Indian intellectual malaise: "... the sense of merit unrecognized, often injured, the consequent obsession with the futility of effort, and the passion to fly, to escape to some happier land elsewhere".[21] Selvon's characters flee Trinidad only to return. "They have found that the bigger world, despite all its glamour, cannot give them what they want, that when all is said and done, an island is a world" (*ibid.*, p. 2). This recalls the conclusion of Naipaul's story "Old Man": Trinidad, "with its burning political problems of no significance, is really the world in small".[22] His world-weariness does not preclude a particular contempt for Trinidad, but he here uses it to symbolize the provincialism of the world at large.

C. L. R. James's *Beyond a Boundary* also includes an account of migration to England. Like the other writers discussed here, James is a product of the colonial education system: he describes himself as "a British intellectual long before I was ten, already an alien in my own environment among my own people, even my own family".[23] He identifies a general tendency to disappointment in those so placed. "People educated as I had been could move rapidly from uncritical admiration of abstractions to an equally uncritical hostility to the complex reality".[24] Reviewing George Lamming's *Of Age and Innocence,* Naipaul discusses the background to what he terms the West Indian quest for identity. "It is not fully realized how completely the West Indian Negro identifies himself with England".[25] The experience of England, however, is "usually traumatic. The foundations of his life are removed. He has to look for new loyalties" (*ibid*). Lamming's novel, *The Emigrants*, dramatizes this process. Lamming's *The Pleasures of Exile*, a cultural and political polemic containing muted autobiographical references, also conforms to this pattern. The West Indian, he asserts, has a relation to "the *idea* of England";[26] he "arrives and travels with the memory, the habitual weight of a colonial relation".[27] He describes the resultant oppressive sense of a "mausoleum of historic achievement",[28] and explores what he terms the "colonial castration of the West Indian sensibility".[29] *The Pleasures of Exile* provides a noteworthy contrast with *The Engima of Arrival* in respect of its confrontational reappropriation of literary allusion: Naipaul writes in the Wiltshire sections as an inheritor of the English literary tradition, finding analogies between Wordsworth's Lake District and his Wiltshire; Lamming rewrites *The Tempest* from the point of view of Caliban, as a narrative of imperial conquest and resistance, with Caliban turning Prospero's gift of language against his master. This is not dissimilar to the project of Rhys's *The Wide Sargasso Sea*, which develops a riposte to *Jane Eyre*, imagined from the point of view of Bertha Mason, Rochester's first wife.

A narrative of partial or total disillusionment with a society and culture familiar to these writers through their education is therefore a consistent feature of these accounts of colonial migration. It is as if there were an inherent connection between the cultural dislocation of the colonial situation, where, in Lamming's words, "education was imported in much the same way that flour and butter are imported from Canada",[30] and the revisions which play such an important part in the drama of *The Enigma of Arrival*. First-hand experience leads to the reassessment of an illusory familiarity, then initial impressions are revised by a more prolonged and deeper acquaintance with the metropolis.

This drama of revised perceptions also characterizes the Wiltshire sections of the work, to which this discussion will now turn its attention. *The Enigma of Arrival* is concerned to record with scrupulous fidelity Naipaul's initial impressions of the Wiltshire landscape, and faithfully recapitulates his every erroneous assumption concerning his new location. The first line of the book introduces the subject of perception which is the work's abiding preoccupation: "For the first four days it rained. I could hardly see where I was" (*EA*, p. 11). The work proceeds to depict with painstaking clarity what it was that Naipaul failed to see, and the process of learning to interpret it: "I saw what I saw very clearly. But I didn't know what I was looking at. I had nothing to fit it into" (*EA*, p. 12).

> Knowledge came slowly to me. It was not like the almost
> instinctive knowledge that had come to me as a child of the

plants and flowers of Trinidad; it was like learning a second language. If I knew then what I know now I would be able to reconstruct the seasons of Jack's garden or gardens (*EA*, p. 32).

Gradually Naipaul masters this second language, and the novel revises its initial impressions. He learns to see his surroundings as constructed rather than inevitable, man-made rather than natural, mutable rather than unchanging. The novel interprets the various strata of historical endeavour legible in the Wiltshire landscape as evidence of a process of change which amounts to a vision of flux rather than of mere decay. A consciousness of prior ignorance and subsequent understanding imparts reminders that the person who writes is distinct, and sees differently, from the person who first arrived in the valley.

In the first section, entitled "Jack's Garden", Naipaul constructs an edifice of assumption around the figure of Jack — perceiving his life as emblematic of a form of timeless pastoral harmony with the land, from which Naipaul feels excluded — only to proceed to expose this pastoral as illusory, but nevertheless to persist in construing Jack's life as the affirmation of an ideal. At first, Jack is no more than "a figure in the landscape" (*EA*, p. 31), but over the course of time, as Naipaul observes him at work in his garden, Jack's diverse activities marking the passing of the seasons, he comes to think of his existence as a living "Book of Hours" (*EA*, pp. 20, 31). A contrasting, retrospective consciousness simultaneously makes itself felt: "Jack lived among ruins, among superseded things. But that way of looking came to me later, has come to me with greater force now, with the writing" (*EA*, p. 19). Naipaul's misapprehension, which he devotes considerable narrative energy to elaborating, consists in seeing Jack's life as a survival of the past, rather than as a matter of choice. Naipaul's reading of the figure is defined in reaction to his own sense of being an intruder: "I felt unanchored and strange" (*EA*, p. 19). He polyphonically interweaves his initial and revised impressions, and distances himself from assumptions he is nevertheless at pains to record:

> Jack himself, however, I considered to be part of the view. I saw his life as genuine, rooted, fitting: man fitting the landscape. I saw him as a remnant of the past (the undoing of which my own presence portended). It did not occur to me, when I first went walking and saw only the view, took what I saw as things of that walk, things that one might see in the countryside near Salisbury, immemorial, appropriate things, it did not occur to me that Jack was living in the middle of junk, among the ruins of nearly a century; that the past around his cottage might not have been his past; that he might at some

> stage have been a newcomer to the valley; that his style of life
> might have been a matter of choice, a conscious act; that out of
> the little piece of earth, which had come to him with his farm-
> worker's cottage (one of a row of three) he had created a
> special land for himself, a garden where (though surrounded by
> ruins, reminders of vanished lives) he was more than content to
> live out his life and where, as in a version of a Book of Hours,
> he celebrated the seasons (*EA*, pp. 19–20).

The emphasis, by the end of the paragraph, is on re-affirming
something akin to the initial impression: scepticism is submerged in
affirmation. He explodes one set of notions about the character, in
order to construct a new set. The musical interplay of inference and
counter-inference, assertion and retraction, continues. Restating
already discredited beliefs about the figure, he likens Jack's garden
to "a medieval village in miniature.... . This was Jack's style, and it
was this that suggested to me (falsely, as I got to know soon enough)
the remnant of an old peasantry" (*EA*, p. 22). The parentheses
indicates the provisionality of the novel's predicates. Naipaul goes on
to question his revised opinion:

> It was his eyes, oddly obstreperous, oddly jumpy, that gave
> him away, that said he was after all a farm worker, that in
> another setting, in a more crowded or competitive place, he
> might have sunk. And the discovery was a little disconcerting,
> because (after I had got rid of the idea that he was a remnant of
> an old peasantry) I had found in that beard of his, and in his
> bearing, his upright, easy, elegant walk, the attributes of a man
> with a high idea of himself, a man who had out of principle
> turned away from other styles of life (*EA*, p. 32).

The work repeatedly recapitulates its progress, summarizes its
discoveries and reminds us of what has gone before. The manuscripts
of the novel show Naipaul busily revising himself in an attempt to
recreate his initial impressions of Wiltshire, and carefully striving to
simulate the casual, natural progress of his thought. Towards the end of
the section, Naipaul reiterates his altered perceptions of Jack:

> Jack himself had disregarded the tenuousness of his hold on
> the land, just as, not seeing what others saw, he had created a
> garden on the edge of a swamp and a ruined farmyard: had
> responded to and found glory in the seasons. All around him
> was ruin; and all around, in a deeper way, was change, and a
> reminder of the brevity of the cycles of growth and creation.
> But he had sensed that life and man were the true mysteries;

and he had asserted the primacy of these with something like religion (*EA*, p. 87).

As a postscript to this apparently definitive and affirmative interpretation of Jack's life, Naipaul appends the discovery that Jack was possibly not the man he has imagined him — that he was perhaps a domestic tyrant. The repeated revision of the work's assertions has the effect of suggesting the provisionality of judgement, as well as hinting at the mystery which surrounds other human beings, and the difficulties of reading a social milieu in relation to which one is an outsider.

Writing about Günter Grass, in terms suggestive of his own work, Salman Rushdie identifies a connection between migration and scepticism which offers itself as also applicable to Naipaul's practices in *The Enigma of Arrival*:

> This is what the triple disruption of reality teaches migrants: that reality is an artefact, that it does not exist until it is made, and that, like any other artefact, it can be made well or badly, and that it can also, of course, be unmade. What Grass learned on his journey across the frontiers of history was Doubt.[31]

Naipaul explains his enterprise in these words:

> I felt that truly to render what I saw, I had to define myself as a writer or narrator; I had to reinterpret things. I have tried to do this in different ways throughout my career. And after two years' work, I have just finished a book in which at last, as I think, I have managed to integrate this business of reinterpreting with my narrative.[32]

He connects the autobiographical impulse with a sense of cultural relativism: the consciousness of straddling two cultures produces the need to explain himself, and to place his perspective for the benefit of his audience.

Jack's case is central to the work: many of the other discoveries Naipaul arrives at concerning the Wiltshire landscape and its inhabitants are anticipated by the first section. In this sense as in others the work can be seen to be organised around a structural principle of recapitulation and revision, and of variation within repetition. In the same way that Naipaul comes to realize that Jack is not as rooted in the land as he had first imagined, so he discovers that the Phillipses, the manor servants, are, like himself, intruders. Neither does Pitton, the gardener, belong: they are all seen by Naipaul as campers in the ruins of the manor.

Naipaul learns to perceive the natural environment as artificially constructed. Human intervention in the landscape is inseparable from the novel's vision of decay: either humans interfere, and the landscape degenerates, or they fail to maintain it, and it goes to ruin. Naipaul is distressed by the fencing in of the droveway: "How sad it was to lose that sense of width and space! It caused me pain. But already I had grown to live with the idea that things changed; already I lived with the idea of decay" (*EA*, p. 26). Jack's death, obliquely hinted at by the observation that the smoke from his chimney one day suddenly stops, is reflected in the way his garden runs wild:

> So much that had looked traditional, natural, emanations of the landscape, things that country people did — the planting out of annuals, the tending of the geese, the clipping of the hedge, the pruning of the fruit trees — now turned out not to have been traditional or instinctive after all, but to have been part of Jack's way (*EA*, p. 47).

The mutability of the world Naipaul observes around him adds to the instability of his conclusions. The work embodies a "sense of what is, wasn't always, has been made, and is about to change again and become something else".[33] Naipaul's perceptions amount to a lesson in impermanence:

> I had seen everything as a kind of perfection, perfectly evolved. But I had hardly begun to look, the land and its life had hardly begun to shape itself about me, when things began to change. And I had fallen back on old ideas, ideas now not so much of decay, as of flux and the constancy of change, to fight the distress I felt at everything — a death, a fence, a departure — that undid or altered or threatened the perfection I had found (*EA,* p. 51).

He suggests that such notions are a form of consolation, a defence against distress.

Revisions impel the drama of *The Enigma of Arrival*, while acting to frustrate the logic of chronological progression: Naipaul repeatedly retraces his steps to reconsider the same events and places from a fresh perspective. The work's repetitions serve to mime the rhythms of the temporal process. Varied agricultural tasks measure the progress of the seasons, and shape the passing of time according to a pattern of cyclical return. Christopher Ricks describes the effects of the novel's style by quoting T. S. Eliot — "With slow rotation suggesting permanence" ("Burnt Norton" III)[34] — and notes the fidelity of Naipaul's prose to the processes of thought, with reference to a quotation from Coleridge about poetic form:

> The reader should be carried forward, not merely or chiefly by the mechanical impulse of curiosity, or by a restless desire to

arrive at the final solution; but by the pleasurable activity of mind excited by the attractions of the journey itself. Like the motion of a serpent, which the Egyptians made the emblem of intellectual power; or like the path of sound through the air, at every step he pauses and half recedes, and from the retrogressive movement collects the force which again carries him onward.[35]

Journeys, as noted below, figure prominently in *The Enigma of Arrival*.

The repetitions of *The Enigma of Arrival* serve as a fixed point against which to measure the unfolding of our own understanding as well as Naipaul's reading of his environment. "For the first four days it rained and was misty; I could hardly see where I was" (*EA*, p. 154). This repeats, with slight variations, the first two sentences of the work. By the time one reads these words again on page 154, however, one has a greater understanding of the route by which Naipaul has arrived in Wiltshire, and of its place in his personal history. He revises one's sense that his arrival in Wiltshire is simply a beginning, by locating it as part of a process: he is constantly arriving in places. In the first section, Naipaul anticipates Pitton's dismissal, and the decline of the manor gardens into dereliction, which is portrayed more fully in "Ivy". The pattern of anticipation and recollection highlights the thematic parallels between the two sections: both detail a series of changes which amount ultimately to a narrative of decay. There is a verbal echo: Pitton is dismissed, and "quite suddenly, from one day to the next, part of the routine of the manor I had grown into, part of my new life and comfort, my private, living Book of Hours, was snapped" (*EA*, p. 247). By the time that Naipaul repeats and develops his account of this event, the reader has a sense of the larger pattern to which it belongs. There is variation within repetition: while Naipaul extrapolates an affirmation from Jack's story, refusing to accept that Jack's labours are mocked by the subsequent destruction of their fruits, the conclusion of "Ivy" might be thought to be more melancholy. Pitton acquires a new life in the town, and eventually ceases to " 'see' " Naipaul (*EA*, p. 255); the estate lapses deeper into decay. The end of "Jack's Garden" anticipates the end of the work, in describing the illness which is to cause Naipaul to move out of the valley, and which puts an end to the period of Naipaul's life described by the work.

The Enigma of Arrival's retractions and repetitions measure the distance between Naipaul's earlier and later self. The writing of autobiography entails a process of self-revision; it involves a distance between experience and the narrative which is constructed out of it. Frank Kermode[36] explores how the difference between the self that recounts and the self that is the subject of the narration is counterbalanced by self-recognition; part of the satisfaction of autobiography lies in its fostering an emergent sense of identity. Kermode notes the significance here of recurrence, which enables authors to persuade us that the self is continuous, and that, in Ralph Singh's words, "The personality hangs together" (*MM*, p. 219). Kermode argues that an autobiography's meaningful moments acquire importance with the advantage of hindsight and through the action of memory. John Sturrock comparably observes that the autobiographer embraces in retrospect accidents that may have seemed painful and unmeaning at the time.[37] Sturrock considers it a feature of autobiography that there should be a life-task waiting to be revealed in the fullness of time and in the light of retrospection. There may be a resultant tendency for the autobiographer to over-rationalize his or her life in an endeavour to coerce it into the required shape, as does Naipaul's mystic masseur Ganesh in his autobiography. He sees the hand of providence in every accident, and good fortune in the fortuitous:

> Everything seemed to be going wrong and Ganesh feared that he had misread the signs of fate. It was only later that he saw the providential pattern of these disappointing months. "We never are what we want to be," he wrote, "but what we must be." (*Mystic*, pp. 69–70.)

His serendipitous failure as a masseur causes him to fall back on writing, and leads ultimately to his successful career as a politician. The narrator treats with irony Ganesh's belief in a personal providence:

> "I suppose", Ganesh wrote in *The Years of Guilt*, "I had always, from the first day I stepped into Shri Ramlogan's shop, considered it as settled that I was going to marry his daughter. I never questioned it. It all seemed preordained." (*Mystic*, p. 41).

The novel plays off Ganesh's glib, retrospectively-imposed narrative against the messy uncertainty of events as they unfold.

Kermode's argument is illustrated with reference to *The Prelude*: he cites the example of Wordsworth's boat-stealing, which is only subsequently construed as a necessary and benign education of the spirit. *The Prelude*'s theme, which is akin to that of *The Enigma of Arrival*, is the birth of the poet's mind. Wordsworth at times offers accounts of his experience that are rather too neat to be true, and are at odds with the detail of the poem's narrative. Naipaul likewise supplies an excessively tidy summary of his personal odyssey: "... writer and man separating at the beginning of the journey and coming together again in a second life just before the end" (*EA*, p. 309). The effort of memory seeks to bridge the chasm which separates past and present, but *The Prelude* draws attention to its failure to achieve this undertaking:

> ... so wide appears
> The vacancy between me and those days,
> Which yet have such self-presence in my mind
> That sometimes when I think of them I seem
> Two consciousnesses — conscious of myself,
> And of some other being.[38]

Naipaul invokes ancestral ideas "not so much of decay, as of flux" (*EA*, p. 51) to account for the changes he observes in the Wiltshire landscape, but it is open to debate whether the perspective of the work may nevertheless be one of decline, and whether Naipaul himself is fully persuaded by the consolations he devises for himself.

> I had lived with the idea of change, had seen it as a constant, had seen a world in flux, had seen human life as a series of cycles that sometimes ran together. But philosophy failed me now. Land is not land alone, something that simply is itself. Land partakes of what we breathe into it, is touched by our moods and memories. And this end of a cycle, in my life, and in the life of the manor, mixed up with the feeling of age which my illness was forcing on me, caused me grief
> (*EA*, p. 301).

The implicit narrative of "Jack's Garden" is one of loss: although Naipaul invests his story with an affirmative significance, Jack falls ill and dies, and his garden is neglected and eventually destroyed. The landscape of *The Enigma of Arrival* is littered with images of deterioration: the changes described do not tend to be for the better. Naipaul's observations record a shifting attitude to the land: the mechanization of farming techniques, which he views as a desecration, is symbolized by the deformed cows which are "the mistakes of an industrial process" (*EA*, p. 16), awaiting death. Naipaul derives from his observations a lament for the passing away of an old, superseded way of life: "The land, for the new workers, was merely a thing to be worked" (*EA*, p. 55).

From the time of his arrival, Naipaul encounters a landscape of dereliction: "Away from the old farm buildings, and down the wide flat way which I thought of as the old road to the farm and Jack's cottage, there were other remnants and ruins, relics of other efforts or lives" (*EA*, p. 16). There is a decaying farmyard, with "antiquated, cumbersome pieces of farm machinery scattered and rusting about the farm buildings" (*EA*, p. 16). The manor, cottages, and farm buildings all show signs of neglect and dilapidation, and are set among older relics. The work supplies an inventory of ruins, in a long passage, culminating in a vision of

> the hill of larks, with the ancient barrows at the top, part of the
> pimpling of the downs as seen against the sky: those rolls of
> hay now as black and as earth-like as the older bales that, at the
> other end of the droveway, had indeed, below their tattered
> plastic sheeting, turned to earth. Grass to hay to earth (*EA*,
> p. 82).

Naipaul's prose has an incantatory quality here.

Transience and mutability are, of course, well-established literary themes. This passage is reminiscent of the theme of George Herbert's "Church-Monuments", in which even the most durable of substances, jet and marble, are imagined crumbling into dust. The poem pictures the monuments of its title,

> When they shall bow, and kneel, and fall down flat
> To kisse those heaps, which now they have in trust?[39]

Distinctions between inner and outer, material and immaterial, collapse in this kinship of mortality. The poem risks reducing everything that it contemplates into an undifferentiated heap of earth and dust:

> flesh is but the glasse, which holds the dust
> That measures all our time; which also shall
> Be crumbled into dust. ("Church-Monuments", 20–22)

Herbert's images of ruin teach a chastening lesson in spiritual humility. The mood of Naipaul's passage is also strongly reminiscent of Walter Ralegh's poetry (Ralegh's futile expeditions to Guiana form the matter of *The Loss of El Dorado* and *A Way in the World*):

> Even such is Time, which takes in trust
> Our youth, our joys, and all we have,
> And pays us but with age and dust;
> Who in the dark and silent grave,
> When we have wandered all our ways,
> Shuts up the story of our days.
> But from which earth and grave and dust
> The Lord shall raise me up, I trust.[40]

The addition of the final couplet removes the impression that the sixth line forms an ending; it recapitulates the imagery of the preceding lines and transforms it into the basis of an affirmation. The assertion of faith in the last line invokes a conception of trust which is distinct from the commercial signification implied in the first line.

The manor, which dominates the Wiltshire sections of *The Enigma of Arrival*, serves, as mentioned above, as a major symbol of decay. Naipaul emphasizes the solidity and durability of its structures, and sets its present decline against the memory of its inception and construction. Beneath the visible neglect is legible evidence of former care:

> The path Pitton had cut, one swathe up, one swathe down, showed grass as tight and fine and level as the grass of a lawn — as though the wilderness was only on the surface and awaited only this cut to reveal the old order and beauty and many seasons' tending that lay beneath (*EA*, p. 181).

Naipaul's Wiltshire, like his Africa, is viewed as liable to the depredations of bush: "Bush inside the great greenhouse, bush outside" (*EA*, p. 186). Perhaps remembering Tennyson's "The woods decay, the woods decay and fall" ("Tithonus"), Naipaul writes: "Every winter and spring created fresh havoc in the manor gardens and water meadows. The bridges over the channels decayed and decayed" (*EA*, p. 190). The chaotic progress of vegetable growth is accelerated in Naipaul's narrative.

> The wind tore the upper branches of one tree free of the wall. The main trunk sagged forward, leaving a ghost-like outline in green-black on the wall; the branches drooped; the tree seemed about to break. But it didn't (*EA*, p. 60).

The final sentence affirms the residual steadfastness of the manor grounds.

A Wordsworthian sense of "a grandeur in the beatings of the heart" (*The Prelude*, 1, 441) would appear to be the effect that Naipaul aims for in his affirmative treatment of Jack's labours and in the celebratory conclusion of the book. In an uneasy appendage to the description of Naipaul's sister's death in "The Ceremony of Farewell", the final section of the work, he contends that her death "showed me life and man as the mystery, the true religion of men, the grief and the glory" (*EA*, p. 318). He refers lyrically to the time of his childhood, itemizing the developments that have ravaged the Trinidadian landscape, and the traditions that are no longer practised:

> None of the Indian villages were like villages I had known. No narrow roads; no dark, overhanging trees; no huts; no earth yards with hibiscus hedges; no ceremonial lighting of lamps, no play of shadows on the wall; no cooking of food in half-walled verandahs, no leaping firelight; no flowers along gutters or ditches where frogs croaked the night away. But highways and clover-shaped exits and direction boards: a wooded land laid bare, its secrets opened up (*EA*, pp. 316–7).

It is open to debate whether Naipaul's jaunty conclusion — "We had made ourselves anew" (*EA*, p. 317) — carries greater conviction than the pervasive sense of loss here. It might be thought that a consciousness of death as the "nullifier of human life and endeavour" (*EA*, p. 97) predominates in *The Enigma of Arrival*, with the work at its most convincing in its depiction of decay. Jack's illness ends in death; and numerous other deaths occur on the periphery of the work: Jack's father-in-law's, Brenda's, Mr Phillips', Naipaul's sister's, and Shiva Naipaul's, which is mentioned only in the epigraph, but casts its shadow over the whole work. "Death was the motif; it had perhaps been the motif all along. Death and the way of handling it — that was the motif of the story of Jack" (*EA*, p. 309). This assertion may appear to be at odds with the work's concern to portray a rebirth, "a second chance, a new life, richer and fuller than any I had had anywhere else" (*EA*, p. 96). Naipaul describes his departure from the valley in terms of the death motif: "And as at a death, everything here that had been a source of pleasure and surprise, everything that had welcomed me and healed me, became a cause for pain" (*EA*, p. 301).

The purpose of autobiography is to defy death — to lend permanence to a transient life, and to make the past live on by means of an enduring record of it. Naipaul has expressed a fear of extinction that can only be combated by the writer's art: death serves as an image of the nonentity of non-achievement. He describes

> the old fear of extinction, and I don't mean of dying. I mean the fear of being reduced to nothing, of feeling crushed. It's partly the old colonial anxiety of having one's individuality destroyed.[41]

Autobiography grows out of and seeks to allay this fear concerning the annihilation of the self.

Naipaul's method has the effect of infusing the details of the scene portrayed with a wider significance: the neglect, for instance, of Jack's garden stands for his illness and death. *The Enigma of Arrival*'s animation of the landscape with human meaning, and the melancholy tone of the work, recall Wordsworth's "The Ruined Cottage". The gradual fading of Margaret's hopes that her husband will return, and the wasting of her life, are depicted indirectly, through the dereliction that befalls her cottage. Margaret's pain is held at a distance, by means of the narrative framing of the poem, and tempered by the consoling beauty of vegetable growth. The drama occurs off-stage:

> 'Tis a common tale
> By moving accidents uncharactered,

A tale of silent suffering, hardly clothed
In bodily form.[42]

The old man who tells the tale asserts a kind of sympathy between places
and those who inhabit them, half-animating the external, physical world.
The ruin of the cottage and garden proceeds in tandem with Margaret's
"heart-wasting" (449), and seemingly in sympathy with it: but there is
also a counterbalancing sense of a natural indifference, in the fecund
growth which continues regardless of Margaret's death. The poet traces

That secret spirit of humanity
Which, 'mid the calm oblivious tendencies
Of nature, 'mid her plants, her weeds, and flowers,
And silent overgrowings, still survived. ("The Ruined
Cottage", 503–6)

"The Ruined Cottage" ends on a somewhat discordant note of
composure which stems from the contemplation of natural processes
that are of a distinct order to the human: the ruins convey

So still an image of tranquillity,
So calm and still, and looked so beautiful
Amid the uneasy thoughts which filled my mind,
That what we feel of sorrow and despair
From ruin and from change, and all the grief
The passing shews of being leave behind,
Appeared an idle dream that could not live
Where meditation was. ("The Ruined Cottage", 517–24)

The complex effect of the poem, which mingles sadness and pleasure, is
akin to that produced by Naipaul's treatment of Jack's life.

The figure of Wordsworth looms large as a literary influence on
The Enigma of Arrival. Naipaul alludes to him on several occasions.
Jack's father-in-law "seemed a Wordsworthian figure: bent, exagger-
atedly bent, going gravely about his peasant tasks, as if in an immense
Lake District solitude" (*EA*, p. 20). "Once I saw him actually with a load
of wood on his bent back: Wordsworthian, the subject of a poem
Wordsworth might have called 'The Fuel-Gatherer' " (*EA*, p. 26).
Naipaul, like Wordsworth, regards the solitary figure with a certain awe
and envy. His solitude mirrors that of the writer, but the inarticulate
solitary exists in a harmonious relation with the natural world to which
the articulate and self-conscious writer can only aspire, and which infuses
the solitary figure with mystery and humble grandeur. There is a similar
sense in Naipaul's as in Wordsworth's treatment of his solitaries — a
sense of the distance between the writer and the silent, inarticulate

characters of whom he speaks. Naipaul, like Wordsworth, invests ordinary human figures with inexplicable power and mystery, while showing little interest in entering into the viewpoint of these figures.

The landscape of *The Enigma of Arrival* is perceived through a filter of literary allusion. Naipaul encounters a sheep-shearing ceremony which is "like something out of an old novel, perhaps by Hardy" (*EA*, p. 18). The sight of hares recalls to him Cobbett's mention of these animals. Naipaul writes that "the view through which I walked, was of a Nature almost unchanged since Constable's day" (*EA*, p. 185). It is as if his observations are validated by what he has read and witnessed on the canvas, and vice versa. This, however, is an impression which is subject to modification. It is his initial belief that he inhabits a literary landscape familiar to him through his education in Trinidad: but the landscape demonstrates, in places, an inability to sustain such references: "No lowing herd winding o'er the lea here, as in Gray's 'Elegy'; no 'sober' herd lowing to meet their young at evening's close, as in 'The Deserted Village' " (*EA*, p. 80). Naipaul's allusions do not only point to particular survivals of the past, but also remember obsolete ways of life, and function as another index of loss and decline. In an early version of *The Enigma of Arrival*, Naipaul unambiguously declared that these allusions were an aspect of the false expectations he entertained of England, and that they impeded his capacity to see it: "These literary influences constantly came to me in England; they came between me and what I saw; it was not easy for me to get rid of them and look directly".[43] This judgement has itself been subject to revision; in the finished version of the work, Naipaul is not so emphatic. "So much of this I saw with the literary eye, or with the aid of literature" (*EA*, p. 22). The allusions are once more invested with a form of validity, and express a truth about the English scene.

An intimate connection between reading the landscape and reading the literature is implied by Naipaul's essay, "Jasmine", where he manifests an equivocal attitude towards his relation to an English literary tradition, hesitating between considering himself as an outsider to it and as an heir. He states that "this literature was like an alien mythology" (*OB*, p. 23), but writes of adapting it to the Trinidadian scene. He seems to distance himself from the politically-motivated argument that English literature referred to a world too remote to be applicable to the Trinidadian situation, an argument illustrated by "Wordsworth's notorious poem about the daffodil. A pretty little flower, no doubt; but we had never seen it. Could the poem have any meaning for us?" (*OB*, p. 23.) Elsewhere he unambiguously asserts: "I cannot myself see why anyone should deny himself the pleasures of any literature or song" (*MP*, p. 65). He concludes the essay, however, with an instance of his inability to connect the wider world with the landscape of his childhood: the name "jasmine" refuses to attach itself to the flower he has known.

In *The Enigma of Arrival*, Naipaul is reborn into a countryside which he has read about from a distance, and the novel records the process of learning to read the landscapes of Wordsworth, Gray and Goldsmith. He associates his rebirth with an ability to put a name to another type of flower: "These peonies of my convalescence, these peonies around my cottage, were my first; and they stood for my new life" (*EA*, p. 180). He implies that he now considers himself an inheritor of the tradition. Derek Walcott contends that, in *The Enigma of Arrival*, Naipaul seeks to inscribe himself in the tradition of English elegiac pastoral, invoked by means of these allusions, as if to signal his arrival in the canon.[44] His relation to English literature is not dissimilar to that of nineteenth- and early twentieth-century American literary migrants in Europe: Pound and Eliot, for instance. Underlying the impulse to declare themselves part of the tradition through a wealth of allusions may be detected an anxiety about not fully belonging. Michael Gorra suggests that the position of the colonial writer is characterized by a sense of belatedness, and of the difficulty of carving out a place in the metropolitan literary culture.[45]

In direct opposition to Walcott's view that Naipaul is unduly deferential towards English culture, Helen Tiffin[46] interprets *The Enigma of Arrival* as a confrontational work, akin to *The Pleasures of Exile* or *The Wide Sargasso Sea*. She implies that merely for a colonial or postcolonial writer to write about the self is to defy the colonizer's definition of the colonial subject: "Post-colonial texts always offer, by their placement in relation to Britain and British literature, sites of resistance to it".[47] She sees *The Enigma of Arrival* as challenging the colonial idea of England, by emphasizing that England's pastoral heartland is subject to decay, and investigating the relativistic and socially-constructed character of perception. Her thesis seems to be based on sweeping assumptions. The notion of Naipaul as cultural incendiary does not ring true, and smacks of an attempt to rescue Naipaul for radicalism.

Naipaul's retractions and revisions have the effect of drawing attention to the impermanence of his perceptions and the instability of judgement. This instability can also be felt in the sense produced by *The Enigma of Arrival* that the author is imprisoned in the solitude of his perceptions, and, despite indefatigable speculation, is unable to penetrate the mystery of others. The work encourages a consciousness of the limitations of the author's vision.

Naipaul encourages an acknowledgement of the subjectivity of perception, and asks us to attend to a questioning of the authority of his own observations. He wonders whether his perceptions correspond with those of others, although he appears comfortable with this state of uncertainty:

> The wet river banks, the downs: everyone saw different things. Old Mr Phillips, with his memories of chalk and moss; my landlord, loving ivy; the builders of the manor garden; Alan; Jack; me (*EA*, p. 268).

Each, as it were, is imprisoned in the solitary confinement of his own consciousness. Naipaul devotes much energy to speculating about his landlord's thought processes:

> What did he see? Sitting there in his canvas-backed chair. Did he see the tall weeds in the solid greenhouse, the tops of some of the weeds flattened against the glass? Was he agitated by the wish to put things right or by the idea of decay and lack of care? Did he see the ivy that was killing so many of the trees that had been planted with the garden? He must have seen the ivy. Mrs Phillips told me one day that he liked ivy and had given instructions that the ivy was never to be cut (*EA*, p. 194).

The insistent repetition of "Did he see" and "ivy" invests this passage with a mildly obsessional quality: the more urgent the questioning, the more enigmatic and elusive the landlord appears. Naipaul derives all his information about his landlord through hearsay. His attempts to infer the nature of the landlord's character from these sources serve as a case study in the enigma that is another's personality, and the obstacles to comprehending it. Naipaul draws attention to the unreliability of his sources, by providing conflicting accounts of the occasion when the landlord fed Pitton champagne. Such is the uncertainty surrounding the character of the landlord, only ever glimpsed from a distance, that Naipaul is unable to offer a physical description of him. Naipaul leads us to doubt the reliability of his perceptions, by detailing the surreal metamorphoses his landlord undergoes in the writer's imaginings. Despite the landlord's elusiveness, Naipaul is nevertheless prepared to make assumptions about his motives. He portrays the landlord as his double, and as sharing his urge to withdraw: "I felt a great sympathy for my landlord. I felt I could understand his malaise" (*EA*, p. 53).

This speculative method, which combines respect for the enigma of otherness with what might be viewed as the antithesis of respect, resembles the artistic practices of Naipaul's friend Anthony Powell. In the person of Jenkins, the narrator of *A Dance to the Music of Time*, Powell tactfully meditates on the limitations to his understanding of the people who surround him, but this respectful approach contrasts with a tendency to satiric reductiveness in the treatment of certain characters. The country house milieu of parts of *The Enigma of Arrival* is closer to that of Powell's novels than any other of Naipaul's works. *The Enigma of*

Arrival also resembles *A Dance to the Music of Time* in the way it constructs patterns across time. It draws parallels, for instance, between the decline and fall of the Roman and British empires, and traces designs in the raw material of Naipaul's life: the motif of the journey, for example, reappears, with repeated journeys back and forth across the Atlantic measuring the progress of his evolution as a writer.

Journeys figure prominently throughout Naipaul's work: he writes of *In a Free State*, "The theme of the journey and flight recurs in my work; in this work the journeys are all final".[48] They are necessarily an important theme and structural device of his travel books. A dance is a more structured, ritualized and orderly form of activity than a journey; the destination of a journey may be planned in advance but nevertheless contain an element of indeterminacy: it may turn out to be other than what was expected, as in the case of Naipaul's journey of development as a writer. The dance forms a closed, repeating pattern: the journey an activity rather more uncertain and formless. *A Dance to the Music of Time* delineates a more orderly and circumscribed world than *The Enigma of Arrival*, although it narrates and laments the destruction of this closed world; the disruption of a social order is further advanced in *The Enigma of Arrival*.

Naipaul's gloomy awareness of the subjection of human life and endeavour to the ravages of time shows certain resemblances with the work of Vladimir Nabokov, a figure who stands closer than Powell to Naipaul's projected condition of permanent placelessness. Both present themselves as solitary, patrician types, disdainful of some of the cultural and political orthodoxies of their time. Nabokov's exile is at once spatial and linguistic, as is emphasized by the multiple textual mutations of his autobiography, *Speak, Memory*: "This re-Englishing of a Russian re-version of what had been an English re-telling of Russian memories in the first place ... "[49] Frank Kermode implies that truthfulness and stylish writing may be incompatible: "Writing well is an activity which has no simple relation to truth".[50] *Speak, Memory* makes no pretence of artlessly relaying events as they unfolded, or as they appeared to Nabokov at the time: the work draws attention to the artistry of its construction. An image of Nabokov's playful aesthetic ideals is provided by the butterflies, whose

> protective device was carried to a point of mimetic subtlety, exuberance, and luxury far in excess of a predator's power of appreciation. I discovered in nature the nonutilitarian delights that I sought in art. Both were a form of magic, both were a game of intricate enchantment and deception (Nabokov, p. 125).

On encountering a general in search of a light who, many years ago, used to perform tricks with matches, Nabokov playfully defines his artistic principles: "The following of such thematic designs through one's life should be, I think, the true purpose of autobiography" (Nabokov, p. 27). *Speak, Memory* is concerned to piece together, from the messy confusion of a life, a fixed, coherent pattern, a process symbolized towards the end of the work by the broken bowl composed of fragments of his past, which Nabokov wishfully reconstructs into an imaginary whole.

In the case of both writers, their response to exile consists in the construction of an imaginary or substitute home in words, and the imposition of order and coherence on fractured and disorderly experiences. Salman Rushdie has described how exile intensifies a tendency to retrospection:

> It may be that writers in my position, exiles or emigrants or expatriates, are haunted by some sense of loss, some urge to reclaim, to look back, even at the risk of being mutated into pillars of salt. But if we do look back, we must also do so in the knowledge — which gives rise to profound uncertainties — that our physical alienation from India almost inevitably means that we will not be capable of reclaiming precisely the thing that was lost; that we will, in short, create fictions, not actual cities or villages, but invisible ones, imaginary homelands, Indias of the mind.[51]

This suggestively defines Nabokov's practice in *Speak, Memory* — his precise recreation of the topography of his perfect childhood — and perhaps accounts for the impulse behind Naipaul's repeated need to look back on and to retell the story of his own life. He thereby constructs out of the "sacred places of [his] childhood" a "fantasy of home" (*EA*, p. 318), as if home were unattainable as anything other than an imaginary construction.

Naipaul has supplied various accounts of his personal history and development as a writer. The idea for *The Enigma of Arrival* was initially conflated with the material of what became "Prologue to an Autobiography". Plans for this work include notes on the ideas: "Mystery of arrival, anxiety to leave, fear of revisiting. Refusing to greet my aunt. Fear of entering the Lion House, Chaguanas".[52] The title of "Prologue to an Autobiography" places the work in a chronologically anterior relation to an autobiography proper. Naipaul's theme in the "Prologue" is his "literary beginnings and the imaginative promptings of my many-sided background" (*FC*, p. 9). The point at which the "Prologue" begins and, tracing a circle, ends, is the writing of *Miguel Street*. Literary influences form the work's ordering principle: it is a foregone conclusion that Naipaul will become a writer. This contrasts with Naipaul's response to a question about what it was that made him pursue a literary career:

These things always appear much more deliberate, much more planned and calculated afterward than they actually are. I went to England in 1950 to go to university and when I came down from Oxford, there was the problem of getting a job. I wanted to go to India, but I couldn't get a job in India, and I found myself hanging around in London and gradually doing radio work. Then I began writing articles and stories, and, finally, books.[53]

This indicates how the narrative of his life could be reshaped according to varying emphases.

In the same way that *The Enigma of Arrival* is strikingly self-effacing as an autobiography, "Prologue to an Autobiography" is less concerned with his own actions or motives than with those of the people who surrounded him as a child: it describes the life of his father and of members of the Hindu community in Trinidad. Naipaul tells his father's story twice in the course of the "Prologue": the first time from the point of view, broadly, of his understanding of events as a child; the second in the light of the "proper wonder at his [Seepersad's] achievement" (*FC*, p. 67) which Naipaul has retrospectively attained. The "Prologue", too, testifies to a distance between the earlier and later opinions of V. S. Naipaul. It stands in a very close relation to *A House for Mr Biswas*, which in a fictional form more fully explores and acknowledges Naipaul's debt of influence to his father: the "Prologue" revisits the autobiographical sources of the novel, and is influenced by the process of the writing of the novel, echoing it in many places. As mentioned above, "Prologue to an Autobiography" did not emerge directly from the writing of *A House for Mr Biswas*, but is a revised version of an attempt to construct a narrative out of his family past, entitled "A Visit to Valsayn Park" (1972–3).[54] "Prologue to an Autobiography" works backwards; "Valsayn Park" starts off with Naipaul's great-grandmother making the Indian middle passage. It constructs a different account of his family's past: "certain things are suppressed" (*ibid*) in family histories, Naipaul remarks; here he relates a story he later excised about his father's flight from his first marriage, which is indirectly recalled in Biswas's initial effort to escape his marriage to Shama. "Valsayn Park" is less concerned than the "Prologue" with Naipaul's development as a writer: its emphasis is on his discovery of a new way of looking at his community, through a reading of his father's journalism.

When planning *Guerrillas*, he experimented with a narrative about a character called Anil whose experiences closely resemble the detail of his own life: ultimately they were ascribed to Indar in *A Bend in the River*. Anil has come to England to study at Oxford. The narrative relates Anil's disappointment with England, and concentrates on his panic at the prospect of job-hunting. He works on a farm: "During this month he learnt the meaning of summer: until then he had been indifferent to the seasons".[55] He turns his experiences into writing, and is astonished

> that experience so recent and painful could be so trans-
> formed. . . . He felt he had pulled off some remarkable piece of
> sleight of hand; and the most remarkable in his judgement was
> the suppression of himself as narrator (*ibid*).

In an abandoned draft of *Guerrillas* (1972–3), Naipaul reworked the ideas, moving in and out of the first person, and ascribing them to a character called Krishan as well as to Anil. These fragments sketch out *The Enigma of Arrival*'s themes of disappointment, false expectations and an initial incapacity to read his environment: "Four years before, . . . Oxford had glittered, and I had felt that I would glitter with it".[56]

> There were no beautiful buildings where I had been born; my
> eye had not developed; and the city that the tourist came to see
> was for me an empty decaying one; as London itself had been,
> melancholy, the scene of past glory, so that again I had the
> feeling, as I always had, of arriving too late everywhere. . . . [T]
> o me grandeur was bigness. . . . [I]t did not occur to me that the
> world which I had hoped to enter was disappearing (*ibid*).

At the beginning of the typescript, Naipaul, somewhat enigmatically, has noted by hand: "The mystery of arrival now inseparable from the impossibility of departure" (*ibid*). The resemblance of this phrase to the title of *The Enigma of Arrival* invites comparisons. The idea that departure is impossible is echoed in the finished work by the reference to the de Chirico painting, which Naipaul interprets as depicting a traveller whose ship has left without him. In another fragment written at this time, Anil has a "confused vision of his own future as one of unending desolation" (*ibid*). Another narrative on this theme intersperses self-pity with social comedy, satirizing one of Anil's interviewers, who appears to lead a circumscribed and secure existence similar to Mr Stone's in *Mr Stone and the Knights Companion*.

The mutability of the identity of the narrator of these experiences can be interpreted as signalling the closeness of the links between Naipaul's fiction and his life. The experiences do not seem to grow out of a conception of a particular character: instead, he gives the impression that he is struggling to find a character to fit the experiences. These plans and fragments indicate the importance of autobiographical material to Naipaul's work, and show a pronounced consistency of purpose — he appears to have meditated on the material of *The Enigma of Arrival* for nearly fifteen years before it appeared in its present form. In a draft of *The Enigma of Arrival*, Naipaul reflected on the nature of identity and on the relations between a writer's work and life:

> It isn't that writers have one story to tell and keep on telling it all their lives. That is nonsense, especially, I think, in my case, where many of the problems of composition and construction have had to do with the assimilation of new material It is, rather, that certain words recur.... . [W]e are made at an early age; there are certain tensions ... that link the elderly man to the middle-aged, the middle-aged to the young, the young man to the adolescent. Our nervous excitations are like finger prints; they remain constant.[57]

This ambivalent passage links such recurrences with the autobiographical sources of his work. Both involve the notion of identity: his works show a consistency in their concerns, among which is found a desire to construct narratives of his own identity. These works furnish modified versions of his own life, and the relations between them are shaped by an interplay of variation and repetition, consistency and change.

This book seeks to show that autobiographical material is at the heart of his fiction and non-fiction. His travel books on India are framed by discussions of his Indian ancestry; *A Middle Passage* begins by examining his relation to the Caribbean. His early fiction foreshadows and paves the way for the overtly biographical *A House for Mr Biswas*. Works which seem to stand in a more obscure relation to his life are obliquely autobiographical. Naipaul contends that *In a Free State*

> distils my own experience of coming to a place like England, in a way it is my own life, you know. This is the essence of writing fiction, one doesn't report one's experience, one distils it, one tries to find ways of expressing it. The beauty of fiction is that one can do it through other people.[58]

Naipaul states that *Mr Stone and the Knights Companion* is a more personal work, and one less concerned with the condition of England than it may appear. He argues that it is concerned with the frustrations of creation and the passing of time.[59] Judith Levy[60] identifies as a fundamental impulse of his work the urge to create an autobiography to serve as a myth of origin. She argues that such a myth is inaccessible to Naipaul as a consequence of his situation of cultural dislocation, and that, as a result, he writes frustrated, indirect and incomplete autobiographies.

Mark McWatt has propounded the view that fictional autobiography is a new form developed in response to the peculiar nature of Caribbean experience, citing *The Enigma of Arrival* as an example.[61] McWatt's contention may be worth comparing with countless assertions on Naipaul's part, from the later part of his career, that the novel is dead — "So that work's been done; the novel has done that elucidation of what it is to be alive in a modern society"[62] — and of a need for innovatory forms to meet the challenges of new experiences and societies: "I hate the word novel. I can no longer understand why it is important to write or read invented stories. . . . I don't see reading as an act of drugging oneself with a narrative".[63]

> The dominant form at the beginning of the nineteenth century was the essay, surely. And then it altered. Because the novel became the way people could deliver truths they couldn't in any other way about society. . . . The novel form has done its work.[64]

He describes

> the feeling of artificiality which was with me at the very beginning, when I was trying to write and wondering what part of my experience could be made to fit the form — wondering, in fact, in the most insidious way, how I could adapt or falsify my experience to make it fit the grand form. . . .

> I have always been concerned about this problem of form, and even of vocabulary, because I fairly soon got to realize that between the literature I knew and read, the literature that seeded my own ambition, between that and my background, there was a division, a dissonance.[65]

Landeg White identifies as a central aesthetic crux in the novels of Naipaul's early and middle period the disparity between the forms he employs and the lives of his characters (White, pp. 13–14). The formal innovations of more recent works, which blend fiction and non-fiction, can be seen as a response to this disparity. Cultural dislocation is not only the subject of *The Enigma of Arrival*, but is reflected in its form. The present discussion raises certain questions regarding the work's form by considering what Naipaul describes as a novel in the context of autobiography. The subtitle signals a desire on his part to absolve himself from any requirement of fidelity to the facts — permitting him to invent, and to preserve his privacy intact. The autobiographical form is widely understood to promise a greater degree of self-revelation than the novel is likely to provide, although the discussions by Kermode and Sturrock show that the artifices of the form may be at odds with a full and honest representation of the self. Naipaul has declared himself reluctant to engage in the pretence of intimate self-revelation that would constitute an autobiography.

Mark McWatt touches on this dialectic of disclosure and concealment in *The Enigma of Arrival*. He sees the work as moving towards increased self-revelation only to undermine the possibility of such knowledge. If the first section focuses on the object of Naipaul's perceptions, an object external to himself, the second section makes the self who perceives the object of his scrutiny. Such is the work's sense of the provisionality of all conclusions, however, that by the end it is not only the personality of others, but of Naipaul himself, which remains an enigma. McWatt concludes that *The Enigma of Arrival* explores "the area of uncertainty and overlap between fiction and the idea of autobiography".[66] It is a commonplace of contemporary thought that the notion of a continuous, coherent self is a reassuring fiction, and one which the autobiographical form serves to promote. This is a respect in which all autobiographies contain elements of fiction.

Naipaul's comments on autobiographies indicate that he finds a thematic patterning, in defiance of the logic of chronology, the most satisfactory approach to the writing of a life. Reviewing Philip Callow's *Native Ground*, he contends,

> The effect is as satisfying as that of a connected narrative; perhaps more so, for autobiographical details easily become blurred, whereas each of Mr Callow's snapshots is wonderfully clear.[67]

"A Handful of Dust: Return to Guiana" revisits some of the themes of Naipaul's portrait of the country in *The Middle Passage*, in order to revise the earlier account. "I wrote more romantically than I actually felt about the African or black racial movement of the late 1950s".[68] Naipaul's views may have changed, but Cheddi Jagan's remain constant; Naipaul argues that such consistency, this refusal to let a changing world unsettle his theoretical beliefs, represents a weakness on Jagan's part. Naipaul treats Jagan's *The West on Trial* as an autobiography, although the book might better be read as a work of political polemic. Naipaul sees analogies between his own situation and Jagan's: he writes of "the *lostness* of a young man in those days coming out of a background without a literary culture".[69] Naipaul argues that, as a result of his background, Jagan lacked the means to see and understand his surroundings when living in the U. S. — a similar analysis to that which he proposes, in *India: A Wounded Civilisation*, for Gandhi's response to England. Of the narrative of the first twenty-five years of Jagan's life, condensed into as many pages, Naipaul judges that "the reader cannot keep it all in his head; he cannot (any more than the writer can) make all the connections".[70]

Naipaul's observations on this text are of interest in view of the influence exerted on *The Mimic Men* by the shape of Jagan's political career. The inspiration for the political action of the novel was furnished by events in what was then British Guiana: the alliance between Indian- and African-backed politicians in an anti-colonial protest which subsequently broke down into racial conflict; the controversies over bauxite royalties and the nationalization of sugar. The tension between British Guiana's East Indian majority and African minority, which reached a crisis at the time of Trinidad's acquisition of independence, served to heighten the fears of Trinidad's Indians about their fate under self-rule, and may have formed part of the background to Naipaul's political views. Jagan's career invited meditation on the nature of power: Jagan describes his People's Progressive Party as, during the period 1957–64, "in office but not in power",[71] since "real power remained in the hands of the Governor" (Jagan, p. 226). While Jagan's contention implies that external interference is the only obstacle to self-government, Naipaul suggests that there is something inherent in the colonial situation which renders independence a farce. Recalling the imagery of *A Flag on the Island* — which suggests that symbols of nationhood are insufficient in themselves to summon a nation into being — and bringing to mind Fanon's proposition that the independence of post-colonial nations risks amounting to no more than a "fancy-dress parade",[72] *The Mimic Men* portrays Singh's power as a fraud, and Isabella's independence as posited on empty signifiers:

> It was part of our innocence that at the beginning we should have considered applause and the smell of sweat as the only source of power. It took us no time to see that we depended on what was no more than a mob, and that our hold on the mob was the insecure one of words. I went a little beyond this. I saw that in our situation the mob, without skills, was unproductive, offered nothing, and was in the end without power. The mob might burn down the city. But the mob is shot down, and the power of money will cause the city to be built again. In the moment of victory we had wondered why no one had called our bluff. Soon we saw that there had been no need, that our power was air (*MM*, p. 245).

The notion of a power based exclusively on the use of words is one that brings to mind the position of the writer. It is through the exercise of the writer's art that Ralph constructs the kind of order which as a politician he was only able to destroy. He provides in his writing the controlled evocation of a collapse into chaos: the narration remains detached from the turmoil depicted. Derek Walcott comments on this disparity between form and content: "Here is a celebration of inertia in a powerful style, a despair that has syntactical confidence".[73]

The West on Trial provides an account of the events which furnished the source of the political action of *The Mimic Men*,[74] but the contrasts between the two works are more noteworthy than their similarities are. While an account of Jagan's political career is at the centre of his book, and his personal life is afforded only an occasional mention, the emphasis is reversed in *The Mimic Men*: the private life is all, and political events — "that period in parenthesis" (*MM*, p. 38) — are relegated to its periphery. In contrast to *The West on Trial*, *The Mimic Men* resolutely resists following the order of chronological succession. It repeatedly returns to the point at which Ralph is writing, in his hotel in the Home Counties. The work begins at the period when Ralph was a student, incorporating the subject of a postwar convergence of peoples on London which, in *The Enigma of Arrival*, Naipaul reproaches himself for not having written about; it shifts to the imaginary island of Isabella, at first in order to depict the period after Ralph's return from England, and then to depict his childhood; it subsequently turns its attention to Ralph's political career, before finally working back to its starting-point — Ralph at the moment of writing. The work is held together by a vision of universal desolation, shipwreck and disorder: a consistency of mood and theme links this disparate and fragmentary material. It is also shaped by the developing sense of a coherent personality. Ralph traces analogies between his childhood and maturity:

> My later career as a public speaker and handler of men surprised many and was seen by some as a violent breaking out of character. It did not appear so to me. The public speaker was only another version of the absurd schoolboy cricketer, self-consciousness suppressed, the audience ignored, at the nets of Isabella Imperial (*MM*, p. 136).

The cohesiveness of Ralph's account of his life bears the imprint of an artful shaping, designed to expel the messy redundancy of life.

The Mimic Men is included in the present discussion by virtue not only of its form — it is a novel masquerading as an autobiography — but also of the analogies between Ralph's life and Naipaul's. As described in chapter one of this book, *The Mimic Men* reworks some of the autobiographical material used in *A House for Mr Biswas*, but in a less respectful and tender manner. Ralph records a sense of the unreality of his education and of his peripheral condition, a sense shared by both Biswas and his author:

> We, here on our island, handling books printed in this world, and using its goods, had been abandoned and forgotten. We

pretended to be real, to be learning, to be preparing ourselves for life, we mimic men of the New World, one unknown corner of it, with all its reminders of the corruption that came so quickly to the new (*MM*, p. 175).

Shipwreck is an image Ralph Singh employs on several occasions in order to express his sense of abandonment: "My own journey, scarcely begun, had ended in the shipwreck which all my life I had sought to avoid".[75] Ralph's sense of shipwreck is echoed by Hok's (*MM*, p. 117), and imaged by some driftwood on a beach (*MM*, pp. 128, 212). This can be compared with the scene depicted in the de Chirico painting, which Naipaul describes as the germ of *The Enigma of Arrival*: a painting which he sees as portraying a traveller who finds that his ship home has departed. This sensation characterizes Ralph's experience of London as well as Isabella.

> Shipwreck: I have used this word before. With my island background, it was the word that always came to me. And this was what I felt I had encountered again in the great city: this feeling of being adrift, a cell of perception, little more, that might be altered, if only fleetingly, by any encounter (*MM*, p. 32).

The Mimic Men anticipates *The Enigma of Arrival* in recording London's failure to live up to Ralph's expectations:

> Here was the city, the world. I waited for the flowering to come to me. . . . Excitement! Its heart must have lain somewhere. But the god of the city was elusive. The tram was filled with individuals, each man returning to his own cell (*MM*, p. 23).

This reiterates the contention of Naipaul's article "London" — an echo which confirms the importance of the autobiographical sources of the novel:

> The privacy of the big city depresses me. There are no communal pleasures in London. . . . However gay the musical or farce, however good the acting, you come out alone into the cold streets, private, sitting in a bus full of grim people who have left their pleasure behind them in the theatre (*OB*, p. 15).

The experience of exile is represented as leading to an enhanced impression of the unreality of the self: Ralph refers to "the injury inflicted on me by the too solid three-dimensional city in which I could never feel myself as anything but spectral, disintegrating, pointless, fluid" (*MM*, p. 61). This is the reverse of Jacobson's notion that his own reality was confirmed by inhabiting a world he had read about. *The*

Mimic Men describes the colonial situation and England in similar terms. "To be born on an island like Isabella, an obscure New World transplantation, second-hand and barbarous, was to be born to disorder" (*MM*, p. 141). England offers no respite, only "the greater disorder, the final emptiness: London and the home counties" (*MM*, p. 11).

The work proposes a connection between displacement and disorder: the attempt to flee displacement by going into exile and exposing oneself to further dislocation is therefore inevitably doomed. Sketching out the concerns of the book he has set out to write, Ralph asserts,

> It was my hope to give expression to the restlessness, the deep disorder, which the great explorations, the overthrow in three continents of established social organizations, the unnatural bringing together of peoples who could achieve fulfilment only within the security of their own societies and the landscapes hymned by their ancestors, it was my hope to give partial expression to the restlessness which this great upheaval has brought about (*MM*, p. 38).

Ralph may feel he has not written this book, but the statement defines the abiding preoccupations of Naipaul's opus. Naipaul portrays the tumult of post-colonial politics as a direct consequence of such uprootings, arguing, through his narrator,

> that in a society like ours, fragmented, inorganic, no link between man and the landscape, a society not held together by common interests, there was no true internal source of power, and that no power was real which did not come from the outside (*MM*, p. 246).

The dereliction associated with placelessness is the antithesis of the harmonious relation to the land which Naipaul sees as symbolized by the figure of Jack — "man fitting the landscape" (*EA*, p. 19) — and into which Naipaul feels he is reborn in Wiltshire, where he finds himself "in tune with a landscape in a way that I had never been in Trinidad or India" (*EA*, p. 157).

Ralph states that his aim is "to impose order on my own history, to abolish that disturbance which is what a narrative in sequence might have led me to" (*MM*, p. 292). Naipaul, comparably, includes among a statement of his artistic goals an aspiration to "reconstruct my disintegrated society, to impose order on the world, to seek patterns".[76] *The Enigma of Arrival* similarly involves an endeavour to eradicate disorder while, by its structural discontinuities, bearing witness to the persistence of that disorder. It at once disowns and asserts a connection with an earlier self, finding it necessary to relegate this self to a section of its own, "The Journey". His multiple reworkings of the materials of his life suggest, moreover, the provisionality of constructions of the self. They lead to the inference that the self is open to variable interpretations, and that the writing of autobiography is for Naipaul an ongoing project of self-reinvention.

Notes

1   Interviewed by Aamer Hussein, "Delivering the Truth", *Times Literary Supplement* (September 2 1994), p. 4.

2   *In a Free State* (London: André Deutsch, 1971), p. 77.

3   "London Letter: The Old Houses Go", *Illustrated Weekly of India*, 85 (April 26 1964), p. 21.

4   "London Letter: The Christmas Spirit", *Illustrated Weekly of India*, 84 (December 22 1963), p. 25.

5   "London Letter: A Return to England", *Illustrated Weekly of India*, 84 (April 14 1963), p. 21.

6   "London: The New Developments", *Illustrated Weekly of India*, 84 (May 12 1963), p. 14.

7   "London Letter: The Christmas Spirit", p. 25.

8   "What's Wrong With Being a Snob?", Hamner, p. 36.

9   *Time of Arrival and Other Essays* (London: Weidenfeld and Nicolson, 1953), p. 37.

10   "Without a Dog's Chance", *New York Review of Books*, 19 (18 May 1972), p. 31.

11   "Without a Dog's Chance", p. 29.

12   "Without a Dog's Chance", p. 29.

13   "Without a Dog's Chance", p. 30.

14   "Without a Dog's Chance", p. 30.

15   *Smile Please: An Unfinished Autobiography* (London: André Deutsch, 1979), p. 63.

16   *Smile Please*, p. 64.

17   *Smile Please*, p. 97.

18   *Smile Please*, p. 142.

19   *Smile Please*, p. 124.

20   *Smile Please*, p. 168.

21   *Caribbean Voices* (May 1 1955), p. 1, BBC Written Archives.

22   *Caribbean Voices* (April 26 1953), p. 11, BBC Written Archives.

23   *Beyond a Boundary* (London: Hutchinson, 1963), p. 28.

24   *Beyond a Boundary*, p. 115.

25   "New Novels", *New Statesman*, 56 (December 6 1958), p. 827.

26   *The Pleasures of Exile* (London: Allison and Busby, 1984), p. 25.

27   *The Pleasures of Exile*, p. 25.

28   *The Pleasures of Exile*, p. 27.

29   *The Pleasures of Exile*, p. 49.

30   *The Pleasures of Exile*, p. 27.

31   *Imaginary Homelands*, p. 280.

32   "Some Thoughts on Being a Writer", *Chronicles: A Magazine of American Culture*, 11, 15 (May 1987), p. 14.

33   Interviewed by Bharati Mukherjee and Robert Boyers, "A Conversation with V. S. Naipaul", *Salmagundi*, 54 (Fall 1981), p. 11.

34 "Version of Pastoral", *London Review of Books*, 9 (April 2 1987), p. 17.
35 Samuel Taylor Coleridge, *Biographia Literaria: or Biographical Sketches of My Literary Life and Opinions,* vol. 2, ed. by James Engell and W. Jackson Bate. *The Collected Works of Samuel Taylor Coleridge*, vol. 7 (London: Routledge and Kegan Paul, 1983; Princeton: Princeton University Press, 1983), p. 14.
36 "Memory and Autobiography", *Raritan*, 15, 1 (Summer 1995), pp. 36–50.
37 *The Language of Autobiography: Studies in the First Person Singular* (Cambridge: Cambridge University Press, 1993), p. 6.
38 *The Prelude*, 1805 text, ed. by Jonathan Wordsworth, M.H. Abrams and Stephen Gill (London: Norton, 1979), Book 2, ines 28–33.
39 *The English Poems of George Herbert,* ed. C.A. Patrides (London: Dent, 1974), lines 15–16.
40 *Sir Walter Raleigh: Selected Writings*, ed. Gerald Hammond (Manchester: Carcanet, 1984), p.61. Nicholas Spice cites this work in a review of *A Way in the World* , in order to illustrate a kinship between the tenor of Naipaul's story concerning Ralegh and that of Ralegh's poetry: "Inspector of the Sad Parade", *London Review of Books*, 16, 15 (August 4 1994), p. 11.
41 Interviewed by Charles Michener, p. 108.
42 "The Ruined Cottage", 231–4, in *William Wordsworth* (The Oxford Authors), ed. by Stephen Gill (Oxford: Oxford University Press, 1984).
43 Notebook containing plans for *EA*, V. S. Naipaul Archive, II, 14:1.
44 "The Garden Path", *New Republic*, 196, 15 (April 13 1987), p. 28.
45 "Naipaul or Rushdie", *Southwest Review* 76, 3 (Summer 1991), p. 382.
46 "Rites of Resistance: Counter Discourse and West Indian Biography", *Journal of West Indian Literature*, 3, 1 (January 1989), pp. 28–46.
47 "Rites of Resistance", p. 39.
48 Blurb for *IFS*, André Deutsch Archive, 96, *IFS* folder.
49 *Speak, Memory: An Autobiography Revisited*, rev. ed. (London: Weidenfeld and Nicolson, 1967), p. 12.
50 "Memory and Autobiography", p. 37.
51 *Imaginary Homelands*, p. 10.
52 Handwritten loose sheets, containing plans for "Prologue to an Autobiography", 1972, V. S. Naipaul Archive, I, 1:3.
53 Interview, "V. S. Naipaul Tells How Writing Changes a Writer", *Tapia* (December 2 1973), p. 11.
54 Typescript, V. S. Naipaul Archive, I, 1:3.
55 Notebook, 1972–4, containing plans for *G*, V. S. Naipaul Archive, II, 3:4.
56 Typed manuscript of an abandoned draft of *G*, 1972–3, V. S. Naipaul Archive, II, 3:5.
57 Notebook, 1984, containing draft of *EA*, V. S. Naipaul Archive, II, 14:4.
58 Interviewed by Margaret Drabble, *Bookcase* (November 26 1971), Transcript of BBC broadcast, André Deutsch Archive, 96, *IFS* folder.
59 Interviewed by Francis Wyndham, *The World of Books* (June 7 1963), BBC Written Archives.
60 *V. S. Naipaul: Displacement and Autobiography* (New York and London: Garland, 1995).
61 "The West Indian Writer and the Self: Recent 'Fictional Autobiography' by Naipaul and Harris", *Journal of West Indian Literature*, 3, 1 (January 1989), pp. 16–27.
62 Interviewed by Andrew Robinson, "Andrew Robinson meets V. S. Naipaul", *Literary Review*, 148 (October 1990), p. 24.
63 Interviewed by Ahmed Rashid, "Death of the Novel", *Observer Review* (February 25 1996), p. 16.

64   Interviewed by Aamer Hussein, p. 3.

65   "Some Thoughts on Being a Writer", pp. 13–14.

66   "The West Indian Writer and the Self", p. 26.

67   "New Fiction", *New Statesman*, 57 (May 16 1959), p. 700.

68   "A Handful of Dust: Return to Guiana", *New York Review of Books*, 38 (April 11 1991), p. 16.

69   "A Handful of Dust", p. 18.

70   "A Handful of Dust", p. 19.

71   *The West on Trial: My Fight for Guyana's Freedom* (London: Michael Joseph, 1966), p. 224.

72   *The Wretched of the Earth*, tr. by Constance Farrington (Harmondsworth: Penguin, 1967), p. 118.

73   "Is V. S. Naipaul an Angry Young Man?", *Trinidad Guardian* (August 6 1967), p. 10.

74   *The West on Trial* was published the year before *The Mimic Men*.

75   *MM*, p. 10; the novel circles back to the image at pp. 134, 141, 214. See also John Thieme, "A Hindu Castaway: Ralph Singh's Journey in *The Mimic Men* ", *Modern Fiction Studies*, 30, 3 (Autumn 1984), pp. 505–18.

76   Interviewed by Adrian Rowe-Evans, p. 52.

* Parts of Chapter 2 appeared earlier in an article entitled "Tradition, innovation and the representation of England in Naipaul's *The Enigma of Arrival*" published in *The Journal of Commonwealth Literature*, XXXII, 2, 1997.

History and repetition in *The Loss of El Dorado* and *A Way in the World*

The epigraph to *A Way in the World* is taken from Tennyson's *In Memoriam*:

> And year by year our memory fades
> From all the circle of the hills. (CI)

Naipaul then adds the stanza which precedes these lines in Tennyson's poem, leading to some confusion of meaning:

> Till from the garden and the wild
> A fresh association blow,
> And year by year the landscape grow
> Familiar to the stranger's child. (CI)

The passage alludes to the Tennyson family's move from Somersby, a site cherished by Tennyson for its associations with the memory of Hallam. *In Memoriam* is broadly analogous in structure with *A Way in the World*: both comprise a sequence of loosely linked material, tied together by verbal echo, and by recurring themes and images; and both look back to the past to seek out evidence of constancy, and continuity, in change. Both works balance linear progression against a circling back on themselves. Naipaul, however, has not tended to represent his native Trinidad as a place where he ever felt at home.

> I had never wanted to stay in Trinidad. When I was in the fourth form I wrote a vow on the endpaper of my Kennedy's *Revised Latin Primer* to leave within five years. I left after six; and for many years afterwards in England, falling asleep in bedsitters with the electric fire on, I had been awakened by the nightmare that I was back in tropical Trinidad (*MP*, p. 41).

One aspect of what Naipaul does in *A Way in the World* is to construct an imaginative homeland of his native land, by means of an excavation of the island's and the author's past.

A Way in the World is concerned, centrally, with revisitings. It begins with a description of the defamiliarizing effect produced by a six years' absence from Trinidad. The second section, "History: *A Smell of Fish*

Glue'', describes Naipaul's progressive alienation from his native land. It portrays Naipaul's first revisiting, when he finds the people and place transformed by agitation for independence: "In some such way every black or African person from my past altered. And I felt a double distance from what I had known".[1] This would appear to account for the allusion to Tennyson. "Now on this return I felt it had passed to other hands" (*WW*, p. 33). Naipaul has repeatedly been drawn to the theme of revisitings: The long short story which provides the title for Naipaul's collection of short stories, *A Flag on the Island*, for example, centres on Frank's return to an imaginary Caribbean island; *The Middle Passage* describes Naipaul's revisiting of the West Indies; *India: A Million Mutinies Now* reconsiders his two earlier books on the subject; "Prologue to an Autobiography" revisits the territory of *A House for Mr Biswas*.

A *Way in the World* reworks material used in other books. It encroaches on the subject-matter of *The Enigma of Arrival*, which also portrays return journeys to Trinidad and imparts Naipaul's feeling of displacement in his native island. More importantly, *A Way in the World* reworks the material of *The Loss of El Dorado* — in particular, its historical fictions concerning Walter Ralegh's and Francisco de Miranda's sojourns in the West Indies. *A Way in the World* interlards these historical episodes with contemporary, non-fictional material, which echoes their themes: the figure of the "revolutionary as damaged man"[2] recurs. Naipaul portrays his revolutionary fraudsters in a manner which, in John Updike's words, "mixes sympathy and irony somewhat enigmatically".[3] Naipaul's sympathy for his subjects, especially Miranda and Lebrun (the itinerant revolutionary theorist in *A Way in the World*), is characterized by a tendency to recognize himself in them: they mirror his own position, as "an exile, a maimed man".[4] *A Way in the World* plays a part in Naipaul's continuing project of self-understanding, and once more reworks the material of his own life.

There is an interpenetration of the personal and the political in *A Way in the World*: self-exploration is implicated in an archaeological process of delving into cultural inheritances, and into the collective memories that are history. The work's characters resemble Blair, who comes "trailing all the strands of his own complicated past" (*WW*, p. 25). A description of the destruction caused by an outbreak of looting in Port of Spain maps out the trajectory of the book.

> You could see down to what might have been thought buried forever: the thick-walled eighteenth-century Spanish foundations of some buildings. You could see the low gable marks of early, small buildings against higher walls. You could look

down, in fact, at more than Spanish foundations: you could look down at red Amerindian soil (*WW*, pp. 40–1).

The sentence is distinguished by a return to the anchors ''You could see'' and ''You could look down''. *A Way in the World* does for Trinidad what *A Turn in the South* earlier did for the American South, exploring the various strata of a complex past: ''I had a sense of the history here resting layer upon layer. The Indians, disappearing after centuries; the poor whites; the blacks''.[5] The inhabitants of both places feel the past as a wound. Naipaul provides another, overlapping account of the shape of *A Way in the World*'s historical explorations, which take as their starting-point the nationalist agitation he refers to as ''the sacrament of the square'':

> There was an immense chain of events. You could start with the sacrament of the square and work back: to the black madmen on the benches, the Indian destitutes, the plantations, the wilderness, the aboriginal settlements, the discovery. And you could move forward from that exaltation and that mood of rejection to the nihilism of the moment (*WW*, p. 40).

Nicholas Spice suggests that *A Way in the World* ''enacts an understanding of history as recapitulation in variation'', and structures its material through ''evolution and return'' (Spice, p. 10). By juxtaposing apparently fragmented material, it encourages the seeking out of connections between its various sections. Echoes, recapitulations and correspondences cut across temporal difference and the various sections of the book; and the work is held together, not by narrative, but by thematic consistency: ''The themes repeat''.[6] Repetition also functions as a stylistic principle in this work. The shape of Naipaul's sentences mirrors the structure of the work as a whole. Its area of interest, and associative logic, are evoked by means of multiplying ramifications:

> As soon as you tried to enter that idea [of a recent, wiped-out past], it ramified. And it ramified more and more as your understanding grew: different people living for centuries where we now trod, with our own overwhelming concerns: different people, with their own calendar and reverences and ideas of human association, different houses or huts, different roads or paths, different crops and fields and vegetation (and seasons), different views, speeds, reasons for journeys, different ideas of the ages of man, different ideas of the enemy and fellowship and sanctity and what men owed themselves (*WW,* pp. 208–9).

The recurring "different" serves, as a constant element, to contain the centrifugal tendencies of the sentence, providing a stable framework on which to hang its propensity for diversification.

The book starts with a seventeen-year-old Naipaul working in the Red House, Trinidad's Registry Office, and repeatedly reverts to this point of departure.[7] The place is a literal repository of the island's history, and the point from which the associations made by the book radiate: "All the records of the colony were there, all the births, deaths, deeds, transfers of property and slaves, all the life of the island for the century and a half of the colonial time" (*WW*, p. 21). This description is recalled at a later point in the work:

> I remembered the smell of the fish glue in which I had worked; and thought of the dimly lit, airless, oddly quiet vault, full of paper, where I had been told all the records of the British Colony were stored, all the records, that is, since 1797, records of surveys and property transactions and then the records, starting later, of births and deaths, together with a copy of everything that had been printed in the colony (*WW*, p. 39).

By the time we read the second passage, it is not only Naipaul, but also the reader, who remembers the Registry Office. The work makes remembering its theme, and is constructed in such a way as to make demands on the reader's memory. Naipaul has stated,

> I like to repeat things in different ways. I like the reader to remember. Miranda's story is done four times. The idea is that an illusion of knowledge makes it easier for the reader to approach unfamiliar material.[8]

The understanding and interpretation of a literary text involve, not only a chronological reading, but also the drawing of non-chronological connections, cutting back and forth across the text, in an effort to apprehend its pattern and underlying structure. The fragmented and disparate elements of *A Way in the World* insistently require that the reader, by means of a tracing of connections within and across sections, furnish the coherence the book's fragmentation may obscure.

The shape of the lives of its characters is also characterized by recapitulation. Naipaul notes that, as he grows old, Lebrun comes to resemble the Spanish-American revolutionaries he has written about in his first book: Naipaul comments on "a circularity in human lives" (*WW*, p. 129). Lebrun, in later years, is prone to the "racial feelings" (*WW*, p. 129) he has earlier sought to flee. It is not only the author who revisits Trinidad; Naipaul pictures the year Miranda spends in Trinidad as a "homecoming" (*WW*, pp. 261, 266), a return to the circumscribed dereliction of colonial society: "It's as if after half a lifetime I have made a circular journey back to what I was" (*WW*, p. 310). Ralegh's life forms a comparable pattern: the story in *A Way in the World* centres on his revisiting of the mouth of the Orinoco after twenty-three years, and his subsequent return to another imprisonment in England. The concluding section of *A Way in the World* ends with Naipaul imagining Blair's body making a "ceremonial return" (*WW*, p. 369) to Trinidad.

In *A Way in the World*, Naipaul reverts to the concerns of *The Loss of El Dorado*, and, although twenty-five years separate the two works, there is more evidence of a steadfastness in Naipaul's views than of any radical shift in emphasis. In *The Loss of El Dorado*, Naipaul elaborated a reading of West Indian history as a history of waste, farce, defeat, fraudulence and dereliction. "How can the history of this West Indian futility be written?" (*MP*, p. 28) Naipaul had asked. "History is built around achievement and creation; and nothing was created in the West Indies" (*MP*, p. 29). *The Loss of El Dorado* makes use of an ironic tone and a fractured structure in order to convey this futility. *The Loss of El Dorado* is divided between two periods when, in Naipaul's view, Trinidad was touched by history, or by contact with a wider world: the first when the island was used as a base by Spanish and English adventurers for the exploration of El Dorado; the second when, under British rule, and on its way to becoming a slave colony, Trinidad was used to foment revolution in Spanish-America. In between and after these episodes, the island drops out of history (*LED*, p. 315), and becomes "an outpost, a backwater" (*LED*, p. 316).

The centrality of the notion of dereliction to Naipaul's rendering of West Indian reality is indicated by the emblematic figure of the old Indian man he encounters in Surinam, described in *The Middle Passage*.[9]

> A derelict man in a derelict land; a man discovering himself, with surprise and resignation, lost in a landscape which had never ceased to be unreal because the scene of an enforced and always temporary residence; the slaves kidnapped from one continent and abandoned on the unprofitable plantations of another, from which there could never more be escape (*MP*, p. 190).

In *The Loss of El Dorado*, as elsewhere in Naipaul's work, the image of shipwreck expresses his sense of the West Indian desolation. He explores the significance of *Robinson Crusoe* — a founding myth of West Indian history: in *A Way in the World*, Miranda is described as a "man marooned" (*WW*, p. 239) on Trinidad; and Lebrun, an educated black man born early in the century, is another of these "shipwrecked men" (*WW*, p. 119). In the years between the two historical periods on which

Naipaul concentrates in *The Loss of El Dorado*, "the Spaniards lived like shipwrecked people, close to nature, concerned only with survival" (*LED*, p. 97). The colony is neglected, a forgotten part of a vast empire: "No Spanish ships came that way. Berrio and his Spaniards, like shipwrecked men, lived off the land" (*LED*, p. 31). The dereliction of the Spaniards is echoed by that of the Chinese, translated to an alien environment as part of a misguided scheme to create a peasantry (*LED*, p. 270). The indentured Indian labourers form "a new human dereliction, in the pattern of what had gone before" (*LED*, p. 318).

Naipaul is sceptical about the belief in Arcadias, but *The Loss of El Dorado* at one point describes the New World as an Arcadia defiled:

> El Dorado, which had begun as a search for gold, was becoming something more. It was becoming a New World romance, a dream of Shangri-la, the complete, unviolated world. Such a world had existed and the Spaniards had violated it. Now, with a sense of loss that quickened their imagination, the Spaniards wished to have the adventure again (*LED*, p. 22).

The work furnishes a narrative of botched actions, of ineptitude, greed and brutality, in tones of sustained irony. Its ironies turn on a disjunction of aspiration from achievement, intention from outcome — a mode dependent on the advantages of hindsight. "Columbus and Crusoe", written in the course of the composition of *The Loss of El Dorado*, prefigures its tone: the Indies, where Columbus "thought he had discovered the Terrestrial Paradise, had become, largely through his example, *anus mundi*" (*OB*, p. 204). Naipaul exercises his ironies at the expense, for example, of Sir Robert Dudley's heroic posturings when he visits Trinidad. He confers with some locals.

> One of the Indians spoke Spanish. A warning sign; but Dudley asked him whether there wasn't a gold mine in the neighbourhood. The Indian said he would lead them to it right away. He led them on an eight-mile walk along the shore to the place where foreigners usually dug for gold. Wyatt and his friends dug up quantities of sand and marcasite. Each man shouldered a load and walked back eight miles to the ship (*LED*, p. 35).

The comedy of this passage results from the cross-cultural misunderstanding, and the disparity between the Englishmen's, and our own, sense of the worth of their actions. Dudley is well-pleased by his achievement, and sets about erecting a plaque to himself. The lengthy description of the associated pomp recalls the detailed and laconic narrative of the absurdly elaborate ceremony of possession by means of which the Spaniards solemnize their appropriation of the island:

> Vera marked out a small square beside the raised cross, calling on the notary to observe and bear witness. Then he drew he drew his sword and said: "I take possession by turf and twig! *Yo corto esta yerba*". He slashed at the branches of the surrounding trees and at the grass, and held up his sword in one hand and cut twigs and grass in the other (*LED*, pp. 23–4).

For all the charade of legality, it is brute force which secures the possession. When Ralegh seizes St Joseph from the Spaniards, he discovers the supposedly acquiescent Indian chiefs imprisoned there, in chains, and scarred by torture. Ralegh styles himself a protector and liberator of the Indians, but having made mischief between them and the Spaniards, leaves them without protection, and does not return for twenty-three years. At the conclusion of the first section, Naipaul asserts that

> the New World as medieval adventure had ended; it had become a cynical extension of the developing old world, its commercial underside. No one would look at Trinidad and Guiana again with the eye of Ralegh or Robert Dudley or Captain Wyatt (*LED*, p. 88).

Naipaul's account has sought to recreate some of the romance of the aboriginal island; the sense of loss, emphasized by the book's title, results not only from the defiling and brutalizing of the island and its inhabitants, but from the loss, also, of this capacity for wonder.

In the third part, "The Torture of Luisa Calderon", Naipaul extracts much comedy from the bunglings of Venezuelan revolutionaries. He portrays "the New World as blood, fraud and make-believe" (*LED*, p. 250).

> Caro, it was said, would be arriving in Trinidad or Venezuela in "a very singular disguise", with a wig that "perfectly simulates the wool of the Negro, and he has stained his face and his body in the same colour with a dye so fast that neither water nor sweat can wash it off". These revolutionaries, and the men who tracked them down, took disguises seriously — even Miranda, an austere man, had his false names and his green glasses — and Caracas sent out orders to officers in all Venezuelan ports that until further notice they should pass their hands "with deliberation", *con detenida pausa*, over the heads of all incoming Negroes (*LED,* p. 139).

It appears to be only the authorities who consider that these revolutionaries pose any significant threat — Naipaul treats them as a joke; and the laugh is as much on the officials as on the revolutionaries. For all the farcical ineptitude, *The Loss of El Dorado* reminds us that genuine suffering and misery result from these antics. Naipaul describes an uprising in Venezuela, in 1797, incited by Mañuel Gual, a retired soldier, and José España, a planter and slave owner:

> The revolution known as the Revolution of Gual and España held much of what was to come: the borrowed words that never matched the society, the private theatre of disguises and false names that ended in blood and the heads spiked in public places (*LED*, p. 153).

Of Miranda's first attempt to stir up revolt in Venezuela, Naipaul writes: ''It had happened again: the revolution that seemed for so long to be just words, the action that was like play ... and then the real blood on the beach and the heads on the highways'' (*LED*, p. 264).

Naipaul is perhaps indebted to the example of Conrad — particularly to *The Secret Agent* and to *Nostromo* — for his mode of savage, bloody farce, accompanied by an irony which unsettles by reminding us of the human costs which comedy generally serves to occlude. Mrs Gould's ruminations establish the tone in which Conrad tends to portray the political goings-on of Costaguana. The novel speaks of ''the constant 'saving of the country', which to his wife seemed a puerile and bloodthirsty game of murder and rapine played with terrible earnestness by depraved children''.[10] It is, in Mrs Gould's view, ''as though the government of the country had been a struggle of lust between bands of absurd devils let loose upon the land with sabres and uniforms and grandiloquent phrases'' (*Nostromo*, p. 88). A combination of fatuity and malevolence marks the behaviour of the Monteros, Guzman Bento, Sotillo and others. Naipaul's unadventurous conquistadors can be seen as the literary descendants of Conrad's imperialist adventurers in *Heart of Darkness* — the name of the group invites the drawing of parallels. Marlow explains:

> This devoted band called itself the Eldorado Exploring Expedition, and I believe they were sworn to secrecy. Their talk, however, was the talk of sordid buccaneers: it was reckless without hardihood, greedy without audacity, and cruel without courage; there was not an atom of foresight or of serious intention in the whole batch of them, and they did not seem aware these things are wanted for the work of the world. To tear treasure out of the bowels of the land was their desire, with no more moral purpose at the back of it than there is in burglars breaking into a safe.[11]

The Loss of El Dorado's ironies also operate in the area of the disjunction between ideals and practice in the early days of British rule in Trinidad. Trinidad became a British colony in 1797, and, while attempting to stir up revolution in Spanish-America, Britain was busy degrading the island into a slave colony, with a legal code more stringent than that favoured by the Spanish empire. Picton, the first governor,

> gave shelter to revolutionaries who spoke the high language of liberty. But the island Picton had inherited was a slave island, where he alone was the law. On his island there was to be order; there was to be no revolution (*LED*, p. 127).

The Loss of El Dorado's depiction of English rule in Trinidad is akin to Salim's sense of the Europeans, in *A Bend in the River*, as people who want at once to possess slaves, and to erect statues to themselves as friends of the slaves. "The radical owned slaves. Quick intellectual confusion awaited the radical from England" (*LED*, p. 170). Naipaul's ironies are complex, though, and he does not simply satirize the profession of ideals, but appears to harbour a lurking affection for those who profess them, regardless of their achievements.

> In 1807 one of the objections from Trinidad to the abolition of the British slave trade was that it was unfair to the Africans, who would now not only be denied civilizing contacts but would also be transported in cruel conditions in foreign ships. The argument, with its remote reference to several ideals, is recognizably English (*LED*, pp. 316–7).

Naipaul laments the subsequent failure of the English in Trinidad to call on such ideals as a sign of the increasing intellectual depletion of the colony: an objection to an 1823 regulation forbidding the whipping of Negroes

> comes from people who have accepted the values of the new society, who have ceased to assess themselves by the standards of the metropolis and now measure their eminence by their distance, economic and racial, from their Negroes (*LED*, p. 317).

The Loss of El Dorado is noteworthy for its even-handedness, demonstrated in a refusal to present its characters as simply heroes or villains. A recurring feature of Naipaul's work is its awareness of the shifting nature of power relations, and of the interchangeability of the roles of exploited and exploiter. It is to this which Updike points, in his observation that the work blends "sympathy and irony somewhat enigmatically" (Hamner, p. 153). The villain of today is liable to find himself the victim of tomorrow, according to Naipaul's rendering of the process of history: "The righter of wrongs, the persecutor, the persecuted, the contemptible, the forgotten: it is like the revenge cycle of an old saga, in which sympathy makes the full circle" (*LED*, p. 278). This statement refers to the progress of Colonel William Fullarton's career: he was appointed First Commissioner of Trinidad in 1803. *The Loss of El Dorado* conveys a sense of the instability of victory and achievement not dissimilar, for instance, to that produced by reading Shakespeare's history plays in sequence.

The cruelty of the Spanish dispossession of the Indians does not preclude a recognition of the pathos of the plight of these Spaniards abandoned at the fringes of empire. Ralegh both trades in and meets with cruelty: his discovery of the death of his son is portrayed with some sympathy. A Spanish historian gloats over the event, and Naipaul writes, "It was the brutality the defeated had to endure. It was the brutality Ralegh himself had dealt in twenty-two years before" (*LED*, p. 85). Ralegh makes a scapegoat of Keymis, who emerges as the victim of his displeasure. The work furnishes a roll-call of the victims of Ralegh's expedition:

> There had only been victims: Guanaguanare in chains in St Joseph, "those poore souldiers" at the Port of Spain landing place who had been "many yeeres without wine", Berrio "stricken into a great melancholy", those bodies among the prickly-pear plants at Cumaná, the rotting men in the ships. The sixteen-year-old boy Ralegh had left behind in the jungle had already died; his English clothes, the Indians said, had astonished and maddened a tiger. And the Indians of St Joseph, roused but unprotected, were presently to be repacified (*LED*, pp. 53–4).

Picton's idea of justice is to rule Trinidad according to a "system of impartial terror" (*LED*, p. 134). His opponents attempt to have him prosecuted for various brutal punishments carried out under his auspices: they seek to make the torture of Luisa Calderon appear more illegal by lying about her age, and thereby compromise their moral superiority. Fullarton, sent out by London in order to limit Picton's powers, instantly endeavours to put an end to the regime of punishment, including torture and mutilation, conducted in the Port of Spain jail. Fullarton, however, is portrayed as pompous, legalistic, and "entangled" (*LED*, p. 198) — he doesn't seek to abolish slavery, merely the brutal punishments — and as losing sight of his cause in his personal feud with Picton. Picton, unexpectedly, is described as a victim: "He was the victim of people's conscience, of ideas of humanity and reason that were ahead of the reality" (*LED*, p. 133). His fortunes improve, ultimately, and he earns military glory at the battle of Waterloo. Fullarton, in contrast, dies, according to Naipaul's account, friendless: "And Fullarton was now quite alone" (*LED*, p. 278). The Venezuelan revolutionaries are not merely ridiculous but pitiable: Naipaul writes sympathetically about Manuel de España, whose participation in the Gual and España revolt was secured by the promise of a general's uniform (*LED*, pp. 146–7). Bizarrely, he even spares a moment's sympathy for the hangman: "He was now old; he had to fight his victim into the noose; no one moved to help him" (*LED*, p. 153). The slaves are subjected to irony for the fact that their planned uprising lacks any programme, but are treated with sympathy as the forgotten victims of Picton's brutality:

> This was the gossip of English outrage: an exclusion from Government House, a widow insulted by black soldiers, a soldier unfairly hanged. The Negroes in Vallot's jail, the dirt-eating Negroes dying from *mal d'estomac*: that appeared to exist elsewhere (*LED*, p. 165).

It is a world where "everyone was guilty" (*LED*, p. 65).

In a discussion of *The Loss of El Dorado*, Naipaul remarked that "anger is far too easy", and can "so easily become a substitute for concern in an attempt to understand".[12] A sense of outrage at the cruelties and brutalities which are recorded is evoked by a use of indirection and by means of a withholding of the expected condemnation. This is the effect of the exploration of the economy of the jail (*LED*, p. 159), or of the inventory of not-yet-paid-for tortures presented to Fullarton. The neutral, banal, bureaucratic associations of the inventory clash with, and intensify, the shock of the items listed: "Hanged and burned at St Joseph's, and head cut off ... 1 man" (*LED*, p. 197).

It is a commonplace of contemporary thought that there are points of contact between the novelist's and the historian's art: the historian, too, tells stories, recasting historical data as narration. The novel, conversely, is distinguished as a literary form by its readiness to accommodate facts in its concern with authenticity. Ian Watt contends that "the function of language is much more largely referential in the novel than in other literary forms; that the genre itself works by exhaustive presentation rather than elegant concentration".[13] Mary McCarthy argues:

> We do really (I think) expect a novel to be true, not only true to itself, like a poem or a statue, but true to actual life. . . . We not only make believe we believe a novel, but we do substantially believe it, as being continuous with real life, made of the same stuff, and the presence of fact in fiction, of dates and times and

distances, is a kind of reassurance — a guarantee of credibility.[14]

Clearly, factual accuracy doesn't in itself make a novel, and there are certain conflicting requirements, such as the need for internal, thematic coherence:

> Our art is occupied, and bound to be occupied, not so much in making stories true as in making them typical; not so much in capturing the lineaments of each fact, as in marshalling all of them towards a common end.[15]

Robert Louis Stevenson views the novel, not as "a transcript of life, to be judged by its exactitude", but as a "simplification of some side or point of his life, to stand or fall by its significant simplicity" (Stevenson, p. 297). *The Loss of El Dorado* combines these contrasting tendencies: it perceives symbolic depth in its historical facts, and marries factual authenticity to thematic unity.

Naipaul's formulations in his reviews can usefully be applied to his own work. He writes, of Alexander Cordell's *Rape of the Fair Country*, "I intend a compliment when I say that his history reads like fiction".[16] *The Loss of El Dorado* is, conspicuously, a novelist's rendering of history. The events it narrates are made vividly present by the use of telling detail and in a novelistic fashion. Naipaul gives an impression of effortless ease in his reconstruction of events from the surviving documents: here, if not elsewhere in his work, there is no room for uncertainty as to what occurred, and the motives of the various participants are seemingly transparent to him. This is in contrast to the way in which some historians acknowledge the difficulties involved in recovering the past, and consider a variety of hypotheses regarding what may have taken place and the protagonists' motives. *The Loss of El Dorado* tells a good story, even if the point it wishes to make about West Indian history, enshrined in the book's fractured structure, is that the story it tells adds up to nothing, and goes nowhere. The work describes no momentous achievements, and its account falls into separate parts. The parts hang together, in so far as they do hang together, not by means of plot, but by virtue of the metaphoric consonance implied by collocation: British plans to stir up revolution in Spanish-America are likened to the pursuit of El Dorado — both are chimeras, motivated by greed, and are doomed to remain ineffectual. This can lead to the impression that, for all the disjunctions, Naipaul's rendering of history fits together almost too well. Naipaul's historical agents — Berrio, Ralegh, Miranda — all re-enact the same narrative of the unscrupulous adventurer and unsuccessful man of action, who devotes his life to the pursuit of an illusory goal, only, at the last, and with apparent indifference or relief, to see his project fail.

The historical sections of *A Way in the World* focus on two of these figures: Ralegh and Miranda. Ralegh made two expeditions to Guiana: the first, in 1595, is described in *The Discoverie of Guiana*. This work was designed to encourage investment in future expeditions, with a view to promoting the establishment of an English empire in South America; it describes Ralegh's delight in Indian customs, and contains tales of gold mines, although Ralegh failed to discover any. Ralegh spent the years between 1603 and 1616 imprisoned in the Tower, charged with treason; he was released in order to find the mines, on the understanding that he would avoid conflict with the Spaniards. The 1617 expedition was plagued with difficulties — including sickness and a calm. Ralegh was too ill to travel up the Orinoco, so he sent an expedition under Keymis. The story concerns itself with Ralegh at this time, as he waits passively on events. The expeditionary force attacked the Spanish settlement of San Tomé; Ralegh's son was killed in the fighting. Keymis failed to find any mines in the area, or when he went up river. Ralegh entertained schemes to turn pirate, but in the event returned to England, in 1618. He was arrested, taken to the Tower, and beheaded. The title of Naipaul's story, "A Parcel of Papers, A Roll of Tobacco, A Tortoise", refers to the meagre plunder that was the result of this second expedition.

The other historical fiction contained in *A Way in the World*, "In the Gulf of Desolation", concerns Francisco de Miranda, seen by Venezuelans as the precursor of Bolívar. Miranda was born in 1750, the son of a Caracas merchant; he served in the Spanish Army, and fought in the American War of Independence. In 1782 an order was made for his arrest on a charge of contraband trading (a charge later disproved); Miranda fled to the U. S., and began to shape his project to effect the independence of Spanish-America with foreign backing. Miranda travelled in Europe, where he reinvented himself as a Count. A charismatic, colourful dandy, he was well-received at the court of Catherine the Great. In 1790, he first tried to interest Pitt the Younger in supporting his scheme — this assistance was to be rewarded with trading rights and money. Pitt toyed with the idea, using Miranda as a pawn in Anglo-Spanish relations: support was called off at times of accommodation with Spain. Miranda, too, tried to play the great powers off against each other: he went to France in 1792 to seek backing there, and served in the French Revolutionary army. He participated in an unsuccessful attempt to take Maastricht; he was exonerated from the charges of military mismanagement which ensued. He was imprisoned by Robespierre. In 1797 he fled France for England, where he again sought backing for his plans. He went to the U. S. in 1805 to try his luck, and in

1806 sailed for Venezuela, where the authorities were expecting him; two ships were captured. Miranda recruited more forces in Trinidad and made a second attempt, during which he took Coro, but the local population offered him no support, suspecting him to be a pawn of the English. Miranda withdrew to Trinidad, where he spent a year; it is this hiatus in his life which affords the substance of Naipaul's story. The long-awaited Venezuelan uprising occurred in 1810; Bolívar urged Miranda to return to Venezuela, and, in 1811, independence was declared. Miranda was a member of the Venezuelan Congress, and commanded troops which brutally suppressed royalist uprisings. In 1812, he was placed at the head of the Venezuelan Army, and increasingly lost ground to royalist forces, capitulating without much of a struggle, as it seemed to his critics. He was handed over to the Spaniards. Miranda was imprisoned and fettered, in Puerto Rico and then in Cadiz, where he died in 1816.

In *A Way in the World*, episodes based on autobiographical material are shaped by comparable preoccupations, and recapitulate the themes of the stories of the lives of these historical characters. The fictional figure of Lebrun is the leading example: he is mentioned in "Passenger: *A Figure from the Thirties*", and dominates the section "On the Run". He is a Panamanian of African descent and Marxist political allegiance who travels the world writing and speaking about politics. His path crosses Naipaul's in England, Africa and the West Indies, illustrating how "people occur in one place, then occur elsewhere in your life".[17] He promotes African nationalism, and remains committed to the idea of revolution despite the failure of some newly-independent countries to live up to the hopes invested in decolonization. He lives to an advanced age, and is canonized by people interested in colonial and post-colonial history.

This character is loosely based on C. L. R. James, a fellow Trinidadian of an earlier generation — he was born in 1901 — who, like Naipaul, was a scholarship boy at Queen's Royal College. (The identification is encouraged by the fact that, in 1992, at the time of the composition of *A Way in the World*, Naipaul told Andrew Robinson that he had been reading C. L. R. James.[18]) James went to England in 1932, where he worked as a cricket correspondent, and became politically radicalized: at this point, he wrote *The Case for West Indian Self-Government, The Black Jacobins* and "A History of Negro Revolt". In response to the Italian invasion of Abyssinia, he formed the International Friends of Ethiopia, and worked to promote African liberation. In 1938 he left for America, where he belonged to small Marxist groups. He returned to Trinidad in 1958, and participated in the agitation for independence: he spoke at political meetings, and edited the People's National Movement's paper. He subsequently fell out with Eric Williams, head of the

P. N. M., and left Trinidad in 1962. He returned to found the Worker's and Farmer's Party, which failed to win any seats in the 1966 elections. His influence was largely indirect: his lodgings served as a meeting-point for African intellectuals and politicians in 1930s London, and, in the London of the 1950s and 60s, for West Indian writers. His contribution to independence struggles consisted in fostering a positive self-image among West Indians and Africans by means of his writings on their culture and history. In later years he was lionized as a grand old man of Marxism, and a living monument.

There is evidence that James and Naipaul were personally acquainted. Naipaul mentions going to a Test Match in the company of a West Indian Marxist, African nationalist and cricket enthusiast.[19] In "All About Cricket",[20] Naipaul echoes James's theories about the significance of cricket in the West Indies, as providing the chief means of West Indian self-assertion: cricketers in the Trinidad of his childhood were actors, he writes; cricket had style, and channelled inter-island rivalries. The thesis is drawn from *Beyond a Boundary*, part-autobiography, part-cricket reminiscence, and a history of social conflict, racial division and political change in Trinidad, as they impinged on the cricket pitch. James presents cricket, at times, as an ideal space — "Here on the cricket field if nowhere else, all men in the island are equal"[21] — and as a source of vicarious pride: the successes of West Indian cricketers "atoned for a pervading humiliation, and nourished pride and hope".[22] Reviewing the book, Naipaul lavished high praise on it: "*Beyond a Boundary* is one of the finest and most finished books to come out of the West Indies, important to England, important to the West Indies".[23] Naipaul's review points to similarities in their situations: "To me, who thirty years later followed in his path almost step by step ... Mr James's career is of particular interest" (*OB*, p. 21). They began from different backgrounds, "but we have ended speaking the same language" (*OB*, p. 22).

The figure of Lebrun, and the way he holds fast to political principles to the end of his life, are also reminiscent of Naipaul's portrait of Cheddi Jagan in "A Handful of Dust: Return to Guiana". Jagan is compared to Tony Last at the end of Waugh's novel, trapped outside time and change in the South American jungle. Naipaul maintains that, for fifty years, and despite the massive political upheavals that have occurred everywhere in the world, Jagan has adhered to the same political position. Through all the corruptions of the Burnham government, Jagan has remained uncorrupted by power, "the possessor of a purer Marxist way, waiting to be called".[24] Naipaul argues that Jagan's politics have offered a means of overcoming the difficulties of his personal situation: "Whatever historical or social bewilderment he may have grown to feel, was submerged in his Marxist ideas of surplus value and the universal class struggle''.[25] Jagan emerged from a rural Hindu background akin to Naipaul's: "I shared to some extent the background of both Burnham and Jagan".[26] Lebrun's name recalls that of Ralph Singh's political associate in *The Mimic Men*, Browne, a figure who plays a role in the political action of the novel broadly similar to Burnham's in Guyana.

Ralegh, Miranda and Lebrun all correspond to the recurring type of the revolutionary maker of mischief, who then moves on, leaving others to face the consequences of his actions. The surgeon who in the Ralegh story speaks as an authorial mouthpiece asserts, " 'You stirred people up, here in this Gulf, and you went away. You stayed away for twenty-three years. You left a lot of people to face the consequences' " (*WW*, p. 173). Lebrun is said to have caused problems in Africa.

> He had always been on the run, a revolutionary without a base, always a failure in one way, in another way fortunate, never having to live with the consequences of his action, always being free to move on (*WW*, p. 155).

Miranda is portrayed as preferring to entertain his eager audience in the salons of Europe with tales of the horrors of the Inquisition, rather than realize his revolutionary schemes. Like Miranda, Lebrun is a "revolutionary without a revolution" (*WW*, p. 12), and without any real support: "Lebrun was an impresario of revolution" (*WW*, p. 107). Ralegh, Miranda and Lebrun are all talkers rather than doers; when called upon to act, to put their money, so to speak, where their mouth is, they prove themselves conspicuously inept. Miranda, in Naipaul's judgement, bungles every opportunity for military command into which he manages to bluff his way. Ralegh is a timorous adventurer — "He longed for the new but was nervous about the unknown" (*LED*, p. 50) — and is, according to Naipaul's account, passive and ineffectual at the last:

> It was better now, after all the years, after the journey out, not to know about El Dorado, Manoa, the mountain of crystal or even the mine. Keymis knew where the mine was. Keymis was to go to look for it (*LED*, p. 78).

He channels all his disappointment, frustration and despair into a hostility towards Keymis. "Incapable of action, as he had been since his release, doubting the value of action, a man withdrawn, prepared for the end, this became all his activity" (*LED*, p. 85). Ralegh and Miranda are as likely to be found in prison as engaged in action: "Prison was perhaps the setting that Miranda, like Ralegh, subconsciously required. It dramatized inaction, failure and the condition of exile" (*LED*, p. 309).

Lebrun is described as one who lives by his wits (*WW*, p. 118), Miranda as a tout for the idea of revolution (*WW*, p. 238). Miranda keeps reinventing himself,

> becoming a lover of liberty among the Americans; a revolutionary among the French; a Mexican nobleman and a count among the grandees of the Russia of Catherine the Great; a ruler in exile among the British (*WW*, p. 241).

This self-recreation carries echoes of the behaviour of Ganesh, in *The Mystic Masseur*, and of Naipaul's portrait of Abdul Malik in "The Killings in Trinidad". Both Malik and Miranda are depicted as performing for a metropolitan audience: Malik is another "leader who had no followers",[27] "made by words" (*REP*, p. 18), and "made in England" (*REP*, p. 29). Miranda peddles myths about his native land, and deludes not only his audience but himself:

> In his projections Venezuela and South America had been steadily adapted to the fantasies of late eighteenth-century European thinkers. . . .
> But the Venezuela in which Miranda now finds himself isn't like that at all (*WW*, p. 241).

Miranda is said to have misrepresented the extent of his importance as leader of the planned revolution, in part because he was cut off and misinformed, before returning to Venezuela and realizing the true state of affairs:

> "For years I had believed — and people like Gual and Caro and Vargas had encouraged me to believe — that when I landed the people would flock to my colours. No one came now" (*WW*, p. 292).

Ralegh also falls prey to delusion: "In the Tower of London these memories were turning to fantasy" (*LED*, p. 69). The pattern of both their stories is the same: "There is this kind of madness and self-deception — followed by surrender" (*WW*, p. 238). At the end of their lives, they find themselves carried along by the momentum of events, and compelled to try to enact chimerical schemes they no longer believe in. Miranda is charged with inconsistency, having traded in slaves at the beginning of his career; both he and Ralegh are described as incongruously patrician agents of revolt, who despise the men who serve under them. Miranda's revolution and Ralegh's dreams of an English empire in South America are depicted as disguising "a dream of a fabulous personal authority" (*WW*, p. 243).

Naipaul's reading of Miranda's life is profoundly indebted to Salvador de Madariaga's *Bolívar*.[28] Madariaga seeks to question the reverence paid to the memory of Bolívar by suggesting that the project of Spanish-American independence emanated from the crazed imaginations of deluded and power-hungry Venezuelans abroad. He implies that Spanish America was better-off under Spanish rule. Madariaga portrays Bolívar as a Don Quixote, tilting at an imaginary tyranny, and Miranda as a "freebooter" of freedom, on an "expedition to smuggle liberty into Venezuela as if liberty were a cargo of British goods".[29] Madariaga makes the connection which is at the heart of *The Loss of El Dorado*: for the British, "the Spanish empire remained an Eldorado as glittering as in the days of Raleigh" (Madariaga, p. 103). Madariaga's analysis of the course of the Venezuelan revolution resembles Naipaul's in certain respects. Madariaga writes: "Venezuela had entered a period of chaos as the outcome of the weakening or disappearance of the only force capable of balancing the anarchical tendencies of the individual — the monarchy" (Madariaga, p. 214). Naipaul writes:

> The pacific, deficient colonial society had become bloody. Spain was now seen to be more than its administrative failures. It was, however remotely, a code and a reference that the colonial society by itself was incapable of generating. Without such a reference obedience, the association of consent, was no longer possible (*LED*, p. 283).

Madariaga's treatment of Miranda ceases to be satirical, and grows almost tender, when he turns to the subject of Miranda's capitulation to royalist forces and subsequent imprisonment in 1812. He infers a desire on Miranda's part to be reconciled with Spain, perhaps wishfully recasting Miranda's actions in conformity with his own political agenda. This may have influenced Naipaul's contention that, at the end, Miranda is resigned to the failure of his cause, and even relieved:

> And then the appalling discovery, at the end of a life, ... that the society was wrong, the cause was wrong, that the good words didn't fit. An appalling discovery ... but it must also have been like reconciliation (*LED*, p. 297).

Miranda's biographer Robertson, in contrast, argues that his intention in capitulating may have been to buy time for retrenchment in order to return to fight again.[30]

Naipaul's treatment of the figure of the opportunist and adventurer, who brags and bluffs only to find himself taken at his word, suggests itself for comparison with Graham Greene's, in *The Comedians*. "Major" Jones's stories about his soldierly exploits in Burma land him a role in a Haitian insurgent group. It is implied, however, that his lies express a kind of truth about himself and his aspirations: " 'I only wanted my chance', he added, and I wondered whether perhaps in all his devious life he had been engaged on a secret and hopeless love-affair with virtue".[31] Put to the test, Jones reveals unsuspected qualities: he couldn't handle arms, but knew how to lead, and "the men loved him" (*The Comedians*, p. 347). Conrad has a rather less benign adventurer of the same name in *Victory*. *The Comedians* begins by contrasting a humble memorial to Jones's heroism, located in Haiti, with grander London monuments to "equestrian generals, the heroes of old colonial wars, and to frock-coated politicians" (*The Comedians*, p. 1). Their achievements may be of as mixed and as dubious a character as Jones's; his achievements may be as worthy of commemoration. There are similarities between Greene's perception of a weak and sinful humanity and Naipaul's perception of a universal delusion and corruption. But the theological basis of Greene's world view would appear to allow for possibilities of redemption inaccessible in Naipaul's world: Greene is readier to forgive human failings, at the risk of a certain sentimentality concerning his sinners with hearts of gold.

Naipaul portrays figures who are becalmed and marooned in the West Indies: the mood of dereliction and desolation is enhanced by the fact that, in *A Way in the World*, these stories are fragments, cut off from the larger historical picture in which, in *The Loss of El Dorado*, they played a part. The stories are set at the end of the characters' lives, as they reflect on the past: this gives them an internal quality which further promotes a sense of isolation. There is little external drama; nor is there a clash of viewpoints. All the characters in these stories speak in Naipaul's voice, and reiterate views expounded in *The Loss of El Dorado*. The surgeon, in the story about Ralegh, serves as a kind of ventriloquist's dummy, whereby Naipaul purveys his interpretations of Ralegh's actions, and the reading of Ralegh's *Discoverie* first proposed in *The Loss of El Dorado*: "In the details of action it [*The Discoverie*] is, fatally, imprecise".[32] Ralegh himself confirms Naipaul's analysis of his passivity: " 'The expedition had its own life. I just surrendered to it' " (*WW*, p. 162). In Miranda's story, Naipaul distributes the material of *The Loss of El Dorado* among a number of characters. Bernard provides an account of the fantasy life of the slaves, imported from the earlier book.[33] Hislop reiterates Naipaul's contention that the supposed radicals who call for a British constitution merely seek to disenfranchise the free people of colour: " 'We use words in a special way here' ".[34] Naipaul also speaks through Level de Goda: Naipaul's judgement that "this kind of place is held together only by a strong external authority" (*WW*, p. 242) is recapitulated in Level's view that " 'the question to ask when you talk about independence is, "Who is going to rule over us?" ' " (*WW*, p. 331.) There is a greater variety of viewpoint in *The Loss of El Dorado*, where Naipaul quotes extensively from his historical sources. In the foreword to *The Middle Passage*, Naipaul contends that "the novelist works towards conclusions of which he is often unaware; and it is better that he should" (*MP*, p. 5). An examination of the historical material of *A Way in the World*, which works towards foregone conclusions, already finalized in the writing of *The Loss of El Dorado*, might be thought to support this proposition.

The figure of the revolutionary mischief-maker as "damaged man"[35] occurs once more in *A Way in the World* in the character of Foster Morris, who appears in the section "Passenger: *A Figure from the Thirties*". This describes how Naipaul's path gradually converges with, and later diverges from, that of an author who has written a travel book about Trinidad. The book is called *The Shadowed Livery*: this title was earlier given by Naipaul to a book by Mr Blackwhite, the confrontational Caribbean writer who appears in *A Flag on the Island*. Foster Morris's book is sympathetic to the 1937 oilfield strikes — an attitude Naipaul considers mistaken. When they meet, Foster Morris informs Naipaul that he thought the strikers were, in fact, racial fanatics, but that he did not say so because of the racism of the social organization they protested against. This identifies him as one of a type which attracts much antipathy in Naipaul's work — the left-wing apologist for the oppressed who treats them as beyond reproach. At first, Naipaul considers Foster Morris a not insignificant literary figure. Foster Morris offers Naipaul advice which he finds useful in the early stages of his literary career. On a second occasion, his advice is merely offensive. Naipaul learns to assess the figure as second-rate: his potential unfulfilled, the man is jealous of more successful contemporaries.

This character is loosely based on Arthur Calder-Marshall. Naipaul describes his dealings with him:

> In 1955 I started another novel. I thought perhaps my duty was to be a very serious writer: I wrote 70,000 words and still hadn't finished the incidents of the first day! I sent these 70,000 words to Arthur Calder-Marshall, who was a contributor to *Caribbean Voices*. He wrote me a long, critical, puncturing but rather *excellent* letter about this very bad MS — so I abandoned it at once. I am very grateful to him. I still have the letter — it's typewritten in red. It set me on the path of finding out about myself.[36]

Calder-Marshall reviewed Naipaul's work: he tempered praise for *A House for Mr Biswas* with the opinion that it is too long.[37] Calder-Marshall visited Trinidad in the wake of the 1937 labour unrest (which James also wrote about, in "A History of Negro Revolt", interpreting it as a necessary stage in the politicization of Trinidadians, which paved the way for a sense of national identity and incited agitation for independence).[38] Calder-Marshall described his travels in *Glory Dead*, a work of political tourism: instead of depicting beauty spots and places of historic interest, Calder-Marshall records visits to Port of Spain tenements, and leavens his text with economic statistics. He writes sympathetically about the living and working conditions of the island's poor, and satirically about its caste-system, based on colour. The book contains an onslaught against the shortcomings of the colonial government — ''Glory dead when white man come'', goes the song which gives the book its title. Calder-Marshall occupied himself during his visit by lecturing unions on the need for self-organization, which is what earns him the status, in *A Way in the World*, of mischief-maker.

The story ''New Clothes'' concerns the doings of another meddlesome intruder, a ''carrier of mischief. A revolutionary of the 1970s, say'' (*WW*, p. 46). He is engaged on a project to stir up revolt among indigenous people in an unnamed South American country which resembles Guyana — the area which Ralegh visited almost four hundred years before. The narrator has not yet arrived at his destination before he resolves on flight: he imagines that the people will remember him as ''the man who stayed long and wasn't straight with them, who promised many things and then went away'' (*WW*, p. 64). The pay-off comes when it emerges that the people recall Ralegh's visit as a recent event, and still await his return: they produce a Tudor doublet, the ''relic of an old betrayal'' (*WW*, p. 67). This is a sour version of the Arcadia myth, which imagines a society untouched by change and external contact, ''a world without time where men live only in the present'' (*WW*, p. 55). The setting suggests generic affinities with the sombre fantasy which concludes Waugh's *A Handful of Dust*, and to which Naipaul alludes in his article about Cheddi Jagan. An incident recorded in *The Loss of El Dorado* would appear to have supplied the origins of the story: fourteen years after Ralegh's first expedition to Guiana, Robert Harcourt visited the area and encountered an Indian chief dressed in tattered English clothes. Harcourt made excuses for Ralegh's failure to return, and was later greeted by Ralegh's Indian interpreter. ''Leonard wanted the English to settle. He showed a site and said it was good for *houses*, and the English word in the South American jungle startled Harcourt'' (*LED*, p. 69). ''New Clothes'' rehearses once more the plot of Ralegh's expedition to Guiana. Its conclusion is preordained: history simply repeats itself across the ages, and an old story appears decked out in new clothes.

Naipaul's portrayal of these revolutionary mischief-makers can be seen in the context of a persistent scepticism in his work regarding the efficacy of political action. Those lines of Conrad's from *Nostromo* which Naipaul quotes in ''Conrad's Darkness'' as particularly resonant for him evoke a widespread pessimism in Naipaul's thought: "Always 'something inherent in the necessities of successful action . . . carried with it the moral degradation of the idea' '' (*REP*, p. 216). This pessimism, in *Mr Stone and the Knights Companion*, extends to literary creation. Mr Stone reflects: "All that he had done, and even the anguish he was feeling now, was a betrayal of that good emotion. All action, all creation was a betrayal of feeling and truth".[39] Naipaul suggests that his fatalistic attitude towards politics is a legacy of his Indian ancestry — rulers were held to be remote and corrupt, and the individual to be without political power: "I have to admit . . . that a lot of Hindu attitudes, the deeper attitudes, are probably also mine — that I probably do have a feeling about the vanity of human action and human life".[40] In *An Area of Darkness*, he identifies an Indian tendency to retreat, in which he participates:

> . . . part of a greater philosophy of despair, leading to passivity, detachment, acceptance. . . . [I]t had convinced me that every man was an island, and taught me to shield all that I knew to be good and pure within myself from the corruption of causes (*AD*, p. 198).

A sense of the corruption of causes informs the presentation of Miranda's story.

All the political uprisings to which *A Way in the World* and *The Loss of El Dorado* allude follow the same pattern. They lack a programme, as in the case of the Gual and España revolt: "It was an absurdity, a 'shouting', as one Spanish official said, for almost everything".[41] This condition is parodied by the slave rebellion, which has no other aim, in Naipaul's view, than to enable its participants to "eat pork and dance" (*WW*, p. 267). These revolts amount to no more than rhetorical flourishes, according to Naipaul's interpretation: the Venezuelans, writes one agent, "believe that it is the same to acclaim independence as to be independent" (*LED*, p. 142). Revolution satisfies needs other than rational, providing a spectacle of destruction. Naipaul describes the agitation for Trinidad's independence by means of religious imagery:

> Now all those private emotions ran together into a common pool, where everyone found a blessing. Everyone, high and low, could now exchange his private emotion, which he sometimes distrusted, for the sacrament of the larger truth.[42]

The energies released by revolt are viewed as threateningly irrational. Later political disturbances (Naipaul appears to refer to the kidnapping in 1990 of Trinidad's Prime Minister and half his cabinet by Black Muslim rebels) are presented as a bacchanal of destruction:

They formed looting gangs. It was of this — of the
inflamed, unrecognizable faces of the looters, the glittering
eyes — as much as of the siege at The Red House that
people spoke when I went back. For six days or so whole
communities had lived with the idea of the end of things, a
world without logic, and they had been lifted out of
themselves (*WW*, p. 40).

History repeats itself across Naipaul's works: the uprisings which
occur in the background of *Guerrillas, A Bend in the River* and *In a Free
State* are presented in similar terms: "The hysteria recurs, but the
situation doesn't change".[43] In *The Mimic Men*, Ralph's father's
movement is another "gesture of mass protest, a statement of despair,
without a philosophy or cause" (*MM*, p. 159). Ralph's own movement
"zestfully abolished an order; we never defined our purpose"
(*MM*, p. 237). Anti-colonial protest in this work is defined as an
expression of the "negative frenzy of a deep violation" (*MM*, p. 245).
Ralph is said to trade in "borrowed phrases" (*MM*, p. 237): he is another
fraud — "We began in bluff" (*MM*, p. 249) — whose bluff is never
called by his colonial rulers.

The background of Naipaul's alienation from agitation for Trinidadian
independence is the history of mutual mistrust between Africans and East
Indians in Trinidad:

The almost religious exaltation of the early days of the black
movement had given way very quickly to the simplest kind of
racial politics. In Trinidad that meant anti-Indian politics and
constant anti-Indian agitation; it was how the vote of the
African majority was to be secured. Though I was no longer
living in Trinidad, I was affected (*WW*, p. 355).

Indians and Africans in Trinidad have maintained a distance from each
other — with the former concentrated in the countryside, while the latter
are congregated in towns, and the former tending to retain their traditions,
while the latter are creolized, after generations in the New World.
Naipaul defines the relations between the two groups:

Trinidad in fact teeters on the brink of racial war. Politics must
be blamed; but there must have been an original antipathy for
the politicians to work on. Matters are not helped by the fierce
rivalry between Indians and Negroes as to who despises the
other more. . . .
   It is sufficient to state that the antipathy exists. The Negro has
a deep contempt, as has been said, for all that is not white; his
values are the values of white imperialism at its most bigoted.

> The Indian despises the Negro for not being an Indian; he has, in addition, taken over all the white prejudices against the Negro and with the convert's zeal regards as Negro everyone who has any tincture of Negro blood. "The two races", Froude observed in 1887, "are more absolutely apart than the white and the black" (*MP*, p. 80).

His voice merges with the tones of Froude's "mid-Victorian certainty".[44] Naipaul looks back to the past, not to measure change, but to seek out evidence of the enduring. Independence and its aftermath did nothing to lessen the division between the groups. The impetus for independence came from the African community, from which the People's National Movement drew its support; East Indians feared that they would be swamped in an independent country. The P. N. M. were perceived by some in the Indian community as black fascists; it is such perceptions which Naipaul echoes in his reference to racial politics. Voting in Trinidad's elections followed ethnic lines; and even though they didn't win an outright majority in the 1956 elections, the P. N. M. were invited to form a government. There were accusations of electoral fraud at the 1961 elections, which the P. N. M. again won, ensuring that they saw the country through independence in 1962; and they remained in power until 1986. For these reasons, East Indians feel excluded from and mistrustful of the political processes of the island.

Naipaul distances himself from his community, describing the Trinidad Indian as "the complete colonial, even more philistine than the white" (*MP*, p. 82). He has stated that "I really find it very hard to put forward the prejudices of a group"[45] — by which he seems to refer to ethnic allegiances. Discussing racial animosity in Trinidad, he describes himself as driven by "the fear of being swallowed up or extinguished by the simplicity of one side or the other, my side or the side that wasn't mine" (*EA*, p. 140). Naipaul, however, has not always avoided making statements which might be seen as consistent with such prejudices. His portrayal of African characters in his fiction has caused offence. He concluded a review of books about Jamaica with the suggestion, "And perhaps — who knows? — a banana a day will keep the Jamaican away".[46] His work has, furthermore, been pressed into service in this racial conflict.[47] In Naipaul's depiction of nationalist agitation and the politics of independent Trinidad, as well as in the portrait of Lebrun, and in the account of the pernicious effects of his views, can be detected the residual traces of ancestral loyalties, and an oblique, attenuated expression of group solidarity.

Naipaul's representation of his native island can be seen to entail conflicting impulses, combining the urge to make Trinidad appear significant with the desire to disown it as "unimportant, uncreative, cynical" (*MP*, p. 41). Some degree of paradox is inherent in the notion of repeatedly proclaiming his distance from his past. In *A Way in the World*, the past comes back to haunt Naipaul: the work shows its recurrence and continuing influence. Naipaul could be viewed as, in this respect, akin to the figure of Lebrun: on the run from the shame of a past which nevertheless reasserts its hold. Naipaul writes that the purpose of Lebrun's book about Venezuelan revolutionaries was

> to lift the islands from the end-of-empire smallness in which they had been becalmed since the abolition of slavery, and to attach them once again to the great historical processes of the continent (*WW*, p. 128).

The description serves equally to define one aspect of the project of *The Loss of El Dorado*, which concerns itself with moments when Trinidad was touched by history and brought into contact with a wider world — a contact which confers on the island the benediction of significance: "The idea behind the book, the narrative line, was to attach the island, the little place in the mouth of the Orinoco river, to great names and great events" (*EA*, p. 142). In *A Way in the World*, Naipaul discusses how the writing of *The Loss of El Dorado* changed his relation to Trinidad, enabling him to recapture the wonder of Ralegh's and Wyatt's response to the island:

> It was easier in London, separated by many years and some thousands of miles from that ground-level view, and while I read in the British Museum and the Public Records Office, to feel the truth of the other, aboriginal island. From that distance, from that other side, as it were, the landscape of the aboriginal island became fabulous (*WW*, p. 209).

Naipaul's representation of his revisiting of the island in the light of this new mode of apprehension reworks a passage from earlier in *A Way in the World*, a passage which attempts to recover Columbus's view of Trinidad: "It was hard to hold on to that romantic way of looking" (*WW*, p. 72). These passages, in turn, return to material used earlier in *The Loss of El Dorado*:

> I wanted to see the island where I had been living in a new way in my imagination for the last two years, the island I had restored, as it were, to the globe and for which now I felt a deep romance.
> I found an island full of racial tensions, and close to revolution. So, as soon as I had arrived at a new idea about the place, it had ceased to be mine (*EA*, p. 145).

Naipaul's opus increasingly appears to form a self-sufficient system, with earlier books providing the matter for later works.

The contrary impulse manifested in Naipaul's writings about his place of origin is to denigrate and disown it. "In the Gulf of Desolation" contains an extensive portrait of the society of colonial Trinidad, reworked from the material of *The Loss of El Dorado*: Naipaul's analysis in these works is consistent with his depiction of contemporary Trinidad in *Miguel Street, The Mystic Masseur, The Mimic Men* and *Guerrillas*. Colonial Trinidad is described as "an outpost, a backwater ... an error and a failure" (*LED*, p. 316). It is a "simple society" (*LED*, p. 283), preoccupied only by "race and money" (*LED*, p. 283). It is a place where metropolitan words and concepts are inappropriate, meaningless and fantastic; fantasy is reproduced and parodied in the night-time world of the slaves, which serves to comment metaphorically on the society at large. The element of unreality can be compared with the dreams of self-transformation entertained by the characters in *Miguel Street*, who model themselves on Hollywood stars. It is a place where newcomers soon shed their ideals. Hislop's lament — " 'I feel I am sinking here. I feel I can no longer see my way' " (*WW*, p. 273) — is echoed by Miranda's: "I feel that, as the world around me gets smaller, I dwindle with it. . . . I cannot hold on to large ideas in this setting" (*WW*, p. 310). Both statements derive from the blueprint furnished by the following passage, in which, describing the intellectual impoverishment of the English, Naipaul elaborately builds up to an anti-climax:

> In the slave society, where self-fulfilment came so easily, this liveliness began to be perverted and then to fade, and the English saw their pre-eminence, more simply, as a type of racial magic. . . . The quality of controversy declined, and the stature of men. What was left was a colony (*LED*, p. 316).

It is a place devoid of justice, where there is yawning chasm between professed ideals and actual practice. It is a society which is said to lack the "association of consent" (*LED*, p. 283), where everyone is out for himself, and revolution merely unleashes chaos, and a decay into "minute egoisms".[48] There is no scope for significant achievement, nor demand for ability or skill:[49]

> "The Spanish empire damaged us in that way. It kept us backward, gave us very little to do. It gave us as men no way of proving ourselves. It never made us believe in human achievement. It made us believe only in luck and birth and influence and theft and getting patents from the king" (*WW*, p. 330).

Such a society calls only for the talents of the trickster, of the type of Ganesh, in *The Mystic Masseur*. This view also fits *The Suffrage of*

Elvira, in which characters are motivated largely by the lure of self-enrichment, to be attained by political chicanery. Naipaul's perception of contemporary Trinidad is consonant with his rendering of the island's past. The present is doomed eternally to repeat the past; the sterile circularity of the repetition enhances the mood of futility.

It can seem that there is a more complex play of attitude in *The Loss of El Dorado*. The notion of the superiority of metropolitan society, implicit in Naipaul's depiction of the colonial world, may appear to be subjected to irony in the contention that, when in Spain, "it excited Level to be close for the first time to the real world and real events, to be in a country that could support classical illusion" (*LED* p. 304). John Updike seizes on this ambiguous assertion, asking, "Illusion or allusion?" (Hamner, p. 157). "Allusion" would appear to be the more natural choice in the context, and the invocation of the notion of illusion detracts from the supposedly superior reality of this world. The same opposing ideas are played off against each other in the statement, "The romance of the real world and real events had begun to fade" (*LED*, p. 305). *A Way in the World* lacks such ironies.

Naipaul portrays both Miranda and Lebrun with a mixture of sympathy, irony and self-recognition. Naipaul writes that he at first saw Miranda in his own image, as subject to

> the deeper colonial deprivation, the sense of the missing real world, that Miranda had spent a lifetime making good. For John Adams, Miranda was "an Achilles, hurt by some personal injury, real or imaginary" (*LED*, p. 266).

In *A Way in the World*, Naipaul repudiates the earlier portrait:

> And when I first read about Miranda and began to look at his papers, I too, but in my own way, thought of him as a precursor. I saw him as a very early colonial, someone with a feeling of incompleteness, with very little at home to fall back on, with an idea of a great world out there, someone who, when he was out in this world, had to reinvent himself.…
>
> I feel now that I was carried away by a private idea of an ancestry (*WW*, pp. 243–4).

Despite the disavowal, however, the later version is not untinged with sympathy, predicated on a sense of kinship. Lebrun is portrayed as a wounded man, crippled by the racial humiliations of the past:

> And now I felt — with shame, grief, sympathy, admiration, recognizing something of myself in his struggle — that, as much as the uneducated old coachman of ninety years before,

and the middle-aged black man in bowler and pinstripe suit
stepping out of the bus queue in Regent Street in 1950 to show
me photographs of his house and English wife, Lebrun had
always needed to find some way of dealing with the past (*WW*,
p. 122).

Lebrun and Miranda are implicated in a project of biographical self-
understanding: they mirror the situation of the author. Naipaul's relation
to his characters unites a disconcerting complex of ironies regarding the
dangerous consequences of their words and actions with a surprising
tenderness and tact, and a reluctance to pass judgement on them.
Nicholas Spice approaches the question from an opposing direction,
observing that "Naipaul's sympathy for the fragile men who populate his
book is tempered by his sense of the harm they are capable of doing"
(Spice, p. 11). Naipaul asks of Lebrun, "How could one enter the
emotions of a black man as old as the century?" (*WW*, p. 129.) This
avowal of the limitations of judgement is parallel to that scene when
Miranda observes some slaves at work outside his room, and is brought
up against the existence of an unknown world, in close physical
proximity to his own: "The strange private language, and the whole
internal, unknowable world it implied, made him consider the faces of
the men" (*WW*, p. 257).

It is given to Miranda to argue that the judgements passed on him by
his detractors are unfair:

> "Of course I know it's strange to be going on a campaign of
> liberation with these French aristocratic adventurers who only
> want land and Negroes. But that's looking at it from the
> outside. I know the logic of what I'm doing. I know how I've
> got here. You know. You and I know all the twists and turns of
> events that have brought me here" (*WW*, p. 264).

While such passages attempt to enter into Miranda's viewpoint, they do
not withhold judgement on him either: the implication is that his cause
has led him to assume an untenable position, and that his self-
justifications express his delusions about himself. Naipaul states that the
story aims "imaginatively to show how you get corrupt, how your cause
remains clear to you, but you make all kinds of adaptations that other
people judge you by".[50]

The manner in which Naipaul simultaneously sympathizes and
condemns on this occasion can be contrasted with Gabriel García
Marquez's treatment of Bolívar in *The General in His Labyrinth*.
Marquez's starting-point is a commitment to a sense of the value of
Bolívar's achievements.

> He was accused of being capricious in the way he judged men and manipulated history, he was accused of fighting Fernando VII and embracing Morillo, of waging war to the death against Spain and promoting her spirit, of depending on Haiti in order to win the war and then considering Haiti a foreign country in order to exclude her from the Congress of Panamá, of having been a Mason and reading Voltaire at Mass but of being the paladin of the Church, of courting the English while wooing a French princess, of being frivolous, hypocritical, and even disloyal because he flattered his friends in their presence and denigrated them behind their backs. "Well, all of that is true, but circumstantial", he said, "because everything I've done has been for the sole purpose of making this continent into a single, independent country, and as far as that's concerned I've never contradicted myself or had a single doubt".[51]

Marquez leaves the last word with Bolívar, and seems to concur in this self-vindication. This long sentence accumulates inconsistencies in a breathless, undifferentiated rush, and in a fashion designed to discourage condemnation: it isn't that his faults are ignored, but that they don't matter. Marquez appears to be happy with inconsistency — his books burst with the varieties of experience and the multitudinous contradictions that human life affords. The contradictions apparent in the treatment of Naipaul's characters are hard to assess in such terms.

Another respect in which Naipaul points to similarities between the character of Lebrun and himself is by ascribing to Lebrun the authorship of a book which closely resembles *The Loss of El Dorado* and *The Black Jacobins* — a book concerning early Spanish-American revolutionaries. This self-referential allusion invites a comparison between C. L. R. James's and Naipaul's treatment of West Indian history. *The Black Jacobins* may be seen to represent an aspect of the intellectual background of *The Loss of El Dorado,* in contradistinction to which Naipaul's views are defined. In a discussion of points of comparison and disagreement between Naipaul and Frantz Fanon, Michael Neill suggests the manner in which opposing political opinions can be perceived as forming a context in which to understand Naipaul's work. He sees the relationship of the two writers as a gradually unfolding argument, and as a preoccupation with common socio-political themes; each writes in an attempt to exorcise the "complex hurt and dislocation imposed by the double exile which was his colonial inheritance".[52] Neill compares their analysis of the empty symbolism of independence, of the political parasitism of elite groups within new nations, and the mistrust of nationalist leaders that can be found in the work of both writers.

Meanwhile, Naipaul's continuing interest in portraying revolutionary violence as senseless, futile and farcical can be seen as driven by a desire to dispute Fanon's notion of the redemptive possibilities of violent struggle.

The Loss of El Dorado is open to interpretation as an ironic riposte to *The Black Jacobins*. While the latter provides a grand narrative of liberation, which suggests a meliorist perspective,[53] the former is fragmented, ironic and discontinuous — a record of botched and incomplete villainies. *The Black Jacobins* concentrates on a successful revolt; *The Loss of El Dorado* on revolutionary failures. *The Black Jacobins* was written with a view to promoting change in a colonial Africa, showing Africans engaged in making their own history. When Naipaul reflects on the past, it is in order to expose the futility of revolutionary posturings and to explode myths of heroism. Even failed revolts are treated by James as a valid response to abuses, laying the foundations for future attempts, while Naipaul views them as crazed absurdities. Naipaul sees significance as conferred by contact with Europe: James argues that European history was determined by the outcome of the revolution in San Domingo, which made possible the French Revolution. Both employ irony as a means of expressing the radical disjunction between professed aspirations and a brutal reality which distinguishes West Indian history. The savage farce of *The Loss of El Dorado* is anticipated by James's description, say, of the Creoles of San Domingo, who form a militia, invent an enemy, and shoot each other by mistake. Naipaul's ironies at the expense of the unforseen consequences of Columbus's discovery can be contrasted with James's treatment of the moment of discovery: "Christopher Columbus landed first in the New World at the island of San Salvador, and after praising God enquired urgently for gold".[54] James's ironies serve a particular political position, and as a way of voicing his indignation: he remarks, of the stated intention of an English commander to betray Toussaint, that it "was in the best tradition of the way in which the higher civilisation uplifts the backward peoples".[55] Naipaul's ironies are more restless and elusive in their effects, denying rectitude to any one political stance or individual.

The portraits of Foster Morris and Lebrun must be seen in the context of Naipaul's hostility to left-wing assumptions. Naipaul's dealings with Lebrun centre on two dinner parties: on both occasions, Naipaul's sense of alienation from his company is crystallized in a fastidious revulsion from the food. At the second, Naipaul is served foo-foo: "A heavy glistening mound ... slimy from the yams.... I thought it awful, the texture, the slipperiness" (*WW*, p. 116). Naipaul resists being co-opted as Lebrun's acolyte: "I began to feel that in their vision I was incidental to

my own work: I was an expression of Lebrun's will'' (*WW*, p. 123).
Naipaul dramatizes a refusal to enter into a Faustian pact with Lebrun's
dangerously seductive audience:

> And they were so nice and attractive, and the house was so
> pleasant, . . . it would have been marvellous, it would have been
> less trouble, if I could have pretended to be a convert. And I had
> a sense that years before, in much harder times, Lebrun might
> have made such a deal, would have shed one smarting skin and
> felt himself reborn in another (*WW*, p. 123).

There is an internal echo here: the occasion recalls Naipaul's dealings
with Foster Morris, and the relief he feels at the termination of their
burgeoning "disciple-guru relationship" (*WW*, p. 97). Membership of a
group is presented as a threat to individual identity: "No other group
would ever again make me an invitation so wholehearted or so seductive.
But to yield was to cease to be myself, to trust to the unknown" (*WW*,
p. 124). Naipaul's reluctance to form part of a wider entity or group, to be
co-opted to serve a cause, forms a motif of *A Way in the World*. He
describes an incident from his childhood, when a friend's father has
spoken mystically about the future of the coloured races, seeking to
include Naipaul in his vision:

> I was moved, but at the same time embarrassed. I understood
> their feelings, shared them to some extent, but I wished, even
> with that understanding, to belong to myself. I couldn't support
> the idea of being part of a group (*WW*, p. 16).

This sentiment is one which Naipaul has expressed throughout his career:
"I find it very hard to join a group and subscribe to everything that the
group believes in".[56]

The dinner party scenes might appear as a sour rewriting of a
eucharistic moment of cross-cultural communion in Colin MacInnes's
City of Spades: the foo-foo eating scene, when the Englishman Pew, the
novel's central character, is attired in African clothes and made an
honorary African. Naipaul has written admiringly of MacInnes's work;
the voices of the two writers merge as Naipaul describes MacInnes's
criticisms of English society: "This reliance on the myth, this refusal or
unwillingness to see, is leading to artistic sterility".[57] Naipaul portrays
MacInnes's project in terms that remind one of his sense of his own: "He
wants people to *see*".[58] There is some irony in this praise, since
MacInnes was later to assume a position which Naipaul devotes much
energy to attacking: he gave his support to Michael X (he worked with
him in Defence, an organization which provided help to blacks who had
been arrested). *City of Spades* depicts the society of Africans and West

Indians in 1950s London as magical; the milieu is viewed through the approving eyes of Pew, who sees it as injecting " 'an element of joy and fantasy and violence into our cautious, ordered lives.' "[59] The novel anticipates and acknowledges possible criticisms of its own position. Karl Marx Bo analyzes the phenomenon Pew represents: " 'You also are what we despise even more than we do those who hate us — you are full-time professional admirers of the coloured peoples, who like us as you like pet animals' " (MacInnes, p. 85). Naipaul's treatment of the life of West Indian immigrants in London, in "Tell Me Who to Kill", is, in contrast, distinctly unmagical: their lives are restricted, isolated and desolate.

Naipaul tends to assume in his readers a sympathy with decolonization struggles and the plight of newly independent countries, and a propensity to idealize them. His work consistently sets itself in opposition to such beliefs, in seeking to expose what he sees as liberal sentimentalities and pieties. (It is the argument of critics such as Chinua Achebe,[60] Selwyn Cudjoe[61] and Chris Searle[62] that his work, however, reinforces an alternative set of assumptions regarding the inability of the formerly colonized peoples to govern themselves effectively.) Naipaul has asserted, "I'm *desperately* concerned about the countries I'm in", but that "there's nothing to be done. Except we mustn't romanticize them".[63] Naipaul inveighs against those whom he terms liberals:

> On a repandu un tas de mensonges sur le réveil des peuples de la brousse et se sont ensuivies de nombreuses catastrophes à cause de ces mensonges. . . .
>
> La dépendance coloniale tout comme l'indépendance ont été déformées, faussées, par le mensonge libéral des grands pays.[64]

The character of Richard, who appears in the final section of *A Way in the World*, set on a university compound in East Africa, seems designed to illustrate the thesis. Richard is an Englishman, and a resident apologist for a less than pleasant regime: "The country was a tyranny. But in those days not many people minded" (*WW*, p. 346). Expatriates are presented as condoning dictatorship and racial hatred in the interests of a spurious socialism; a special antipathy is excited by Richard, whose role is to police the thoughts of the expatriates on the compound. Naipaul sees him as interested only in possessing politically correct views, and as oblivious to the human cost of the implementation of such views. "That again was like Richard, still concerned only with the rightness of his principles, and somehow still safe" (*WW*, p. 369). As an expatriate, he is not required to live with the consequences of his politics.

Naipaul's sense of the prevalent orthodoxies of his audience would appear to have been shaped in part by the reception of his early works, summarized here by his friend Francis Wyndham:

> During the Fifties it was considered rather bad form, in literary circles, to approach an "underdeveloped country" in a spirit of sophisticated humour.... . Well-meaning British reviewers — whether in sheer ignorance of the background, or else unconsciously reflecting the prevalent attitudes of neo-colonialist embarrassment — responded to *The Mystic Masseur*, *The Suffrage of Elvira* and *Miguel Street* in dismayed tones of patronizing rebuke. They would have preferred a simple study in compassion where a clear distinction is made between oppressors and the oppressed, or a "charming" exercise in the *faux-naif*, or a steamily incoherent drama of miscegenation and primitive brutality. [65]

This passage closely corresponds to various statements made by Naipaul himself about the pressures of audience expectation in relation to West Indian literature. Reviewing Samuel Selvon's *Turn Again Tiger*, Naipaul condemned the work for being " 'angled' in the light of the current vogue for Race, Sex and Caribbean writing", and dismissed Tiger's affair with an Englishwoman, "with its obsolete hints of racial oppression and revenge",[66] as out of keeping with Selvon's earlier work. He contends that his own reading of West Indian literature has taught him to avoid certain themes (poverty, death, melodrama and miscegenation).[67] He asserts, regarding a publisher who described him as a West Indian writer: "I've been breaking away from that tag all my life".[68] Naipaul's own work, however, shows a certain compliance with this tendency: as discussed elsewhere in this book, interracial sex and violence form the subject of *Guerrillas, In a Free State* and *A Bend in the River*.

"So often with West Indian writing one gets the impression that the whole thing is being done for alien approval: there must be explanations, apologies, or defiance",[69] Naipaul argues. It is this literary trend which Naipaul parodies in the lead story of *A Flag on the Island*. A work particularly popular with the tourists is *I Hate You*, by Mr Blackwhite:

> "I am a man without identity. Hate has consumed my identity. My personality has been distorted by hate. My hymns have not been hymns of praise, but of hate. How terrible to be Caliban, you say. But I say, how tremendous" (*FI*, p. 129).

The reference to Caliban brings to mind George Lamming's *The Pleasures of Exile* (1960), which, as noted previously, appropriates *The*

Tempest as a defining myth of West Indian reality by rewriting it, confrontationally, from the point of view of Caliban. Lamming attacked Naipaul for his "castrated satire";[70] the figure of Mr Blackwhite is perhaps Naipaul's rejoinder to the attack. There may also be an element of self-caricature to the portrait: *The Shadowed Livery*, the title of one of his books, was the name of Naipaul's first novel, written as an undergraduate. The literary mutations of Blackwhite, formerly H. J. B. White, distil a parodic history of West Indian literature: he begins by writing about absurdly incongruous and anachronistic subjects (romances concerning the English nobility); at Frank's suggestion, he makes the everyday life of the island his theme; his work grows increasingly confrontational; and this manner finds favour not only with the tourists but with foreign foundations, eager to encourage their own idea of an "authentic" tradition, specially packaged for external consumption. Naipaul's analysis is the same in the case of African literature, seen as satisfying a European thirst for confrontational images of the periphery. Of the stay in Uganda on which the final section of *A Way in the World* is loosely based, Naipaul recalls "foreign publishing houses seeking African markets; the whole bogus European-managed cultural thing, creating a kind of bogus man, acting for the expatriate".[71] Naipaul's sense of the characteristic themes of West Indian literature was informed by his role as editor of the BBC World Service's *Caribbean Voices* programme, which was designed to encourage new writing from the Caribbean; at one point he announced that he thought the programme should reassess its policy, and instead discourage Caribbean writing.[72] West Indian literature serves, therefore, as another context which, both directly and indirectly, exerts an influence on his work. Naipaul's treatment of the Lebrun character, and the portrayal of his dealings with Lebrun's powerful patrons, particularly at the second dinner party, might be interpreted as an allegory of his refusal to succumb to the pressures of audience expectation.

E. H. Carr, in a well-known formulation, described history as "an unending dialogue between the present and the past".[73] Not only does Naipaul see the present as doomed to repeat the past: "Miranda's failure is still relevant, and the whole business of New World slavery is still with us. The borrowed revolutions of South America are also still with us".[74] His perception of the past is, in addition, shaped by his sense of the present. His depiction of the failures which have attended West Indian history is a response to what he perceives as

> the new politics, the curious reliance of men on institutions
> they were yet working to undermine, the simplicity of beliefs
> and the hideous simplicity of actions, the corruption of causes,

half-made societies that seemed doomed to remain half-made
... (*REP*, p. 216.)

A tendency to see patterns in history is enhanced also by his practice of self-reference: both history and Naipaul repeat themselves.

Notes

1 *A Way in the World: A Sequence* (London: Heinemann, 1994), p. 32.
2 Interviewed by Aamer Hussein, p. 3.
3 "Fool's Gold", *New Yorker* (August 8 1970), *Critical Perspectives on V. S. Naipaul*, p. 153.
4 *The Loss of El Dorado: A History* (London: André Deutsch, 1969), p. 266.
5 *A Turn in the South* (New York: Alfred A. Knopf, 1989), p. 35.
6 *REP*, Author's Note
7 *WW*, pp. 17, 21, 39, 84, 149, 353.
8 Interviewed by Aamer Hussein, p. 4.
9 This is noted by David Ormerod, "In a Derelict Land: The Novels of V. S. Naipaul", Hamner, p. 161.
10 *Nostromo* (London: Dent, 1957), p. 49.
11 *Heart of Darkness* (Harmondworth: Penguin, 1983), p. 61.
12 Interviewed by Julian Mitchell, *The Arts This Week* (October 29 1969), p. 2, BBC Written Archives.
13 *The Rise of the Novel* (London: Chatto and Windus, 1957), p. 30.
14 *On the Contrary* (London: Heinemann, 1962), pp. 262–3.
15 Robert Louis Stevenson, "A Humble Remonstrance", *Memories and Portraits* (London: Chatto and Windus, 1888), p. 284.
16 "New Novels", *New Statesman*, 57 (January 17 1959), p. 79.
17 Interviewed by Andrew Robinson, "Stranger in Fiction", *Independent on Sunday* (August 16 1992), p. 23.
18 *Ibid.*
19 "London: A Case for Future Historians", *Illustrated Weekly of India*, 84 (July 28 1963), p. 15.
20 *Illustrated Weekly of India*, 84 (September 29 1963), p. 15.
21 *Beyond a Boundary*, p. 61.
22 *Beyond a Boundary*, p. 99.
23 "Cricket", *Encounter* (September 1963), in *OB*, p. 22.
24 "A Handful of Dust", p. 15.
25 "A Handful of Dust", p. 15.
26 "A Handful of Dust", p. 16.
27 *The Return of Eva Perón: With the Killings in Trinidad* (London: André Deutsch, 1980), p. 23.
28 This work is mentioned in the bibliography of *LED*.
29 *Bolívar* (London: Hollis and Carter, 1952), p. 92.
30 William Spence Robertson, *The Life of Miranda* (Chapel Hill: University of North Carolina Press, 1929), vol. 2, p. 248.
31 *The Comedians* (London: Bodley Head and Heinemann, 1976), p. 329.
32 *LED*, pp. 88, 51; *WW*, pp. 165, 177.
33 *WW*, p. 309; *LED* pp. 254–5.

34   *WW*, p. 276, which repeats *LED*, pp. 166, 209.
35   Interviewed by Aamer Hussein, p. 3.
36   Interviewed by David Bates, p. 13.
37   *Talking of Books*, Transcript of BBC broadcast (November 24 1961), André Deutsch Archive 95, *HB* folder.
38   *Fact* (September 1938), p. 79.
39   *Mr Stone and the Knights Companion* (London: André Deutsch, 1963), p. 149.
40   Interviewed by Charles Wheeler, p. 537.
41   *LED*, p. 136; echoed in *WW*, p. 331.
42   *WW*, p. 29. The image is repeated at pp. 32, 36, 40, 150.
43   Interviewed by Adrian Rowe-Evans, p. 51.
44   "The Little More", Hamner, p. 13.
45   Interviewed by Walter Allen, *The World of Books* (October 24 1961), p. 6, BBC Written Archives.
46   "Where the Rum Comes From", *New Statesman*, 55 (January 4 1958), p. 21.
47   An instance is furnished by an anonymous pamphlet, "Naipaul and the Blacks", which has accused Naipaul's critics of racism, in terms which are unambiguously racist (*New Voices*, 3, 7 & 8 (1976), pp. 19–23, 62–4, 87).
48   *LED*, p. 301; see also *MP*, p. 72.
49   A view of colonial society also presented in *MP*, p. 42.
50   Interviewed by Aamer Hussein, p. 4.
51   *The General in His Labyrinth*, tr. by Edith Grossman (London: Jonathan Cape, 1991), pp. 202–3.
52   "Guerrillas and Gangs: Frantz Fanon and V. S. Naipaul", *Ariel* 13, 4 (October 1982), p. 23.
53   As argued by Edward Said, *Culture and Imperialism*, p. 30.
54   Prologue, *The Black Jacobins: Toussaint L'Ouverture and the San Domingo Revolution*, rev. ed. (New York: Vintage, 1963), p. 3.
55   *The Black Jacobins*, p. 212.
56   "V. S. Naipaul Tells how Writing Changes a Writer", p. 11.
57   "England, Half-English", *Listener*, 66 (September 7 1961), p. 358.
58   "England, Half-English", p. 358.
59   *City of Spades* (London: MacGibbon and Kee, 1957), p. 69.
60   *Hopes and Impediments: Selected Essays 1965–87* (London: Heinemann, 1988).
61   *V. S. Naipaul: A Materialist Reading* (Amherst: University of Massachusetts Press, 1988).
62   "Naipaulicity: A Form of Cultural Imperialism?" *Race and Class*, 26, 2 (Autumn 1984), pp. 45–63.
63   Interviewed by Charles Michener, p. 109.
64   Interviewed by Bernard Geniès and Nicole Zand, "*Un Observateur Féroce du Tiers-Monde*", *Le Monde* (26 June 1981), p. 20.
65   "V. S. Naipaul", *Listener,* 86 (October 7 1971), pp. 461–2.
66   "New Novels", *New Statesman*, 56 (December 6 1958), p. 827.
67   *Caribbean Voices* (August 31 1958), p. 2, BBC Written Archives.
68   Interviewed by Charles Michener, p. 108.
69   *Caribbean Voices* (September 16 1956), p. 4, BBC Written Archives.
70   *The Pleasures of Exile*, p. 225.
71   *A Congo Diary* (Los Angeles, Sylvester and Orphanos, 1980), p. 36.
72   *Caribbean Voices*, (September 16 1956), p. 3, BBC Written Archives.
73   *What is History?* (Harmondsworth: Penguin, 1964), p. 30.
74   Letter from V. S. Naipaul to Diana Athill, (December 5 1968), André Deutsch Archive, 95, *LED* folder.

4 | Naipaul's changing representation of India: autobiographical and literary backgrounds

Naipaul's three Indian books span the course of his career. He begins by writing a travel book and comedy of manners in *An Area of Darkness.* In *India: A Wounded Civilization,* he appears in the guise of a prophet of doom, and has excited hostility by assuming the position of one who knows more about India than Indians do, and by forecasting an impending chaos in Indian civilization, while satirizing the progress of Indian self-rule. In *India: A Million Mutinies Now*, Naipaul is reborn into a new persona: accepting and tolerant, he listens to characters as they recount the narrative of their own lives, and he refrains from offering overt authorial judgements. His writings on India show an interplay of consistency and self-divergence: his preoccupations remain constant, while the response they produce is subject to change. The Indian books, although atypical in not including any fiction, are shaped by characteristic concerns. Throughout his opus, he reworks his own material. His life functions as a primary source of material in all his works, and his Indian books are suffused with a sense of the personality of the writer and with autobiographical detail.

Naipaul's connection with the Indian cultural heritage adds interest to these works, although it is open to question whether it assists or impedes his understanding of India. In *India: A Wounded Civilization*, he defines the problems it poses:

> India is for me a difficult country. It isn't my home and cannot be my home; and yet I cannot reject it or be indifferent to it; I cannot travel only for the sights. I am at once too close and too far.[1]

He is therefore able to base his investigation of the society on the traces of India he carries within.

> And though in India I am a stranger, the starting point of this inquiry — more than might appear in these pages — has been myself. Because in myself, like the split-second images of infancy which some of us carry, there survive, from the family

rituals that lasted into my childhood, phantasmal memories of old India which for me outline a whole vanished world (*IWC*, p. 9).

The notion of this subjective, internal starting-point contrasts with the emphasis placed on the value of objective examination of empirical data. It also corresponds to a tendency which Naipaul identifies and excoriates in Indians:

> But to know India, most people look inward. They consult themselves: in their own past, in the nature of their caste or clan life, their family traditions, they find the idea of India which they know to be true, and according to which they act (*IWC*, p. 130).

Naipaul's analysis of Indian attitudes gives the impression that his arguments are projections of his own internal drama, and, with an irony evident intermittently to Naipaul and his readers, are applicable to his own artistic practices.

> And in India I was to see that so many of the things which the newer and now perhaps truer side of my nature kicked against — the smugness, as it seemed to me, the imperviousness to criticism, the refusal to *see*, the double-talk and double-think — had an answer in that side of myself which I had thought buried and which India revived as a faint memory (*AD*, p. 38).

This can be seen to belong to an established tradition of representing the exotic, which treats other societies and landscapes as a backdrop for a playing-out of the traveller's own psychological conflicts, and for a definition and analysis of the self. In *Heart of Darkness*, to which the title of *An Area of Darkness* is likely to allude, Marlow similarly discovers in the course of his journey distant ancestral affinities with the locals.

An Area of Darkness begins by identifying Naipaul's position as an observer, through an exploration of the autobiographical dimensions of his relation to India. It traces the progress of his grandfather's migration from India to Trinidad, where he recreated a simulacrum in miniature of his lost Indian world. His was a family circle enclosed in a community based on a denial of the adopted country. It goes on to describe the gradual contraction and disruption of the seemingly complete world of Trinidad's Little India. India functioned for Naipaul as a "resting-place for the imagination". "It was the country from which my grandfather came, a country never physically described and therefore never real, a country out in the void beyond the dot of Trinidad" (*AD*, p. 29). India's unknown character is symbolized by a similar image to that which

Naipaul uses in *A House for Mr Biswas* to evoke abandonment and desolation, as if to suggest Naipaul's sense that, cut off from the land of his ancestors, he is, figuratively speaking, an orphan. India was imagined by him as shrouded in darkness, ''as darkness surrounds a hut at evening, though for a little way around the hut there is still light'' (*AD*, p. 32). In contrast to the notion that he can find India by looking within himself, and in an admission that his journey to India has been a disappointment, he asserts:

> And even now, though time has widened, though space has contracted and I have travelled lucidly over that area which was to me the area of darkness, something of darkness remains, in those attitudes, those ways of thinking and seeing, which are no longer mine (*AD*, p. 32).

According to this opposing motif, India remains to an important degree elusive, mysterious and unknown.

An Area of Darkness therefore forms a narrative of unfulfilled expectations. It records Naipaul's failure to discover in India the ancestral homeland he had imagined it to be:

> India had not worked its magic on me. It remained the land of my childhood, an area of darkness; like the Himalayan passes, it was closing up again, as fast as I withdrew from it, into a land of myth (*AD*, p. 266).

Naipaul's situation is analogous to that of the Indian repatriates from Trinidad who flock to India, find they no longer have a home there, then besiege the ship, begging to be taken back to Trinidad. He sees them as symbols of the placelessness of the Trinidad Hindu community (*FC*, p. 61). Naipaul discovers that his conception of an Indian identity has no echo in the minds of those he meets, whose identity is defined in terms of region or caste.

> A colonial, in the double sense of one who had grown up in a Crown colony and one who had been cut off from the metropolis, be it either England or India, I came to India expecting to find metropolitan attitudes. I had imagined that in some ways the largeness of the land would be reflected in the attitudes of the people. I have found, as I have said, the psychology of the cell and the hive. And I have been surprised by similarities. In India, as in tiny Trinidad, I have found the feeling that the metropolis is elsewhere, in Europe or America. Where I had expected largeness, rootedness and confidence, I have found all the colonial attitudes of self-distrust (*OB*, p. 44).

Some of the bitterness of Naipaul's account of Indian society can be ascribed to this disappointment.

In his first two books, Naipaul oscillates between presenting himself as an insider and as an outsider in relation to Hindu society. This ambivalence in Naipaul's travelling persona is noted by Rob Nixon.[2] Nixon argues that Naipaul moves between contradictory modes: at times he styles himself distanced and analytic; at other times, as subjectively entangled. Nixon locates the literary antecedents of his travel writing in the confident tones of Victorian travellers, the supposed impartiality of ethnography — which reduces the other to object — and the confessional mode which promises an honest declaration of the writer's involvement.

Naipaul writes that he bears traces of a vestigial Hinduism, attenuated to "that sense of the difference of people, which I have tried to explain, a vaguer sense of caste, and a horror of the unclean" (*AD*, p. 35). A sense of the difference between people works against the perception of kinship or solidarity. Such is his sense of alienation that Trinidad is atypically (for Naipaul) represented as a homeland, against which is measured his distance from India: "I had learnt my separateness from India, and was content to be a colonial, without a past, without ancestors" (*AD*, p. 266). As a vestigial Hindu, he is able to enter into Hindu habits of thought. As an outsider, he possesses the necessary critical distance for judicious observation: he presents himself as better able to comprehend the state of Indian society than Indians themselves are. This dual perspective is not exclusive to his writings on India: it has attracted comment in other works of his. It is also apparent in *Guerrillas*, as will be argued in Chapter 5. Naipaul identifies a similar dichotomy in his father's writings (*FC*, p. 70), and employs this divided perspective in his own treatment of the Trinidad Hindu community.

An important aspect of Naipaul's analysis of the Hindu character — the very effort to think in such general terms might appear bound to slip into caricature — is his notion that Indians are incapable of perceiving in an objective way the world about them. He attaches a complex of assumptions to this proposition, arguing that Hindus lead instinctual lives governed by magic and ritual and by caste, lives characterized by self-absorption and social indifference. Naipaul expounds and illustrates his contention with reference to Gandhi's *The Story of My Experiments with Truth*. Gandhi repeatedly detects in his experience the hand of God, who intervenes to rescue him from the commission of various sins. The book is shaped by an interplay of indeterminacy and structure which is the result of occasional divergences between Gandhi's will and the divine scheme. Naipaul finds the book deficient as an autobiography; it is lacking in observed detail of English and African life, he contends:

The inward concentration is fierce, the self-absorption complete.... . The London of 1890, capital of the world — which must have been overwhelming to a young man from a small Indian town — has to be inferred from Gandhi's continuing internal disturbances, his embarrassments, his religious self-searchings, his attempts at dressing correctly and learning English manners, and above all, his difficulties and occasional satisfactions about food (*IWC*, p. 98).

This is in direct contrast to the terms in which *An Area of Darkness* had chosen to commend Gandhi's capacity to look at India: he saw it, Naipaul argues, "as no Indian was able to; his vision was direct, and this directness was, and is, revolutionary. He sees exactly what the visitor sees; he does not ignore the obvious" (*AD*, p. 77). Naipaul ascribes this capacity to Gandhi's residence in South Africa: "Contrast made for clarity, criticism and discrimination for self-analysis" (*AD*, p. 78). An implicit parallel is established between Gandhi's and Naipaul's position.

From his reading of Gandhi's book in *India: A Wounded Civilization*, Naipaul identifies a Hindu "need constantly to define and fortify the self in the midst of hostility" (*IWC*, p. 100). As is the case with other aspects of his analysis of the Hindu psyche, Naipaul's comments can be read as contrasting with, and, at a deeper level, as corresponding to, his own position. The ironies inherent in his analysis are a function of the ambivalent stance Naipaul adopts towards his subject. Although his descriptions of the Indian scene proliferate in detailed observation of his external surroundings, they give the impression that they are impelled by personal needs. They speak of a hysterical sense of embattled individuality, akin to what he defines as "the always desperate Hindu sense of the self, the sense of encircling external threat" (*IWC*, p. 45). He writes that in India, for the first time, he does not stand out from the crowd; his singularity is threatened. "It was like being denied part of my reality. Again and again I was caught. I was faceless. I might sink without a trace into that Indian crowd" (*AD*, p. 46).

The threat goes deeper. People are reduced in Naipaul's descriptions to a faceless mass of emaciated bodies, or to the status of animals or objects:

> ... like the squatters in the ruins outside the living Vijayanagar temple, slipping in and out of the decayed stone façades like brightly coloured insects, screeching and unimportantly active on this afternoon of rain (*IWC*, p. 17).

The dehumanization is intended to reflect the attitudes of a society in which the individual is supernumerary — as in the case of a woman sweeping the dam in Rajasthan with a rag, whom Naipaul perceives as denied humanity by the nullity of her labour: "She is hardly a person" (*IWC*, p. 75). Such figures appear to constitute for Naipaul a threat to his own sense of self and of human possibility.

> Men had been diminished and deformed; they begged and whined. Hysteria had been my reaction, and a brutality dictated by a new awareness of myself as a whole human being, and a determination, touched with fear, to remain what I was (*AD*, p. 16).

His outrage at this reduction of human possibility expresses itself in a manner whereby sympathy becomes virtually indistinguishable from revulsion: "It was compassion like mine, so strenuously maintained, that denied humanity to many" (*AD*, p. 263).

> I had seen Indian villages: the narrow, broken lanes with green slime in the gutters, the choked back-to-back mud houses, the jumble of filth and food and animals and people, the baby in the dust, swollen-bellied, black with flies, but wearing its good-luck amulet. I had seen the starved child defecating at the roadside while the mangy dog waited to eat the excrement. I had seen the physique of the people of Andhra, which had suggested the possibility of an evolution downwards, wasted body to wasted body, Nature mocking herself, incapable of remission. Compassion and pity did not answer; they were like refinements of hope. Fear was what I felt (*AD*, p. 48).

The starved child could be any child, or a composite figure. This passage suggests the motif of the traveller discovering within himself atavistic impulses.

Naipaul's horror of the unclean, legacy of ancestral attitudes, leads to a fascinated dwelling on this subject. A preoccupation with bodily functions, the potency of Naipaul's disgust, and his obsessive return to what has excited a negative reaction, suggest themselves for comparison with Swift. While *An Area of Darkness* is concerned to reproduce the initial experience of the visitor to India, when India may be felt "only as an assault on the senses" (*OB*, p. 41), *India: A Wounded Civilization* expounds a general thesis about Indian society, but it would appear to be at variance with the values of balanced and rational assessment which Naipaul advocates in this work that it should contain descriptions in which observation seems to dissolve into nightmare and phantasmagoria.

Naipaul's fear is openly avowed:

> The poverty of the Indian streets and the countryside was an affront and a threat, a scratching at my old neurosis. Two

generations separated me from that kind of poverty; but I felt closer to it than most of the Indians I met (*IMMN*, p. 8).

An instinct for survival on his part leads to the fending-off of any sense of kinship, and indirectly manifests itself in fascination, horror and rejection. Comparably, in *The Mimic Men* Ralph's motivation suggests the condescension and reductiveness which may be implicit in humanitarian concern. Opposing attitudes are fused: as a politician, Ralph might be among those who stand for the "dignity of distress" (*MM*, p. 237), but he views his supporters with fear and contempt. Political movements which claim to represent the oppressed, Naipaul suggests, risk diminishing the objects of their concern by treating them purely as ciphers or passive victims:

> There is more to people than their distress. . . . And unless you understand that everyone has cause for self-esteem, you make a terrible political error. The Marxists tend to reduce people to their distress, or to their economic position.[3]

A former Naxalite later interviewed by Naipaul confirms his proposition, noting a tendency in his organization to conceive of the people as "objects, not living subjects making their own lives — and history in that process" (*IMMN*, p. 323). The technique of *India: A Million Mutinies Now*, in which characters speak for themselves, as here, seems designed to avoid treating its subjects as the passive objects of scrutiny, although Naipaul tends to interview people who have transformed their lives in some way, and the faceless hordes of the poor exist only on the periphery of the book.[4]

The difficulties involved in the representation of the oppressed are suggested by Mulk Raj Anand's *Untouchable*, which shifts between treating its untouchable hero as a degraded victim of his environment, and as miraculously rising above it.[5] The humanitarian impulse might, in general, be thought both to imply and to be sabotaged by a deterministic view of social environment. Bakha is shown as degraded in order to demonstrate the way in which the caste system degrades. At the same time, Anand endeavours to engage our sympathy for the hero by presenting him as superior to his environment, in defiance of his degraded social position. Anand seeks to display Bakha's untapped potential, by dwelling on the "nobility" of his physique, in "contrast with his filthy profession and with the sub-human status to which he was condemned from birth",[6] by referring to his pent-up resources (Anand, p. 14), and by delineating his aspirations, if only to emulate the ways of the sahibs. His brother, in contrast, is simply a victim: "His listless, lazy, lousy manner was a result of his surroundings" (Anand, p. 69). A similar contradiction may be seen to define Dickens's orphans: Jo, in *Bleak House*, seems to have emerged relatively unscathed from the noxious environment by which others are vitiated. *A House for Mr Biswas* strikes the difficult balance involved in portraying its hero as vulnerable and yet not altogether a victim, nor miraculously superior to his circumstances.

Contempt or compassion, curiosity or indifference, could all be seen as threatening to reduce the Indian people to a colourful backdrop in Western imaginings of India. In Kipling's *Kim,* certain individuals are picked out of the crowd, given a name and a face, and used to represent the Indian people — to form a recognizable community that can be contained within the novel. In the background, life goes on:

> "All castes and kinds of men move here. Look! Brahmins and chumars, bankers and tinkers, barbers and bunnias, pilgrims and potters — all the world going and coming. It is to me as a river from which I am withdrawn like a log after a flood."
>
> And truly the Grand Trunk Road is a wonderful spectacle. It runs straight, bearing without crowding India's traffic for fifteen hundred miles — such a river of life as nowhere else exists in the world.[7]

The Indian population is viewed accordingly both by Kim and by the narrator:

> This was seeing the world in real truth; this was life as he [Kim] would have it — bustling and shouting, the buckling of belts, and beating of bullocks and creaking of wheels, lighting of fires and cooking of food, and new sights at every turn of the approving eye (Kipling, p. 103).

The human agents who initiate the activity are passed over in this account. Naipaul departs from Kipling's example in that, instead of portraying the mass of the population as a picturesque and vibrant spectacle, he elaborates an infernal vision of human degradation. He has written about Kipling, perhaps inversely defining his own sense of being without a community in his analysis of the manner in which Kipling's writing is shaped in communication with the attitudes of his Anglo-Indian audience, which make possible Kipling's "allusive, elliptical prose, easy but packed" (*OB*, p. 72).

Naipaul quotes from E. M. Forster in *An Area of Darkness* in order to illustrate his contention regarding the development of an English national consciousness: and there are further echoes of *A Passage to India* in the failures of understanding which characterize Naipaul's relations with Aziz in this work, and in his failure to achieve mystical transfiguration in a cave, when he makes the pilgrimage to Armanath. In *A Passage to India*, Adela Quested is engaged on a quest to "see the *real* India".[8] She seeks to resist the reduction of Indian life to a remote, colourful "frieze" (Forster, p. 37), but in the process is the cause of mischief. Forster portrays her urge to see and to know India as proceeding from idle curiosity, and indulged at the expense of individual Indians. It is posited on a lack of engagement with the object of her scrutiny. In her perception, Aziz is made falsely representative: she imposes on him the burden of signifying the "real" India. Aziz, in his later, bitter guise, thinks: "This pose of 'seeing India' ... was only a form of ruling India; no sympathy lay behind it" (Forster, p. 267). Kim's urge to see India, as Edward Said has pointed out,[9] harmonizes with and serves the Indian Survey Department's job of controlling India: knowledge is power.

Kipling's tone is that of one who has "mastered his subject and [who] knows his audience" (*OB*, p. 73). Mastery is implied by his many confident assertions concerning "the Oriental character", which, as Said remarks, imply that it is a fixed entity, distinct from the European, yet fully known to the author. Forster is also the legatee of such imperial confidence: he understands Indian customs better than his English characters do, and translates for his readers the difference between what is said by his Indian characters and what is meant. While Indian and English characters misinterpret each other, Forster is able to move between the two worlds and to rise above the confusion. A resemblance to Kipling's manner might be detected in the claim:

> Suspicion in the Oriental is a sort of malignant tumour, a mental malady, that makes him self-conscious and unfriendly suddenly; he trusts and mistrusts at the same time in a way the Westerner cannot comprehend (Forster, p. 243).

This Westerner, however, appears to have no difficulty in comprehending it.

Although there are fundamental similarities, Forster's and Kipling's approaches embody contrasting trends in the depiction of other cultures. Forster depicts India as essentially unknowable. At the centre of the book is the excursion to the Marabar Caves, around which a ponderous edifice of symbolism is constructed. The experience of the caves is figured as a kind of encounter with cosmic emptiness and the indifference of matter in the raw, a perception of which lies outside the safety of habitual modes of apprehension. This notion might be placed in a different tradition — one which treats the experience of India as testing the limits of the wisdom of Western society. The caves are empty, waiting to be filled with meaning by the visitor or by Forster, and their interior is smooth, reflecting back the image of the observer, in a manner which suggests the circularity of attempts to find a meaning in such things. The caves give Mrs Moore a sense of the muddle of life as viewed under the aspect of eternity: they murmur, " 'Everything exists, nothing has value' " (Forster, p. 128). Mrs Moore experiences in them a negative epiphany, a confrontation with horror, which recalls the dénouement of Marlow's journey to the Congo, although it does not fulfil the function of a climax in Forster's novel.

Forster subsequently suggests that the caves do not sum up Indian reality; the landscape addresses Mrs Moore on her departure, " 'So you thought an echo was India; you took the Marabar caves as final?' " (Forster, p. 182). However, the overriding impression created by the book is that India is inconceivable by the outsider: "How can the mind take hold of such a country? Generations of invaders have tried, but they remain in exile" (Forster, pp. 116–7). India dissolves into the outsider's failure to comprehend it. It is debatable whether this mode is any more respectful than that involving generalizations about "the Oriental character". Such discourse comes close to slipping into the stereotype of the mysterious and inscrutable which informs Forster's portrayal of Godbole. It is a moot question whether this is a more insulting portrait than that of Aziz, which enters into the character's play of mind, and finds in it instability and a subjection to the rule of emotion. In general, attempts to represent other cultures can be seen as bedeviled by hazards on both sides. To assume too ready a familiarity with a character's motives is to presume, or to risk simplification and the reproduction of a standard version of the alien, whereas not to attempt to do so is to portray the other as closed to rational inquiry, in the manner of Conrad's Africans in *Heart of Darkness*: mere projections of European fears and guilt about the imperial project.

Naipaul's depiction of India in his first two books favours an approach closer to Kipling's certainties: he assumes a tone of easy mastery and magisterial control. His generalizations, delivered with absolute authority, imply a conviction that he has the measure of India, and that it can offer no surprises that would unsettle his formulations. Such confidence is implied by the audaciously encompassing scope of Naipaul's statements: "Insecurity merged with the Indian intellectual failure and became part of the Indian drabness" (*OB*, p. 85). With the help of a psychotherapist, Naipaul seeks to incorporate his observations in a thesis about the Indian character, which he defines as possessing a childlike perception of reality, and an underdeveloped ego, as prone to a purely instinctual life governed by ritual and magic, and as devoid of self-consciousness (*IWC*, pp. 102–3). Failures of understanding on Naipaul's part do not undermine his confidence in his capacity to generalize:

From whatever point they started ... there always came a moment when Indians, administrator, journalist, poet, holy man, slipped away like eels into muddy abstraction. They abandoned intellect, observation, reason; and became "mysterious" (*OB*, p. 79).

In this way, the trope of mystery is assimilated to the discourse of authoritative pronouncement. Naipaul's prose expresses confidence concerning his familiarity with particular Indians and Indian social types, and an enjoyment of the occasion to display it:

Bunty comes of a "good" family, Army, ICS; he might even have princely connections. He is two or three generations removed from purely Indian India; he, possibly like his father, has been to an Indian or English public school and one of the two English universities, whose accent, through all the encircling hazards of Indian intonation, he strenuously maintains (*AD*, p. 62).

Another respect in which Naipaul's definition of the Hindu character reads as an exercise in self-exploration, and his criticism of India as self-definition, concerns his description of

the Indian ability to retreat, the ability genuinely not to see what was obvious: with others a foundation of neurosis, but with Indians only part of a greater philosophy of despair, leading to passivity, detachment, acceptance. It is only now, as the impatience of the observer is dissipated in the processes of writing and self-inquiry, that I see how much this philosophy had also been mine (*AD*, p. 198).

This may seem a surprising assertion, in view of his portrayal of himself as in a position to see what Indians cannot, as one who applies the "straight simple vision of the West" (*AD*, p. 78), and in view of the absence of acceptance in his relation to India. Detach himself is what he does, both literally and metaphorically, by fleeing India, in the last chapter of *An Area of Darkness*, entitled "Flight". He has asserted that

I long to find what is good and hopeful and really do hope that by the most brutal sort of analysis one is possibly opening up the situation to some sort of action: an action which is not based on self-deception.[10]

It can more often appear that, by reducing all forms of human activity to a perception of futility, Naipaul expresses a resigned sense of the hopelessness of any attempt at change. *India: A Wounded Civilization* is prone to prognostications of impending doom: the conflict between archaic and modern currents in Indian life, Naipaul contends, has "cracked the civilization open" (*IWC*, p. 18). From a Narayan novel, Naipaul infers that retreat is a repeated occurrence in Indian history: "Retreat from a world that is known to have broken down at last, ... a retrogression to an almost African night... . It is the death of a civilization, the final corruption of Hinduism" (*IWC*, p. 43). Writing of Indian civilization in a manner which suggests that it has fixed and immemorial characteristics, he makes use of the *Kama Sutra* in his analysis of contemporary Indian society, asserting that "no Indian manual is so old that it has ceased to be relevant" (*AD*, p. 81). Naipaul remarks that the subject which furnishes his theme was also that of Raja Rammohun Roy, the Bengali reformer, 150 years ago, and of the Buddha 2,500 years before: "It is depressing, this cycle of similar reform and similar relapse" (*OB*, p. 91). Ironically, such a view is not remote from a concept he detects in Narayan's novels, and sees as related to a shortcoming of Hindu society at large: that of the "Hindu equilibrium" (*IWC*, p. 27), the notion that "life goes on, the past continues. After conquest and destruction, the past simply reasserts itself" (*IWC*, p. 15). Naipaul reduces Indian history to a pattern of vulnerability, defeat and withdrawal: past failures cast their shadow over present and future efforts. Naipaul argues that India's "crisis is not political or economic" (*IWC*, p. 18), but is due to the inadequacies of its civilization. Naipaul resolutely ascribes to India responsibility for its problems: "The faults lie within the civilization itself" (*IWC*, p. 148). His intention, presumably, is to refute those who see India's problems as arising from conquest: "I can't bear the account of people who have been done to. Better to blame the civilization that bred us".[11] The analysis implies the inevitability of defeat rather than proposing the means of producing an effective transformation.

Naipaul's emphasis on his own reactions as an observer can serve to impede the attempt to understand others: Naipaul turns misunderstanding and frustration into the occasion for self-reproachful comedy. The emphasis is on his own reactions in the description of a visit to his ancestral village which ends "in futility and impatience, a gratuitous act of cruelty, self-reproach and flight" (*AD*, p. 277). Self-involvement here precludes sympathy, and external incidents provide an occasion for a probing of the author's own sensibility.

The manner in which Naipaul's writings on India, with the exception of his most recent book, foreground the personality of the observer as much as the objects of his scrutiny is in conformity with various assertions on Naipaul's part that travel books are more interesting and more truthful for so doing. Reviewing a travel book by Harold Nicolson, he argues that the interest "does not lie so much in Sir Harold's inquiry as in Sir Harold himself. . . . Sir Harold has the good essayist's gift of unembarrassing self-revelation"; Nicolson is "entertaining when he is moved by prejudice".[12] In describing the mode of the Victorian travel book, Naipaul would appear to be defining the effect he himself aims for:

> A travel book which is not strictly an account of exploration or discovery succeeds or fails according to the personality of the traveller. And the Victorians were, of course, privileged: they were free to express their most outrageous prejudices.[13]

Naipaul regrets being unable to emulate Trollope's manner. He explains that he felt this mode to be unattainable by him: "Of course I'd read the great European travel books, . . . but how was a man from Trinidad to view the world?"[14] Rob Nixon, however, has argued that Naipaul is indeed indebted to the Victorian travel book: he examines the way *The Middle Passage* enters into dialogue with Froude's and Trollope's writings on the West Indies, and harks back to their style. The Darwinian image, in *The Middle Passage*, of Trinidad's various ethnic groups — "like monkeys pleading for evolution, each claiming to be whiter than the other" (*MP*, p.80) — suggests as much. Naipaul commends Trollope's "unapologetic display of outrageous prejudices ('I hate Baptists like poison'), that fairness, that cruel humour, without a tinge of self-satire".[15] He elaborates a contentious idea of the compatibility of objectivity and prejudice: "For works to last, they must have a certain clear-sightedness. And to achieve that, one perhaps needs a few prejudices".[16] In his view, however, only certain prejudices are acceptable. Earlier in his career, he declared that he wished to dissociate himself from group prejudices of the type espoused by other West Indian writers, by which he presumably refers to ethnic allegiances.[17] Nevertheless, the instances he supplies of Trollope's supposed fairness include the following examples:

> Who today, discussing race relations, will begin a paragraph: "But to get back to our sable friends"? . . . Who . . . will describe a foreign territory as a "Niggery-Hispano-Dano-Yankee-Doodle place?"[18]

A more recent model for the stance of the lone voice in the wilderness, interestingly and gruffly opinionated, may have been furnished by Nirad Chaudhuri. In his *Autobiography of an Unknown Indian*, Chaudhuri portrays himself as occupying the position of one who is at once an insider and an outsider to his society. He can claim sufficient intellectual distance from it to view it critically, but knows it well enough to be able to describe its daily life in the minutest detail. Chaudhuri examines, records and explains the rituals associated with his childhood in the manner of an anthropologist visiting his past: "It was only my subsequent stay of thirty-two years in Calcutta which made me truly aware of Kishorganj".[19] "Perhaps the process of detachment from environment which began with my coming to Calcutta sharpened my perceptive faculties" (*AUI*, p. 257). Chaudhuri's observations on Indian life are saturated in the personality of the writer, to the point that the distinction between external and internal becomes blurred:

> I have only to look within myself and contemplate my life to discover India; my intellect has indeed at last emancipated itself from my country, but taking stock of all the rest I can say without the least suggestion of arrogance: *l'Inde, c'est moi* (*AUI*, p. 461).

This is an attitude which Naipaul at once dissects, condemns and replicates — discovering Indian attitudes within himself.

Chaudhuri's *Autobiography* charts the development not simply of an individual, but of an altogether singular one, whose singularity is belied by the work's ironic title:

> Kishorganj, Banagram and Kalikutch are interwoven with my being; so is the England of my imagination; they formed and shaped me; but when once torn up from my natural habitat I became liberated from habitat altogether; my environment and I began to fall apart; and in the end the environment became wholly external, a thing to feel, observe, and measure, and a thing to act and react on, but never to absorb or be absorbed in (*AUI*, pp. 257–8).

Once Chaudhuri leaves the native element of his ancestral village, he tends to portray himself as on poor terms with his environment, his opinions running against the grain. He is consistently critical of the values of Hindu society, yet despite pitting himself against its mainstream, contends that his autobiography amounts to "more of a national than personal history" (*AUI*, p. 456).

Chaudhuri is a product of the cultural synthesis of empire — specifically, "of a synthesis of the values of the East and the West, which passes under the name of the Indian Renaissance" (*AUI*, p. 179). His tone, like Naipaul's, often tends towards the patrician, in its detachment from and lofty disdain for the mass of humanity. Naipaul has written of Chaudhuri with respect and sympathy. In his review of *The Continent of Circe*, it is at times hard to determine where Chaudhuri's views stop and Naipaul's begin.

But this is the theme of his polemic: that tropical India is the continent of Circe, drugging and destroying those whom it attracts, and that the Aryans, now Hindus, were the first to be lured from a temperate land, ''denatured'' and destroyed. Their philosophy is the philosophy of the devitalized. It is rooted in secular distress, the anguish of flesh on the Gangetic Plain.[20]

This coincides with Naipaul's own views about the depletion and petrifaction of Hindu civilization. Both view Indian society as existing in a state of bondage to its past, while remaining for the most part ''incapable of contemplating and understanding it'' (*AUI*, p. 428). Chaudhuri, like Naipaul, notes the paradox that nationalist pride in ancient Indian traditions is indebted to the scholarship of Western orientalists. While Naipaul contends that ''India, it seems, will never cease to require the arbitration of a conqueror'' (*AD*, p. 213), Chaudhuri asserts that ''there has never been any civilization in India which has not had a foreign origin'' (*AUI*, p. 469). Chaudhuri's analysis of Gandhi's message and legacy is also closely analogous to Naipaul's. He believes, for instance, that Gandhism was a ''descent towards the old rancorous and atavistic form of Indian nationalism'' (*AUI*, p. 431), and that his message was vitiated by its popular reception: the people of India ''accepted only their own version of Gandhism and made it serve their own ends'' (*AUI*, p. 432). Chaudhuri interprets the quality of Indian life with reference to India's geography: ''The unbroken flatness of the plain finds its counterpart in dullness of the mind, monotony of experience, and narrowness of interests'' (*AUI*, p. 493). Naipaul similarly writes, ''The poverty of the land is reflected in the poverty of the mind'' (*IWC*, p. 172). In view of this affinity, it is disconcerting to read Naipaul's references to the ''misunderstandings and futility of the Indo-English encounter''.[21] Naipaul does exempt Chaudhuri from the prevailing futility: *The Autobiography of an Unknown Indian*

> may be the one great book to have come out of the Indo-English encounter. No better account of the penetration of the Indian mind by the West — and by extension, of the penetration of one culture by another — will be or can now be written (*OB*, p. 59).

Chaudhuri might be seen as an exception to the rule — he certainly presents himself in such terms — but the importance which can be ascribed to such an exception surely calls into question the generalization.

A motivation of travel is to experience things at first hand, or at least to put expectation to the test of empirical observation. Naipaul's response to India is shaped by a dialogue between experience and expectations.

These expectations were partly formed by the novels of R. K. Narayan. Naipaul writes that he was familiar with Narayan's work before he travelled to India, but "the India of Narayan's novel is not the India the visitor sees. He tells an Indian truth. Too much that is overwhelming has been left out; too much has been taken for granted" (*AD*, p. 228). There are notable similarities between Narayan's work and Naipaul's early Trinidadian novels: both portray, in complex shades of irony, their chosen social milieux, detailing clashes between the traditional and modern, or the intrusions of a wider world into a circumscribed community. Naipaul tends to write satirically and from a viewpoint external to that of his characters. Narayan's attitude to his subjects is generally more elusive and shifting, but he clearly writes from within his community, and his ironic method assumes, on the part of his readers, a shared store of cultural references and responses, even though, writing in English as he does, he is accessible to an international audience. *India: A Wounded Civilization* further elaborates Naipaul's response to Narayan, partially qualifying the favourable assessment contained in *An Area of Darkness*. Naipaul now sees Narayan's novels less as "the purely social comedies I had once taken them to be than religious books, at times religious fables, and intensely Hindu" (*IWC*, p. 21). Naipaul reads Narayan's work as illustrating his own thesis of a crisis in Indian civilization. He contrasts *Mr Sampath* (1949), which he interprets as manifesting a Hindu sense of acceptance, indifference, and of a cosmic equilibrium with *The Vendor of Sweets* (1967). Naipaul considers that, in the latter novel, this sense of equilibrium is under attack; unsustainable, it collapses into despair. According to Naipaul's reading of the novel, the hero's retreat at the end is not a gesture of calm renunciation, but an attempt to flee "from a world that is known to have broken down at last" (*IWC*, p. 43). Perhaps Naipaul overstates Narayan's sympathy for his somewhat sanctimonious hero, complacent upholder of the ossified old ways: "*The Vendor of Sweets*, which is so elegiac and simplistic, exalting purity and old virtue in the figure of Jagan ..." (*IWC*, p. 42). Narayan mocks the hollow traditionalism of Jagan, with his avarice, his unctuous references to the *Gita*, and faddish theories:

> He was opposed to the use of a toothbrush. "The bristles are made of the hair from the pig's tail", he declared. "It's unthinkable that anyone should bite a pig's tail first thing in the morning". It was impossible to disentangle the sources of his theories and say what he owed to Mahatmaji and how much he had imbibed from his father, who had also spent a lifetime perfecting his theories of sound living and trying them on himself, his coconut trees, children and wife.[22]

This mockery is not devoid of a form of affection. Here it is combined with a sense of the pathos of the father's misplaced solicitude for, and inability to communicate with, his son:

> He noticed that Mali wore socks under his sandals, and wanted to cry out, "Socks should never be worn, because they are certain to heat the blood through interference with the natural radiation which occurs through one's soles, and also because you insulate yourself against beneficial magnetic charges of the earth's surface. I have argued in my book that this is one of the reasons, a possible reason, for heart attacks in European countries ... " While he was busy with these thoughts, he was also dimly aware that Mali had been talking. He had been aware of the sound, but he had missed the substance of the words.[23]

Jagan's conflict with his son, newly returned from America with a Korean-American mistress and plans to manufacture a novel-writing machine, is viewed from Jagan's perspective. Naipaul argues that

> the lack of balance in *The Vendor of Sweets*, the loss of irony, and the very crudity of the satire on "modern" civilization speak of the depth of the violation Narayan feels that that civilization — in its Indian aspect — has brought to someone like Jagan (*IWC*, pp. 41–2).

Narayan's ironies are complex, and serve both to confirm and to refute Naipaul's reading.

To turn Narayan's output into a narrative of irreversible breakdown is to discount the possibility of the restoration of the equilibrium in Narayan's later works. *The Painter of Signs* (1976) reworks the plot of *Waiting for the Mahatma* (1955); in both, the routine life of a thoughtless hero is subjected to the disturbance of passion, and he chases around the country after the woman he loves, engaging in her chosen field of political activity — either birth control or nationalist agitation. A progressive darkening of Narayan's vision could perhaps be inferred from the differing endings of the novels. The earlier work concludes with a marriage: individual desire is reconciled with the framework of social sanction and necessity.[24] But the tone of reconciliation is precarious, marred by the assassination of Gandhi, which occurs in the background. The later novel ends in frustration: the hero returns with some bitterness to the safety of the rituals of his life before the disturbance. *The Painter of Signs* is not constructed around a central clash of the old and the new; if the heroine, Daisy, is an advocate of modern methods of birth control — a means by which life will be prevented from simply going on, regardless

— Raman, too, thinks of himself as a representative of modern values, as a rationalist, in contrast to his traditionalist aunt. His aunt withdraws to end her days in Benares, partly in response to the threat posed to her by Raman's affection for Daisy, partly because she feels it to be appropriate: "I have done my duty".[25] Daisy approves of his aunt's withdrawal, which echoes and contrasts with her own: prior to the action of the novel, she has fled a projected, uncongenial marriage, as at the end she flees from marriage with Raman, contracting out of "the normal drive of a force which kept the whole world spinning".[26] Daisy is portrayed by Narayan from the outside, and as an enigma — not altogether human. A conception of cosmic equilibrium is propounded in the novel, but only in the debased form of the ranting of a local eccentric and soap-box mystic: "Past is gone, present is going, and tomorrow is day after tomorrow's yesterday. So why worry about anything? God is in all this".[27] His message, *"This will pass"*,[28] makes Raman feel light at heart, though, and prefigures the limited consolations of the novel's conclusion.

Richard Cronin argues that Naipaul's interpretation of Narayan is borne out by an examination of these novels: Narayan, in *Waiting for the Mahatma,* defuses Gandhi's political message, by depicting him as a saint, and celebrates India's independence in terms of its changing nothing (Cronin, pp. 54–5). In *The Painter of Signs*, Cronin contends, Narayan rejects politics and change (Cronin, p. 59), and celebrates the forces of continuity as represented by marriage and reproduction (Cronin, p. 56). This interpretation is partly in conflict with Naipaul's view that Narayan's work bears witness to a crisis in the continuity and equilibrium of Hindu society: as in the case of *The Vendor of Sweets*, Narayan's ironies operate in such a way as to make it possible convincingly to argue either case.

Trivial events in the lives of Narayan's characters are invested with significance: the symbolism of his stories is neither overt or ponderous. Chaudhuri declares a preference for "differentiation and complexity" (*AUI*, p. 439). He presents these as opposed to the mainstream of Hindu thought, which tends "towards the simpler in preference to the more complex, towards the unemerged in preference to the emergent, and towards the general in preference to the particular" (*AUI*, p. 439). His autobiography, concerned to map the development of an individual self, manifests a respect for particularity in its method, which consists in a careful accumulation of detail.

The detail of Naipaul's works does not always form an adequate basis for the generalizations it is intended to sustain. Not only does it give the impression of being highly coloured by the preoccupations of the observer, but it also appears to have been selected in order to illustrate a thesis, with a consequent exclusion of contrary evidence. The sparer and more selective earlier books contrast in this respect with the copiousness which distinguishes *India: A Million Mutinies Now*. The multiplicity of narratives which make up this work demonstrates the variousness of Indian reality and the many forms in which individuals seek self-realization: ''All over India scores of particularities that had been frozen by foreign rule, or by poverty or lack of opportunity or abjectness had begun to flow again'' (*IMMN*, p. 6). ''People everywhere have ideas now of who they are and what they owe themselves'' (*IMMN*, p. 517). *An Area of Darkness* encompasses a wider range of mood than *India: A Wounded Civilization*; it includes a comic pastoral interlude in Kashmir, and a softening of approach towards its conclusion. The impulse of the Kashmiri interlude is rather to entertain than to analyze or satirize. Comedy is derived from the smallest incidents of Naipaul's daily life in Kashmir. The focus is on Naipaul's dealings with the staff of the hotel where he is staying — specifically, on the dynamics of his relation with Aziz. This serves as a study in the shifting power relations of master and servant. ''To possess a personal servant . . . is painlessly to surrender part of oneself. It creates dependence where none existed'' (*AD*, p. 121). Ultimately, Aziz takes possession of Naipaul: the economic dependence of servant on master is mirrored by the emotional dependence of master on servant. The mode of the work at this point is that of the comedy of cross-cultural misunderstanding, with Naipaul cast in the role of outsider. He speculates, ''Did I fully know Aziz?'' (*AD*, p. 174). The question, which is central to his treatment of India in general, remains unresolved to the last: ''I could not be sure that he had ever been mine'' (*AD*, p. 192).

India: A Wounded Civilization, in contrast, is constructed exclusively around Naipaul's proposition that there is a crisis in Indian civilization: it contains no explicit information about his travels in India, and the detail serves to support his thesis, rather than to complicate or to unsettle it. It reads as a polemic rather than a travel book, although Naipaul described it as full of jokes and humour.[29] At the conclusion of this work, Naipaul quotes from his article, ''A Second Visit'',[30] written approximately nine years before:

> ''The crisis of India is not political: this is only the view from Delhi. Dictatorship or rule by the army will change nothing. Nor is the crisis only economic. These are only aspects of the larger crisis, which is that of a decaying civilization, where the only hope lies in further swift decay.'' I wrote that in 1967; and that seemed to me a blacker time (*IWC*, p. 174).

The final sentence implies a certain distance from his earlier conclusion, but there is also a consistency in his views: he does not appear to think the earlier opinion worthless, to judge by the fact that he reminds us of it.

Much of the argument of *India: A Wounded Civilization* is anticipated by "A Second Visit": it touches on the subjects of magic, dependence, simplicity, borrowed ideas, self-absorption; an absence of intellect and of the idea of service. One can see Naipaul reaching for the formulation, "The poverty of the land is reflected in the poverty of the mind" (*IWC*, p. 172), in the slightly looser equation, "And the physical drabness itself, answering the drabness of mind: that also held the Indian deficiency" (*OB*, p. 85). The argument about Gandhi's autobiography in *India: A Wounded Civilization*, on which Naipaul bases his contention regarding an Indian egotism that precludes a capacity to see the external world, was first expounded in 1965,[31] ten years before he began to write *India: A Wounded Civilization*. This suggests that Naipaul's argument was already formed before the visit on which the book was based.

There is further evidence that his views on India were formulated long in advance of his visits to the country. In 1950, he wrote to his sister Kamla, then studying in India, about Beverley Nichols' *Verdict on India* (1946):

> He went to India in 1945, and saw a wretched country, full of pompous mediocrity, with no future. He saw the filth; refused to mention the "spiritualness" that impresses another kind of visitor. Of course the Indians did not like the book, but I think he was telling the truth.[32]

This sketch closely corresponds to Naipaul's response to India in his first two books. In another letter he asks Kamla to look for support for his contention that Indian culture is dead: "This is the picture I want you to look for — a dead country still running with the momentum of its heyday".[33] These statements give the impression that he travelled to India with a view to confirming his thesis about the society.

He advocates the application of methods of observation and rational analysis to the Indian scene, but the apparent vindictiveness of some of his comments can suggest that he is writing out of a desire to wound Indian sensibilities, partly as a result of disappointment at India's failure to correspond to his expectations. Furthermore, the notion that Naipaul wishes to encourage Indian self-scrutiny is in conflict with the stance he frequently adopts of one explaining Indian customs for a Western audience. This raises the question of the nature of the audience he sets out to address. In an article first published in *The Illustrated Weekly of India*,[34] and therefore directed at an Indian audience, Naipaul adopts a slightly more conciliatory tone. He writes that any impression of depletion and decay is merely superficial, the initial response of an observer, for whom India is felt as "an assault on the senses" (*OB*, p. 41). A more prolonged acquaintance with the country leads him to see it differently:

And where before I would have sensed only despair, now I feel that the despair lies more with the observer than the people. I have learned to see beyond the dirt and the recumbent figures on string beds, and to look for the signs of improvement and hope, however faint: the brick-topped road, covered though it might be with filth; the rice planted in rows and not scattered broadcast; the degree of ease with which the villager faces the official or the visitor. For such small things I have learned to look: over the months my eye has been adjusted (*OB*, p. 42).

These assertions imply that, after all, the grounds for hope are limited. Nevertheless, a revision of the initial assessment is required. This was written in 1962, in his first article on India, but the two books which follow once more depict the experience of the country as an overwhelming assault on the senses. The views expounded in this article are not simply superseded; the inclusion of the article in *The Overcrowded Barracoon* (1972) — published subsequently to *An Area of Darkness* (1964) — implies a continuing commitment to its propositions on Naipaul's part. The date of publication of these works reverses the order of composition, and produces the paradoxical impression that "In the Middle of the Journey" provides a more considered, later account. His revisions of opinion do not serve to negate earlier statements, so much as to assemble a variety of perspectives, which make of his work a complex, in some measure a self-contradictory, whole.

Further insight into the processes according to which Naipaul selects his evidence in order to confirm a thesis is furnished by the manner of the incorporation of the material of the article "The Election in Ajmer"[35] into *India: A Wounded Civilization*. The details of the election the article describes resemble the plot of *The Suffrage of Elvira*, with its shifting alliances between politicians, who depend on a support base determined by communal allegiances; there is also the seeming irrelevance, to the politicians, of any political programme; together with the importance of tangible rewards for the electors, and of the symbolic dress of the politicians. For Mr Mukut, standing for the old Congress, it is enough that he is a good Gandhian and has "achieved merit through service and sacrifice" (*OB*, p. 117). There is the same sense in the novel and in the article of the machinations of the election agent, who claims to be able to determine the result of the election: " 'I could swing the election in certain districts without leaving this room' " (*OB*, p. 126). The electorate is not deluded by the symbolism of homespun, however, and votes for the candidate who represents Indira's Congress Party, with its slogan "Remove Poverty" (*OB*, p. 101). The article ends on an upbeat note, with the result seen as a vote for modernity and change.

> "Give me seven minutes," Mr Kudal said, and disappeared
> into the crowd. When he came back his clothes and hair and
> face were satisfactorily stained with red. Red the colour of
> spring and triumph, and sacrifice (*OB*, p. 138).

This passage participates in the mood of celebration. When the episode is
incorporated into *India: A Wounded Civilization,* however, Naipaul
resolutely refuses to draw hope from it; he dwells on the resentment of
the defeated candidate, and surmises the existence of an Indian dark age.

> Blind to his own political nullity, the idle self-regard of his
> own Gandhian concept of service, he was yet half right about
> India, for a reason he would not have understood. "Archaic
> emotions", "nostalgic memories": when these were awa-
> kened by Gandhi, India became free. But the India created in
> this way had to stall. Gandhi took India out of one kind of *Kal
> Yug,* one kind of Black Age; his success inevitably pushed it
> back into another (*IWC*, pp. 151–2).

A sense that Naipaul wishes to wound might also be occasioned by the
perception that his criticisms of India are in some measure contradictory.
On the one hand, he presents India's modernity as purely superficial, and
recommends the application of Western methods of inquiry and
assessment to the Indian situation. These form the basis of the contrast
between Indian and Western thought he wishes to establish:

> When caste and family simplify relationships, and the sanctity
> of the laws cannot be doubted, when magic buttresses the laws,
> and the epics and legends satisfy the imagination, and
> astrologers know the future anyway, men cannot easily begin
> to observe and analyse. . . . It is always there, this knowledge of
> the other, regulated world, undermining, or balancing, intellect
> and the beginnings of painful perception (*IWC,* p. 112).

On the other hand, Naipaul indicts Indians of a confusion of values:

> The mimicry changes, the inner world remains constant: this is
> the secret of survival. . . .
>   Mimicry might be too harsh a word for what appears so
> comprehensive and profound. . . . Schizophrenia might better
> explain the scientist who, before taking up his appointment,
> consults the astrologer for an auspicious day (*AD*, p. 60).

Indians are accused of a "craze for foreign" (*AD*, p. 90) — as
symbolized by the tastes of Mrs Mahindra, with whom Naipaul stays in
Delhi as a paying guest — and of having insufficiently assimilated

foreign ideas. This paradox informs Naipaul's representation of various areas of Indian life: "Complex imported ideas, forced through the retort of Indian sensibility, often come out cleansed of content and harmless" (*IWC*, p. 121).

> Naxalism was an intellectual tragedy, a tragedy of idealism, ignorance, and mimicry: middle-class India, after the Gandhian upheaval, incapable of generating ideas and institutions of its own, needing constantly in the modern world to be inducted into the art, science and ideas of other civilizations, not always understanding the consequences, and this time borrowing something deadly, somebody else's idea of revolution (*IWC*, pp. 92–3).

When Naipaul first portrays the figure of Bunty the Calcutta box-wallah, in the article "Jamshed into Jimmy" (1963),[36] it is in tones of mingled mockery and approval. He is seen as the representative of a cultural synthesis: "Enough has been said to show how admirable, in the Indian context, he is. . . . East and West blend easily in him" (*OB*, p.53). When Naipaul reworks the material in *An Area of Darkness*, the construction he places on it is rather more hostile; he finds not synthesis but mimicry:

> It is with this gossip that one begins to doubt what Bunty and Andy show of themselves and one begins to feel that they are not what they seem, and that there are areas to which they can retreat and where they are hard to get at. . . .
> Somewhere there has been a failure of communication, unrecognized because communication seems to have been established (*AD*, p. 65).

Naipaul's notion of an Indian tendency to mimicry might be compared with Kipling's in *Kim*. Hurree Babu, an educated Bengali who aspires to the possession of European learning, is portrayed as absurd. His pretensions to membership of the Royal Society are mocked: "It is an awful thing still to dread the magic that you contemptuously investigate — to collect folk-lore for the Royal Society with a lively belief in all Powers of Darkness" (Kipling, p. 257). Hurree Babu's success as a British agent depends on his ability to perform the role assigned to him by the French and Russian spies, which is not dissimilar to the part in which Kipling casts him: "An oily, wet, but always smiling Bengali, talking the best of English with the vilest of phrases, was ingratiating himself with two sodden and rather rheumatic foreigners" (Kipling, p. 337). The laugh is on the foreigners, but also on Hurree Babu, who is trapped in his role; Kipling always insists on the idiosyncrasies of his use of English. Naipaul, too, has been seen as something of a *renonçant* — "an excellent French word that describes the native who renounces his own culture and strives towards the French" (*OB*, p. 45). He, too, has fled to the West, of which he writes at times in excessively reverential terms.

He dismisses as mythical the notion that there was ever a time when India was complete and unviolated: "That Indian past! That fantasy of wholeness and purity, confusing the present" (*IWC*, p. 143). Elsewhere, he has stated, "Culture is like language, ever developing. There is no right and wrong, no purity from which there is decline" (*OB*, p. 36). His invocation of the concept of mimicry, however, presupposes that an authentic, indigenous culture is being travestied, with cultural synthesis, as mentioned subsequently in this discussion, viewed as an affront and an act of violence: "I felt the coming together of England and India as a violation" (*AD*, p. 201). The comparative vantage-point which Naipaul occupies is described in similar terms: "To look at themselves, to measure themselves against the new positive standards of the conqueror, Indians had to step out of themselves. It was an immense self-violation" (*AD*, p. 223).

The fact that "the themes repeat"[37] also suggests the extent to which Naipaul's analysis is driven by his own preoccupations. The complex of ideas which Naipaul associates with mimicry of Western ways — a parasitic dependence on Western technology, a countervailing faith in magic, a thraldom to ritual, and a decay into barbarism — is one he has applied also to African, Islamic and South American countries. He asserts, for instance, that only under British rule did India enter the course of history:

> To read of events in India before the coming of the British is like reading of many pieces of unfinished business; it is to read of a condition of flux, of things partly done and then partly undone, matters more properly the subject of annals rather than narrative history, which works best when it deals with great things being built up or pulled down (*IMMN*, p. 144).

This is in the spirit of his declaration in *The Middle Passage* that "history is built around achievement and creation; and nothing was created in the West Indies" (*MP*, p. 29). He finds in Argentina a "collective refusal to see" (*REP*, p. 115), and a belief in magic, as, in *Among the Believers*, he accuses Iranians of a failure to understand their historical situation and of a technological dependence on a society they reject. "African" is a word which can be used by him in a sense virtually synonymous with barbarism:

... a retreat from civilization and creativity, from rebirth and growth, to magic and incantation, a retrogression to an almost African night, the enduring primitivism of a place like the Congo (*IWC*, p. 43).

What is unique to his treatment of India is the intimacy with the subject-matter, and the sense that he feels its condition to be a personal affront.

India: A Million Mutinies Now represents a departure from the techniques of the earlier works, in that it is not governed by an overweening authorial voice which issues judgements and directs responses. Instead, a composite portrait of the multifariousness of Indian reality is assembled by means of an accumulation of the varied viewpoints of Naipaul's numerous interviewees. Naipaul is not, of course, absent from the book; he seeks to relate his interviewees' experience to his own, occasionally interposing personal observations. He casts himself in an editorial role in relation to his material: he asks questions and connects the various strands. His own views are implied by the nature of his inquiries.

Perhaps, I said to Arati, the flaw had lain in that very idea of revolution, that idea of a particular moment when everything changes and the world is made good, and men are made anew.

She didn't take the point up (*IMMN*, p. 317).

Naipaul's views also surface in the linking passages between interviews:

To awaken to history was to cease to live instinctively. It was to begin to see oneself and one's group the way the outside world saw one; and it was to know a kind of rage. India was full of this rage. There had been a general awakening. But everyone awakened first to his own group or community; every group thought itself unique in its awakening; and every group sought to separate its rage from the rage of other groups (*IMMN*, p. 420).

This passage bridges the transition from an examination of Indian women's magazines to a treatment of Sikh fundamentalism. Naipaul's interest in the latter can be seen in the context of a recurring fascination with protest movements and with religions, which he conceives of as articulating irrational and frenzied views of the world: this fascination encompasses Islam of *Among the Believers*, the anti-colonial protest of *A Way in the World*, or *The Mimic Men*, and the political disaffection in *Guerrillas*.

The sprawling and miscellaneous form of *India: A Million Mutinies Now* suggests itself for comparison with Rushdie's endeavour to create in

Midnight's Children a work which embodies some of the plurality and diversity of the Indian scene. The form of this novel, Rushdie contends, mimics "the Indian talent for non-stop self-regeneration. . . . The form — multitudinous, hinting at the infinite possibilities of the country — is the optimistic counterweight to Saleem's personal tragedy".[38] The novel portrays this diversity by making reference to a multitude of minor characters who clamour and jostle for attention, refusing to be relegated to its periphery: "And there are so many stories to tell, too many, such an excess of intertwined lives events miracles places rumours, so dense a commingling of the improbable and the mundane!"[39] The absence of punctuation evokes a breathless, multifarious bustle of interconnected stories, and the sense in the novel that relations stop nowhere. An absence of punctuation is a feature of Rushdie's style,[40] apparent, for instance, in the exclamation: "How many things people notions we bring with us into the world, how many possibilities and also restrictions of possibility!"[41] It is consistent with the novel's blurring of the boundaries between material and immaterial, fact and fiction, and between individual identities. Identity is imaged as spilling over into the lives which surround the individual.

> I am the sum total of everything that went before me, of all I have been seen done, of everything done-to-me. I am everyone everything whose being-in-the-world affected was affected by mine.[42]

Rushdie's prose withholds the distinctions implied by commas: it also pulls things together by means of hyphens. Identity, in the novel, is seen as fluid and mutable:

> Because a human being, inside himself, is anything but a whole, anything but homogeneous; all kinds of everywhich-thing are jumbled up inside him, and he is one person one minute and another the next.[43]

This is reflected in the plot of the novel — in the twist of events by means of which Saleem discovers that he is not the child of those whom he has believed to be his parents.

The children's conference serves as an image of the diversity of the Indian nation. Centrifugal forces rapidly disrupt the gathering, and distinctions and differences assert themselves:

> As the prejudices and world-views of adults began to take over their minds, I found children from Maharashtra loathing Gujuratis, and fair-skinned northerners reviling Dravidian "blackies"; there were religious rivalries; and class entered our councils.[44]

Like Saleem's life, the conference serves as a mirror of the progress of the new Indian nation, the birth of which is simultaneous with Saleem's. He, too, claims to be falling apart as he writes his narrative.

Michael Gorra[45] contrasts the way in which Naipaul views cultural hybridity as an aspect of the loss and violation which are the legacy of empire, with the manner in which Rushdie's work celebrates the subversive potential of mimicry, the creative possibilities of hetero-geneity, and the liberating aspects of inconsistency and contradiction. Rushdie's ebullient sense of the fluidity of identity encompasses his attitude towards his own cultural background. He suggests that cultural dislocation has compensations, and that there are gains to balance losses: "It is normally supposed that something always gets lost in translation; I cling, obstinately, to the notion that something can also be gained".[46] Displacement produces a stereoscopic vision, combining the advantages of the insider and the outsider. He furthermore contends that "it is perhaps one of the more pleasant freedoms of the literary migrant to be able to choose his parents".[47]

Naipaul has written disapprovingly of magic realism; he condemns a "fantastic and extravagant" way of writing about "degrading and corrupt countries" as evasive and as "empty, morally and intellec-tually.... [I]t makes writing an aspect of the corruption of the countries out of which it issues".[48] It is a question that remains open to debate whether magical literature is subversive; the mode is not intrinsically inhospitable to the dissection of political corruption: Gabriel García Marquez, for instance, employs the technique to this effect in *The Autumn of the Patriarch*, an anatomy of the dynamics of dictatorship. Rushdie argues that to redescribe the world is to remake it, and to challenge the politicians' version of it: "Writers and politicians are natural rivals. Both groups try to remake the world in their own images".[49] *Midnight's Children* is at pains to condemn political abuses: Saleem's sterilization serves to symbolize some of the outrages committed under the Emergency declared by Indira Gandhi in 1975. Naipaul is notably forgiving of Mrs Gandhi's faults; he sees her as a modernizer. *India: A Wounded Civilization*, written at the time of the Emergency, has little to say on the subject. He declares that India's crisis is not political, that the Emergency merely formalizes a state of social breakdown (*IWC*, p. 45), and implies that foreign notions of the rule of law do not answer in the Indian situation; allegations of torture amount to no more than complaints about caste pollution, in his view (*IWC*, p. 115).

Magic realism is a mode appropriate to the representation of societies where "the truth is what it is instructed to be", and, in consequence, "reality quite literally ceases to exist, so that everything becomes possible except what we are told is the case".[50] This would appear to be the implication of Rushdie's portrait of political misrepresentation in Pakistan, where there is a "divorce between news and reality".[51] The war between India and Pakistan is concealed behind a barrage of propaganda issuing from both sides: "Nothing was real; nothing certain".[52] The Pakistani bombers are, fittingly, named Mirages and Mystères.

The high ratio of detail to generalization in *India: A Million Mutinies Now* contrasts with that found in Naipaul's other books; and the view of India which it presents is very different: the society is seen as dynamic, rather than as static or tending to decay. The India this book portrays is more prosperous and confident, a condition reflected in its "freeing of new particularities" (*IMMN*, p. 9). It has undergone economic and social upheaval; people are breaking new ground; the society is no longer portrayed as held in the deathly grip of a decayed civilization: "All was fluid" (*IMMN*, p. 4). Many of the people he interviews have achieved things undreamt of by their parents. Naipaul derives hope, for instance, from the change in the self-conception of those formerly known as untouchables:

> There had also come the group sense and political conscious-
> ness. They had ceased to be abstractions. They had begun to do
> things for themselves. They had become people stressing their
> own particularity, just as better-off groups in India stressed
> their particularities (*IMMN*, p. 4).

In a notable contrast with the other Indian books, he does not seek to satirize his interviewees, or to turn cultural difference and failures of understanding into comedy, but is prepared to give his interlocutors a fair hearing, and to make an effort of sympathy with their viewpoint, however uncongenial. The people of India are given an identity and a chance to speak. The inhabitants of a Bombay slum are not treated merely as victims of their material circumstances. Naipaul is consider-ably more sympathetic to the founder of the Dalit Panthers than he was, in the essay "Power?", towards the Black Panther movement on which they were loosely modelled.

The germ of this book, which is encapsulated by its title, is hinted at in *India: A Wounded Civilization,* where Naipaul asserts: "And out of this prodigious effort [of development and independence] arose a new mutinous stirring, which took India by surprise, and with which it didn't know how to cope" (*IWC*, p. 167). A negative connotation is apparent in a similar passage — "stirring" is common to both — which talks of

> a populist-religious appeal to Hindus, a word of threat to
> minorities, part of the intellectual confusion, the new

insecurity, the blind dredging up of dormant fantasies and obsessions, the great enraged stirring from below (*IWC*, p. 137).

Such movements are, in contrast, awarded a positive value in his most recent Indian book.

India: A Million Mutinies Now produces the impression that it is not so much India which has changed as Naipaul's attitude towards it, and his method of depicting it. The interpretation of his material has undergone a startling reverse: what in the past would have met with condemnation is now viewed with acceptance. The fundamentalist rage which has accompanied the "awakening" (*IMMN*, p. 420) described by Naipaul is presented, not as evidence of irrationality and of an impending chaos, but as contributing to a positive exercise in self-understanding and self-assertion on the part of the people of India. The material conditions of the India he portrays are in many instances not significantly different from those of the country he describes in earlier books. Similar phenomena elicit contrary inferences, as if Naipaul, having attended to his critics, and wishing to compensate for the offence caused by his earlier books, were seeking to relinquish the persona he has previously cultivated — of the disgruntled and solitary mouthpiece of unpopular and wounding truths — but was not sure of what to substitute in its place. He gives the impression that he is not altogether persuaded by his own arguments: nor does he provide the grounds to justify them.

The manner in which relatively undigested data furnish the matter of the book, and in which the author refrains from judging his interviewees, is directly in conflict with statements of his conception of artistic responsibility, formulated early on in his career. A resistance to the documentary mode is expounded in a review of Isherwood: "The camera describes; it never illuminates. It also never changes".[53] A similar view is also stated in the pronouncement that

> the artist who, for political or humanitarian reasons, seeks only to record abandons half his responsibility. He becomes a participant; he becomes anonymous. He does not impose a vision on the world. He accepts; he might even make romantic; but he invariably ends by assessing men at their own valuation.[54]

Although Naipaul is not altogether anonymous in *India: A Million Mutinies Now*, this assertion indicates how radical is the rift between Naipaul's earlier and later aesthetic. Ironically, the charge that Naipaul has taken his subjects at their own valuation was one made by Nissim Ezekiel against *An Area of Darkness*. He argued that Naipaul had been unduly credulous of characters whose stories form an insufficient basis for the generalizations he makes them sustain.[55]

This reversal in Naipaul's artistic method can also be seen in *A Turn in the South*. Through visiting a part of the world he had not before written about at length, Naipaul says, he discovered how to travel in a new way, letting the people he met shape the book.[56] In this work, Naipaul tends to take people at their own estimate, and to show an unheralded and undisguised sympathy for the victims of history, writing lyrically on the unpromising subject, say, of rednecks. Naipaul states that *A Turn in the South* was the model for the form and method of *India: A Million Mutinies Now*. Tolerance and respect for his subjects, and for the issues which concern them — race, religion, and a sense of the past — are translated from the American to the Indian scene.

Nissim Ezekiel, writing on *An Area of Darkness*, expressed his dissent not so much from Naipaul's conclusions as from the mode of argument by which he arrives at them. The same analysis, the same concern with a gap between conclusions and evidence, can also be directed at *India: A Million Mutinies Now*, despite the fact that, unlike the earlier work, its detail massively outweighs its generalizations. The main body of the book does not substantiate Naipaul's conclusion that India is held together by a "central will, a central intellect, a national idea" (*IMMN*, p. 518). Naipaul attempts to resolve the diversity and heterogeneity he has recorded into a perception of unity, as embodied in the "Indian Union" he speaks of; the material, however, manifests centrifugal tendencies. He has earlier in this book suggested that the existence of this central, secular state may be endangered by the sectarian excess he describes:

> What was unexpected in Gurtej's account of his life and beliefs was how much he took for granted. The constitution, the law, the centres of education, the civil service with its high idea of its role as guardian of the people's rights and improver of their condition, the investment over four decades in industrial and agricultural change — in Gurtej's account, these things, which distinguished India from many of its neighbours, were just there.
>
> ... Gurtej had turned to millenarian politics. It had happened with other religions when they turned fundamentalist; it threatened to bring the chaos Gurtej feared (*IMMN*, p. 445).

Yet, at the risk of laying himself open to the charge of illogicality, Naipaul argues that India's intellectual life is not negated, but reinforced, by extremist religious, sectarian and regional allegiances. The affirmative generalizations with which Naipaul concludes the book sit uneasily with the portrait of the society he has provided: at a time when resurgent fundamentalisms threaten to fragment the secular Indian state, it appears wishful thinking to claim that "many of these movements of excess strengthened the Indian state, defining it as the source of law and civility and reasonableness" (*IMMN*, p. 518). This assertion carries as little conviction as Naipaul's claim that his difficult personal relationship with the country is now resolved: "In 27 years, I had succeeded in making a kind of return journey, shedding my Indian nerves, abolishing the darkness that separated me from my ancestral past" (*IMMN*, p. 516). The earlier books do more to attempt to confront these difficulties.

Naipaul suggested, after his first visit, that Indian society lacked the capacity for self-assessment: "There is never a type of detached intelligence at work on anything".[57] The fussy nervousness and self-preoccupation of his earlier writing on India call into question his own capacity for detachment; he advocates there an objectivity which his own work of the time does not sustain. The earlier emphasis on his own viewpoint, based on the assumption that it is more truthful to reveal his stake in the subject, given that objectivity is unattainable, conflicts with the methods of assessment he recommends to Indians. His writings on India can be viewed as a site for the playing out of the tensions caused by his personal and ancestral involvement with the country.

Notes

1   *India: A Wounded Civilization* (London: André Deutsch, 1977), pp. 8–9.
2   *London Calling*, pp. 18, 67–8.
3   Interviewed by Bharati Mukherjee and Robert Boyers, p. 21.
4   As observed by Karl Miller, "Elephant Head", *London Review of Books*, 12 (September 27 1990), p. 11; Bikhu Parekh, "From India With Hope", *New Statesman and Society*, 3, 3 (October 5 1990), p. 34.
5   Naipaul refers to the work in the course of a discussion of books about race: "To be successful, these chronicles of oppression must have clear oppressors and clear oppressed. This is not easy for an Indian. The most he can manage is something like Mulk Raj Anand's *Untouchable*" (*OB*, p. 13).
6   *Untouchable: A Novel* (London: Hutchinson, 1947), p. 18.
7   *Kim* (London: Macmillan, 1949), p. 81.
8   *A Passage to India* (London: Dent, 1942), p. 16.
9   Introduction to *Kim* (Harmondsworth: Penguin, 1987), pp. 32–6.
10 Interviewed by Adrian Rowe-Evans, p. 51.
11 Notes containing plans for "Prologue to an Autobiography", V. S. Naipaul Archive, I, 1:3.
12 "Insider Out", *New Statesman*, 54 (December 21 1957), p. 859.
13 "Trollope in the West Indies", *Listener*, 67 (March 15 1962), p. 461.
14 Interviewed by Andrew Robinson, "Going Back For a Turn in the East", *Sunday Times* (September 16 1990), 8, p. 14.

15   "The Little More", *Times* (July 13 1961), Hamner, p. 13.
16   Interviewed by Elizabeth Hardwick, "Meeting V. S. Naipaul", *New York Times Book Review* (May 13 1979), p. 36.
17   Interviewed by Walter Allen, *The World of Books* (October 24 1961), p. 6, BBC Written Archives.
18   "The Little More", Hamner, p. 13.
19   *The Autobiography of an Unknown Indian* (Berkeley and Los Angeles: University of California Press, 1968), p. 36.
20   "The Last of the Aryans", *(OB*, p. 66).
21   "Indian Autobiographies", *New Statesman* (January 29 1965), *OB*, p. 57.
22   *The Vendor of Sweets* (London: Heinemann, 1980), p. 26.
23   *The Vendor of Sweets*, pp. 74–5.
24   As pointed out by Richard Cronin, "Quite Quiet India: The Despair of R. K. Narayan", *Encounter*, 64, 3 (March 1985), p. 56.
25   *The Painter of Signs*, (Harmondsworth: Penguin, 1982), p. 123.
26   *The Painter of Signs*, p. 78.
27   *The Painter of Signs*, p. 23.
28   *The Painter of Signs,* p. 25.
29   Letter from V. S. Naipaul to Diana Athill (February 24 1977), André Deutsch Archive, 96, *IWC* folder.
30   *Daily Telegraph Magazine* (11–18 August 1967), collected in *OB*.
31   "Indian Autobiographies"
32   *Letters Between a Father and Son*, p. 5.
33   *Letters Between a Father and Son*, p. 9.
34   "In the Middle of the Journey", (October 28 1962), collected in *OB*.
35   *Sunday Times Magazine* (August 15–22 1971), collected in *OB*.
36   "Jamshed into Jimmy", *New Statesman* (January 25 1963), collected in *OB*.
37   *REP*, Author's Note.
38   *Imaginary Homelands*, p. 16.
39   *Midnight's Children* (London: Jonathan Cape, 1981), p. 11.
40   As pointed out by Michael Gorra, in "Naipaul or Rushdie", p. 376.
41   *Midnight's Children*, p. 108.
42   *Midnight's Children*, p. 370.
43   *Midnight's Children*, p. 230.
44   *Midnight's Children*, p. 248.
45   "Naipaul or Rushdie".
46   *Imaginary Homelands*, p. 17.
47   *Imaginary Homelands*, pp. 20–1.
48   "My Brother's Tragic Sense", p. 23.
49   *Imaginary Homelands*, p. 14.
50   *Midnight's Children,* p. 315. The case is argued by Michael Gorra, *After Empire*, p. 125.
51   *Midnight's Children*, p. 323.
52   *Midnight's Children*, p. 329.
53   "Images", Hamner, p. 32.
54   "The Documentary Heresy", *Twentieth Century*, 173 (Winter 1964–5), Hamner, p. 24.
55   *Selected Prose* (Delhi: Oxford University Press, 1992), p. 91.
56   Interviewed by Andrew Robinson, "Going Back for a Turn in the East", p. 14.
57   Interviewed by John Morris, *The World of Books* (October 5 1964), p. 3, BBC Written Archives.

5 | Fact and fiction in *Guerrillas*

The murders of Gale Benson and Joe Skerritt by Abdul Malik (alias Michael de Freitas and Michael X) and his associates in Trinidad in 1972 form the factual germ of the events portrayed in *Guerrillas*. The discussion in this chapter seeks to investigate the nature of Naipaul's interest in the story, and the emphasis he brings to the writing of it. It explores the interaction between documentary sources and literary influences in the shaping of *Guerrillas*. It examines how Naipaul's article "Michael X and the Black Power Killings in Trinidad" played a part in the genesis of the novel — how, through the writing of the article, he developed a narrative technique and attitudes towards the characters which anticipate, in places, those of the novel.

For an account of the career and activities of Malik, this discussion is indebted to Derek Humphry and David Tindall's *False Messiah: The Story of Michael X*.[1] As the title of the book suggests, their intention is to discredit what they show to be Malik's spurious claims to represent the interests of West Indians in England — to explode the myth that he was a Black Power leader, and to expose the credulity of those who lent him their support. They record Malik's extensive range of criminal activities, as a gangster, conman, pimp, hustler, drug dealer, brothel-keeper, blackmailer, extortioner and property racketeer. Malik's own autobiography, *From Michael de Freitas to Michael X*,[2] admits to certain of these activities. It describes his days as a hustler, from the point of view of a subsequent political awakening and conversion to Islam, but obscures the extent of his links with Rachman, the property racketeer. Humphry and Tindall provide evidence to suggest that Malik's claims to be a reformed criminal were inauthentic, and that he merely continued his career of crime in a new area of operation, with Black Power proving the most lucrative hustle of them all.

Malik flourished in the second half of the 1960s, in the aftermath of the 1958 Notting Hill race riots, which were perceived at the time as indicating the existence of a race problem in the U.K., and which brought to public attention the associated issues of discrimination in housing and in employment. Riots in the U. S. at this time served to place racial matters high on the agenda of the liberal and socially-concerned.

Humphry and Tindall point to the added factor of a racial guilt deriving from Britain's colonial history.[3] These factors combined to make it possible for Malik to find a gullible audience and credulous backers, and the media also contributed to these developments, by representing him as a spokesperson for the immigrant community. Publicity fed on publicity, and, as Malik revealingly remarks in his autobiography, "We were in business" (Malik, p. 148). Malik was adept at eliciting funds to support projects that failed to materialize, the most important being the Black House in Islington, a cultural, educational and information centre: Malik appears to have pocketed the greater part of the proceeds of his aggressive fund-raising. Malik basked in the reflected glory of eminent Afro-Americans, associating with Muhammad Ali, modelling himself on Malcolm X, and earning himself a prison sentence under the Race Relations Act in 1967 by endeavouring to emulate the American Stokely Carmichael's brand of militancy.

In 1971, he fled England for Trinidad to evade an impending trial for robbery and demanding money with menaces. There, he styled himself as spearheading a peaceful revolution based on a return to the land. Malik wrote to Eric Williams, Trinidad's Prime Minister, to say, "There is no revolution without land",[4] and declared that people should be encouraged to "love and plant the land and love one another".[5] His political following in the island was negligible, and he declared that, in his view, Black Power was irrelevant to its problems.

In October 1971, Hakim Jamal and Gale Benson arrived in Trinidad. Jamal was a figure not dissimilar to Malik: a former Bostonian hustler, and a convert to Islam, with a distant connection to Malcolm X, who was proficient at extracting money for good works which existed largely on paper. Benson was the daughter of an inventor and former Conservative MP: she had met Jamal in London and become his Moslem wife, and was prepared to play along with his delusions of his divinity. They went to stay at Malik's commune, where tensions rapidly emerged. Malik was suspicious of Benson, and attempted to drive a wedge between the couple. The motives for Benson's murder are obscure. Malik's intentions may in part have been to cement a bond of fear among his entourage by securing their complicity in the crime. He is reported as having asserted: " 'I want blood. That is the only thing that will keep us together'".[6] After the killing, he told the members of his gang: " 'You are members for life and cannot resign' ".[7] Malik may have wished to exact a deferred revenge on the vulnerable representative of a class — the privileged white female — which he resented for his dependence on it. At the same time that he had excluded whites from membership from his organization, the Racial Action Adjustment Society, he was receiving donations from a wealthy white woman with whom he was sleeping. His autobiography provides an insight into his sense of his position, reminiscent of his "old poncing days":

> It was only then that I saw the real effect the ghetto had achieved in reducing my humanity and enabling me to look on a woman as a commodity. The pressures in the ghetto are so hard that they dehumanise people (Malik, p. 160).

Their roles are reversed: it is he who emerges as the victim of the situation, rather than the woman he uses. Malik continues by observing that

> my speeches became more and more bitter. They reached a new peak of being anti-white. I was terribly hard on poncing and the selling of bodies; I had a lot to say about the awful traps black men fell into, which were terribly degrading for them. I was quite nasty about the women involved. It was myself I was flaying (Malik, p. 160).

The degradation of the women concerned elicits only rage against them, and their exploitation by their ponces is represented as the white race's exploitation of these ponces.

Malik was not present at Benson's murder, but it was conducted under his orders. He kept Jamal occupied while Benson was cut at with a cutlass then buried in a hole that had been prepared in the garden for that purpose. Not long after, Malik engineered and participated in a similar murder of Joe Skerritt, an unemployed Trinidadian cousin of Malik's. Malik went to Guyana, and when the bodies were discovered attempted to flee for Brazil. He was found guilty of the murder of Skerritt; the trial of Benson's murderers followed, but Malik, already under a death sentence, was not tried for Benson's murder. His trial, in 1972, attracted widespread international publicity, and his appeal against the death sentence enhanced his status as a liberal *cause célèbre*. His case was likened to instances of human rights violations in the U. S., such as the imprisonment of Bobby Seale, Angela Davis and the Wilmington Ten, and George Jackson's death in custody. In 1973, the International Committee to save Michael X was formed; it included among its members Kate Millet, William Kunstler, John Lennon, Yoko Ono and Leonard Cohen.

Humphry and Tindall are journalists; Tindall reported on Malik's trial. They argue that Malik, by his duplicity, criminality and fraudulence, besmirched a cause that merited worthier advocates. They emphasize that if Malik was able to obtain support among the West Indian community in Britain, it was because the problems faced by them — lack of representation, discrimination in housing and in employment — were by no means imaginary. Furthermore, they are careful not to tar all black militant and self-help organizations with the same brush they apply to Malik's. They note that some of his associates and other groups were eager to distance themselves from Malik when they realized that he was a fraud. In the run-up to Malik's trial, the National Joint Action Committee, which had led the 1970 Black Power revolt in Trinidad — in so far as this uprising was subject to leadership — declared that it had never had anything to do with him. It argued the massive publicity that the murders were attracting, and the bias evident in the reporting they received, served particular political ends. They asserted that the emphasis laid on Malik's links to Black Power "can leave people with a false impression about the ideology of Black Power".[8]

Before reshaping Malik's story in *Guerrillas,* Naipaul wrote a non-fictional account of events, in "Michael X and the Black Power Killings in Trinidad". In this journalistic feature, he adopts a narrative technique which partly prefigures that employed by the novel, involving a dialectic of certainty and uncertainty: certainty is implied by the assumption of a narrative stance undeceived by Malik's fraudulent claims; uncertainty is evoked by the difficulty of determining what actually occurred, and of plumbing the obscure depths of Malik's motivation. The novel derives much of its atmosphere of menace from the deployment of a strategic epistemological incertitude, which, as in the article, is set off by a contradictory refusal to be taken in by Jimmy's impersonation of a revolutionary leader.

Naipaul's contempt for Malik arises from Malik's self-avowed early criminality, and Naipaul's sense that his political activities were in themselves a confidence-trick. Malik was, Naipaul contends, an entertainer, playing to a gallery, entirely derivative in his ideas; and his publicity was unsupported by any achievement. He is described as

> a Carnival figure, a dummy Judas to be beaten through the streets on Good Friday. Which was all that he had been in London, even in the great days of his newspaper fame as the X: the militant who was only an entertainer, the leader who had no followers, the Black Power man who was neither powerful nor black (*REP*, pp. 22–3).

Naipaul quotes liberally from Malik's writings — "Malik was made by words, his and other people's" (*REP*, p. 51); his fashionable jargon and publicity for non-existent projects are mercilessly juxtaposed with the reality or nullity of his achievement. Inverted commas signal Naipaul's unrelenting scepticism:

> Malik's "commune" was a residential house in a suburban development called Christina Gardens. . . . On this land, with

its mature fruit trees, Malik and his commune did "agriculture." Or so Malik reported to old associates in England and elsewhere (*REP*, p. 3).

A religious-political "conversion" had followed, and Michael de Freitas had given himself the name Michael X. He was an instant success with the press and the underground. He became Black Power "leader," underground black "poet," black "writer" (*REP*, p. 4).

When Naipaul refers to Malik's associate, Steve Yeates, he similarly adduces Yeates' sonorous titles: "Muhammed Akbar, Supreme Captain of the Fruit of Islam, Lieutenant Colonel of Malik's Black Liberation Army, the foreman of the Malik Commune, Malik's bodyguard and familiar".[9]

Imitation is a target for Naipaul's opprobrium throughout his work. Cultural interchanges and interpenetration are perceived by him, as earlier mentioned, not as part of a stimulating process of exchange, but as an affront to cultural integrity. The profession of Western ideas is depicted by him as a form of imitation common to African and Islamic societies:

> I had heard similar words from young Muslim fundamentalists in Malaysia: ecological, Western romance bouncing back like a corroborating radio signal from remote, inactive worlds (*FC*, p. 152).

In Zaire, he notes "African art imitating itself, imitating African-inspired Western art".[10] Imitation characterizes the course of West Indian history, as he portrays it: mimicry of the "revolutionary politics of France"(*LED*, p. 116), and of "Britishness", seen "as an ideal of justice and protection" (*LED*, p. 227). The influence of the U. S. promotes the emulation of inappropriate models in contemporary Trinidad: "Trinidadians of all races and classes are remaking themselves in the image of the Hollywood B-man" (*MP*, p. 61). Mimicry is, in particular, associated by Naipaul with the adoption of radical or left-wing ideas. Of a slogan glorifying revolutionary violence in Argentina, he states, "So, in sinister mimicry, the South twists the revolutionary jargon of the North".[11] His analysis of Argentinean society recalls his treatment of Malik.

> So many words have acquired lesser meanings in Argentina: *general, artist, journalist, historian, professor, university, director, executive, industrialist, aristocrat, library, museum, zoo;* so many words need inverted commas (*REP*, p. 153).

Naipaul most prominently refers to this notion in the title of *The Mimic Men*, which appears to consign all colonial societies to a condition of incompleteness and unreality: "We pretended to be real, to be learning, to be preparing ourselves for life, we mimic men of the New World" (*MM*, p. 175). Naipaul later comes to acknowledge that

> history is an interplay of various peoples, and its [borrowing] has gone on for ever. I can think of no culture that's been left to itself. It's a very simple view that borrowing just began the other day with the European expansion.[12]

His previous statements on the subject of imitation tend to suggest that, on the contrary, ideas are non-transferable, and ridiculous except when applied in anything other than their country of origin.

Naipaul also dwells on the role of audience expectation in shaping Malik's performance: "Malik's Negro was, in fact, a grotesque: not American, not West Indian, but an American caricatured by a red man from Trinidad for a British audience" (*REP*, pp. 31–2).

> He was the total 1960s Negro, in a London setting; and his very absence of originality, his plasticity, his ability to give people the kind of Negro they wanted, made him acceptable to journalists (*REP*, p. 23).

Naipaul sets himself above the limited and provincial understanding of 1960s Londoners. There is an impression of exhilaration and enjoyment in Naipaul's satirical rendering of Malik's beliefs:

> In Malik's system, the Negro who had not dropped out, who was educated, had a skill or a profession, was not quite a Negro; there was no need for anyone to come to terms with him. The real Negro was more elemental. He lived in a place called "the ghetto," which was awful but had its enviable gaieties; and in the ghetto the Negro lived close to crime. He was a ponce or a drug peddler; he begged and stole; he was that attractive Negro thing, a "hustler." The police didn't like the real Negro; and now this Negro was very angry. The real Negro, as it turned out, was someone like Malik; and only Malik could be his spokesman (*REP*, p. 33).

Humphry and Tindall's book provides a chronological account of Malik's life, and gives a comforting sense that the truth of this life is wholly accessible to investigation. Naipaul's narrative is polarized between, on the one hand, a knowing superiority of tone, and a refusal to be numbered among Malik's gulls, and, on the other, the withholding of a relation of certainty regarding the events narrated. The account starts, arrestingly, *in medias res*, with the detail of the file that is used to murder Benson — "A corner file is a three-sided file, triangular in section, and it is used in Trinidad for the sharpening of cutlasses'' (*REP*, p. 3) — a detail to which the narrative repeatedly returns.[13] Naipaul's technique of focusing on the detail of the narrative of the murders, while refusing to supply any explicit moral condemnation — which is in contrast with his account of Malik's career — prefigures the mode in which the outrages committed in *Guerrillas* are recounted.

> She had to be stabbed nine times. It was an especially deep wound at the base of the neck that stilled her; and then she was buried in her African-style clothes. She was not yet completely dead: dirt from her burial hole would work its way into her intestines (*REP*, pp. 6–7).

The reference to Benson's African-style clothes may be intended as a reminder of her absurdity, but also has some pathos. The police inventory of her possessions, which Naipaul repeats without comment — the hippy bag, silver bracelets and rings, face cream and assorted bric-à-brac — likewise suggests her vulnerability. The emotionless, forensic exactitude of the narrative might be thought to imply the moral outrage it refuses explicitly to state.

Naipaul's practice on this occasion could be interpreted as going against the profession contained in his essay ''The Documentary Heresy'', referred to in the previous chapter, which discusses the artistic representation of violence: ''The violence some of us are resisting, . . . is clinical and documentary in intention and makes no statement beyond that of bodily pain and degradation''.[14] The representation of such violence is presented as a dereliction of artistic responsibility; nevertheless, the manner in which the novel and article depict the killings is indeed clinical and documentary. *Guerrillas* would appear to be at odds with Naipaul's stated intentions regarding his novelistic practice in other respects, too. Discussing his limited readership and his tactics for enlarging it, in ''London'' (1958), Naipaul considers but dismisses the possibility of writing about race or sex: ''But I cannot write Sex'' (*OB*, p. 13). And the issues are too complicated for him to write about race, he contends. Another technique, he writes, would be to structure the narrative around an English or American figure. The possibilities he dismisses here are, however, used in *Guerrillas, In a Free State* and *A Bend in the River*.

The article's concentration on the detail of the murders, tersely narrated — on the busy comings and goings, the digging of the hole in preparation — and on the implements with which the crime is performed, together with the circularity of the narration, all recall something of the labyrinthine intricacies and impenetrabilities of a Robbe-Grillet novel. Having begun with the detail of the murders, then moved back in time to explore their background, then returned again to the killings, Naipaul's account attains a moment of contemplative calm, with a quotation from Lamartine. But the lengthy postscript, which incorporates evidence that only emerged in the later trial for Benson's murder, rehearses once more the details of the killings from a slightly altered perspective. This fractured, repetitive structure embodies a response to new evidence and is consonant with the circular structure of the main body of the account. The repetitions are also a consequence of the fact that the essay was first published in two parts. They have the effect of miming the difficulties of providing a satisfactory and full account of events. They contrast with the straightforward, chronological narration employed by Naipaul in *Guerrillas*: the article is the more complex work, in terms of its narrative technique.

For all the reiterated detail of the murders, their motivation remains obscure. Naipaul implies that Benson's murder represents Malik's response to bearing the "wound of England" (*REP*, p. 64): he "had begun to secrete a resentment, soon settling into hatred, not of white people or English people, but of the English middle class he had got to know" (*REP*, p. 37). The crimes exceed, however, such purported motives: to assert that the murder, like Malik's fiction, was a settling of scores with the English middle class (*REP,* p. 73), or a means of entrapping his followers in a bond of fear, seems insufficient and abstract. Naipaul would seem to abandon the attempt to explain Skerritt's murder: "And then, for no reason except that of blood, and because he was now used to the idea of killing with a cutlass, he killed Joseph Skerritt" (*REP*, p. 89).

"Michael X" also anticipates *Guerrillas* in its distribution of authorial sympathy among the characters. The novel's generosity towards the character of Jimmy and hostility towards Jane are prefigured by Naipaul's antipathy, in the journalism, towards Benson and the milieu of which he treats her as representative, and in the manner in which his contempt for Malik is tempered by compassion. His sympathy is manifest in the exploration of Malik's primal shame concerning his mother, which Naipaul portrays as having determined the course of his subsequent career:

> This letter is the truest thing Malik ever wrote, and the most moving. It explains so much: the change of name from de Freitas to X, the assumption of so many personalities, the anxiety to please. A real torment was buried in the clowning of the racial entertainer (*REP*, p. 28).

Naipaul argues that Malik didn't plead insanity, which might have saved him from the death sentence, because "a plea of insanity would have made nonsense of a whole school of theatre. . . . So Malik played out to the end the role that had been given him'' (*REP*, p. 91). In depicting Malik as a victim, Naipaul might appear to reproduce the passivity which he has noted in Malik's own narrative of his life: ''Events accumulate confusedly around him'' (*REP*, p. 25). Naipaul's sympathy for Malik draws attention to certain similarities in their positions, as Trinidadians in London. The expectations of Malik's audience exert pressure on Naipaul's work, too; it is felt in his readiness to dispute their beliefs.

Another respect in which Malik's own opinions, for all Naipaul's evident distance from them, are paralleled by Naipaul's is in regard to their shared mistrust of Malik's supporters. Underlying his casting of Malik as victim, and of Benson as responsible for her fate, is Naipaul's animosity towards the milieu which enabled Malik to flourish. If Malik's crime was an exacting of revenge on the English middle class in the person of Benson, whom he treats merely as a symbolic representative of this milieu, Naipaul's account could be said to perceive her in the same way. The animosity with which Naipaul portrays Benson appears to be in excess of its object: Naipaul gives expression through the portrait to his contempt for the revolutionary sympathizers of 1960s London, and like Malik withholds respect for her individuality, reducing her to little more than a cipher.

Naipaul, as mentioned above, holds that Malik could not have existed without his audience: ''For people like Malik there was no point in being black and angry unless occasionally there were white people to witness'' (*REP*, pp. 5–6). It is Naipaul's view that they were guilty of fostering in him delusions of grandeur:

> England made things easy for Malik. But England in the end undid him. . . .He failed to understand that section of the middle class that knows only that it is secure, has no views, only reflexes and scattered irritations, and sometimes indulges in play: the people who keep up with ''revolution'' as with the theatre, the revolutionaries who visit centres of revolution, but with return air tickets, the people for whom Malik's kind of Black Power was an exotic but safe brothel (*REP*, p. 29).

This characterization of the type acts as a blueprint from which Naipaul draws the figure of Jane. The logic behind the distribution of responsibility is akin to that of the passage from Malik's autobiography quoted earlier, regarding his speeches on pimping:

> Malik was uneducated, but people in England had told him that he was a writer; and he did his best to write. There were also people who had told him — ponce, con man — that he was a leader (though only of Negroes). (*REP*, p. 18.)

This passage illustrates the rapidity with which Naipaul's ironies shift between subjects, targeting Malik at one moment, the audience that supported him at the next. The press is charged with a substantial complicity in the creation of Malik: Naipaul persuasively illustrates his point by quoting from an article by Jill Tweedie, who takes Jamal at his own valuation, as " 'excruciatingly handsome, tantalisingly brown, fiercely articulate' " (*REP*, p. 35). This is another of the details of Malik's story that has its direct counterpart in *Guerrillas*.

Naipaul's peroration invokes Conrad's "An Outpost of Progress", which he describes as

> a story of the congruent corruptions of colonizer and colonized, which can also be read as a parable about simple people who think they can separate themselves from the crowd. Benson was as shallow and vain and parasitic as many middle-class dropouts of her time; she became as corrupt as her master; she was part of the corruption by which she was destroyed. And Malik's wife was right. Benson was, more profoundly than Malik and Jamal, a fake. She took, on her journey away from home, the assumptions, however little acknowledged, not only of her class and race and the rich countries to which she belonged, but also of her ultimate security (*REP*, p. 71).

Guerrillas, he contends, has "very hard things to say about people who play at serious things, who think they can always escape, run back to their safe world".[15] It is difficult to see why Naipaul should lay such stress on her security, since her privileged social background did not prevent her murder.

Naipaul has consistently defined the identity of colonizer and colonized in terms of this issue of security. He told Ian Hamilton that, when he first came to England, he thought that "to be a colonial is, in a way, to know a total kind of security. It is to have all decisions about major issues taken out of one's hands" (Hamner, p. 39). Now, however, in 1974, he thinks that "I am the insecure person and that people here are the totally secure" (*ibid*). In *The Enigma of Arrival*, Naipaul's landlord is portrayed as reduced to a self-destructive accidia by his "very great security" (*EA*, p. 193). In *A Way in the World*, the roles are reversed in the story about Ralegh and the Amerindian he brings back to England, who has "turned out to be safer than all the people he served".[16]

Benson remains untouched by Naipaul's sympathy. In a letter to Diana Athill, his editor at this time, Naipaul chillingly wrote: "People like that create endless trouble for other people in other countries, encouraging the simple-minded".[17] An acquaintance of Benson's, Athill felt that the article misrepresented her:

> Poor Gale was the only white person it [Jamal's behaviour] excited, and her reaction to it was not an example of the secure middle-class white being given the negro she wanted, but of the extremely insecure and empty person being given the *possessor* she wanted. She'd have gone for anyone sexy who offered her a cult. . . . [T]he point you are making her prove is a valid one. But you *are* making her prove it — you are cutting your cloth to fit your pattern.[18]

Athill provides a more sympathetic account of these events than Naipaul's in *Make Believe*: she portrays Benson as compelled to fill an inner vacuum by an act of self-immolation, and Jamal as deformed by the pain of his childhood: "a loving child unloved, a beautiful child made to believe he was ugly, a clever child starved into a process of desperate self-invention".[19] Malik, in contrast, she represents as no more than a cynical and violent gangster.

Naipaul's allusion to "An Outpost of Progress" is of interest for the lack of resemblance between its plot and the events of Benson's life. The story serves as a trial run for *Heart of Darkness*, but lacks the novella's ponderous weight of metaphysical mystification. It describes the gradual degeneration of the morals and sanity of two Belgians in the Congo, and the processes by which, remote from their native society, they accommodate themselves to a compromising of their conventional principles. In the absence of external checks, they come to behave without restraint: one kills the other in an argument over some sugar, and then goes mad. The analogies with the story of Kurtz — "civilized" man reverting to "savagery" in the wilderness — are confirmed by the way that the name of the protagonist, Kayertz, prefigures that of the later work. The early stages of the story are in the manner of a Flaubertian satire on complacent bourgeois stupidity, Bouvard and Pécuchet in the Congo:

> They did not know what use to make of their faculties, being both, through want of practice, incapable of independent thought. . . . But the two men got on well together in the fellowship of their stupidity and laziness.[20]

The alternative to their cosy complacency which is presented in the tale is reversion to an essential evil, symbolized in this story, as in *Heart of Darkness*, by means of a depiction of the landscape that is its backdrop, and of its indigenous inhabitants:

> But the contact with pure unmitigated savagery, with primitive nature and primitive man, brings sudden and profound trouble into the heart . . . a suggestion of things vague, uncontrollable,

and repulsive, whose discomposing intrusion excites the imagination and tries the civilized nerves of the foolish and the wise alike.[21]

Their moral degeneration is shown in the rapidity with which they reconcile themselves to having been the passive beneficiaries of an act of slave trading, despite the fact that they initially condemn such acts, in conventional phrases:

> "Slavery is an awful thing," stammered out Kayertz in an unsteady voice.
> "Frightful — the sufferings," grunted Carlier with conviction.
> They believed their words. Everybody shows a respectful deference to certain sounds that he and his fellows can make.[22]

By the next day, they accept the deal as a *fait accompli*, and their fate is sealed:

> It was not the absolute and dumb solitude of the post that impressed them so much as an inarticulate feeling that something from within them was gone, something that worked for their safety, and had kept the wilderness from interfering with their hearts.... And out of the great silence of the surrounding wilderness, its very hopelessness and savagery seemed to approach them nearer, to draw them gently, to look upon them, to envelop them with a solicitude irresistible, familiar, and disgusting.[23]

Benson's situation had little in common with that of Carlier and Kayertz. The corruption of the protagonists of Conrad's story seems authentic enough, but the Benson of Naipaul's article is more misguided than corrupt.

Naipaul uses his article on the murders as an opportunity to inveigh against the Black Power movement in the Caribbean, even though Malik's connections with the 1970 revolt in Trinidad were, in fact, negligible. For three months, young people, radicals, students and the unemployed took to the streets, calling for greater participation in power, an end to government corruption and to concessions to foreign investors. The uprising was largely undirected. There was some arson and looting. When a general strike threatened, the government called a State of Emergency. Members of the armed forces mutinied. The government response was to request the assistance of the Americans. The Americans declined to intervene, but the Venezuelan military put on a show of force to assist in the restoration of civil order. Malik was passing through Trinidad at the time, and was photographed participating in a march to the sugar-growing areas, designed to encourage the East Indian community to join the ranks of the protesters, but he had no significant influence on political events on the island.

To treat Malik as the leader of a Black Power movement is implicitly to collude in his delusion that "words and publicity made real the thing publicized" (*REP*, p. 38). Naipaul would appear to take Malik at his word,[24] in presenting Malik as the fraud who is not the exception but the rule, and whose story provides an opportunity to denounce what he argues is a fraudulence inherent to the Black Power movement:

> Malik's career proves how much of Black Power — away from its United States source — is jargon, how much a sentimental hoax.... . It perpetuates the negative, colonial politics of protest. It is, in the end, a deep corruption: a wish to be granted a dispensation from the pains of development, an almost religious conviction that oppression can be turned into an asset, race into money. While the dream of redemption lasts, Negroes will continue to exist only that someone might be their leader (*REP*, p. 70).

The analysis recalls the arguments made in the article "Power?" (1970). This article likens Black Power to the lunacy and fantasy of Carnival, which is described as "the original dream of black power, style and prettiness" (*OB*, p. 247), underlying which he perceives a "vision of the black millennium" (*OB*, p. 247). He dismisses the movement as lacking a programme, as articulating only discontents, as mere "rage, drama and style" (*OB*, p. 248). Details of the article are incorporated in *Guerrillas*: the apocalyptic, millennial mood, the slogans, and the prognostication of impending chaos and external intervention.

Naipaul's generosity in *Guerrillas* towards the figure of Jimmy Ahmed has been noted by a number of critics.[25] Naipaul eschews even such disdain as had informed his portrait of Jimmy's prototype, by failing to scrutinize Jimmy's earlier career, and by not ascribing to him the variety of criminal activities with which Malik had been associated, though there is mention of a rape charge in England — which anticipates the novel's dénouement. To a tendency towards self-pity in Jimmy's letters the novel responds with an absence of irony, surprising in view of Naipaul's customary opinions concerning revolutionaries and the inadvisability of taking them at their own estimate. Jimmy writes: "*I am dying alone and unloved and I will die in anger, no other way is possible now*".[26] His expressions of self-pity are endorsed by Jane's sympathy for him, which would also appear to be the author's.

> "And now you'll just leave Jimmy out there for those people to kill. Who's going to give him a job? So Jimmy's right.

You've all turned him into a 'playboy.' A plaything. And now you're throwing him to Meredith" (*G*, p. 224).

As in the case of Malik, sympathy for his plight is seen as validated by Naipaul's disdain for those who, meddlesomely, made Jimmy their protégé and then dropped him. His expression of a sense of betrayal is consistent with the opinions of his author:

> *The people who will win are the people who have won already and they're not taking chances now, like the liberals. You know better than I how they let me down when the crisis came, you would think that after making me their playboy and getting me deported from England they would leave me alone. But they do not. Even here they are coming after me, well I ask you. These liberals who come flashing their milk white thighs and think they're contributing to the cause* (*G*, p. 42).

He is also the plaything of a local firm which sponsors ill-judged good works as a public relations exercise. The responsibility, therefore, for the farcical pretence of a commune at Thrushcross Grange does not rest solely with Jimmy's delusions.

Naipaul is scornful of Malik's attempts to write, and Jimmy is endowed with a literary style far superior to Malik's: "*The corridor of time is now a room of mirrors*," he writes (*G*, p. 227). Words of his provide the epigraph to the book, forecasting the social chaos that temporarily erupts in violence: "When everybody wants to fight there's nothing to fight for. Everybody wants to fight his own little war, everybody is a guerrilla". This is indirectly echoed in Harry de Tunja's account of the revolt: the police "don't know who they fighting or who they fighting for. Everybody down there is a leader now" (*G*, p. 185). Jimmy's words, borne out by the course of events, are given the benediction of authorial sanction.

It is Jane who bears the brunt of the author's opprobrium, which manifests itself with a disproportionate virulence: Naipaul discharges onto the character, as he does onto Benson, the burden of embodying all the features that he finds contemptible in wealthy sympathizers with radical protest. The novel's plot most obviously diverges from the events that inspired it in the way that it engineers sexual relations between the murderer and his victim.[27] Naipaul condenses the roles of Jamal and Malik into the figure of Jimmy. One of the consequences of this is that Jimmy's revenge appears less impersonal and irrational than Malik's murder of Benson. The first sex scene provides a kind of a motivation: Jane is presented as assuming an unduly active, masculine role — as promiscuous and provocative. In its presentation of Jane, Naipaul's prose makes evident his disgust:

> The flowered blouse, through which her brassiere could be seen, the tight trousers that modelled stomach, groin and cleft in a single, sudden curve: that could pass in the city and in the shopping plaza of the Ridge would be hardly noticeable, but here it seemed provocative, over-casual enough to be dressy: London, foreign, wrong (*G*, p. 14).

Naipaul's attitude is echoed by Mrs Stephens' more forthright pronouncement: " 'Parading through the town with their tight pants sticking up in their crutch. They *stink*, Mr Roche. They stink like rotten meat self' " (*G*, pp. 111–2). Jane's "gobbling talk and nervous manner, which now began to appear strident and hysterical" (*G*, p. 99) are contrasted, in a scene at Mrs Grandlieu's, with the demure propriety of a pretty brown-skinned local woman, neat in a tight dress and make-up, whose disapproval of Jane manifests itself in a frozen aloofness. Jane disconcerts Jimmy by seizing the initiative: "Her speed alarmed him; he feared he was losing the moment again" (*G*, p. 78). Her movements are described as sudden, "violent," and unsuitable:

> That drawn up leg, so slender above the knee, and held slightly to one side: there was something masculine about the posture, something masculine about the hand that stroked that leg now (*G*, p. 80).

His sense of being under threat is given expression in a defensive, misogynistic disgust: "The cleft was like a dumb, stupid mouth" (*G*, p. 78). The sex scene reads as an undisguised and brutal power struggle.

John Mellors has suggested that an effect of the novel's dependence on real events for its plot is to deprive the characters of autonomy, to subject them entirely to the constraints of a foregone conclusion.[28] There are many premonitions of the novel's ending scattered through the work: in the story of the gang-raped white girl which Jimmy incorporates into his wish-fulfilment fantasy novel, as an incident involving Clarissa, who is a parallel figure to Jane — white, wealthy, and drawn to Jimmy like a "*mesmerized rabbit*" (*G*, p. 64). Jane's mouth is said to suggest to Jimmy a "healed wound" (*G*, p. 70), which prefigures the violence that is to be done to her, already metaphorically inscribed on her body. Jane may be unduly domineering in bed, but she becomes a more passive figure than Benson was at the time of their respective murders, and she is portrayed throughout as "surrendering to events" (*G*, p. 162): she is an archetypal victim, whose end is entailed by her own character.[29] The language Naipaul uses to denounce the security he sees as conferred by her social background carries an ominous anticipation of her ultimate fate. He contemplates Jane's past through the disenchanted eyes of Peter Roche, with whom her relationship has gone sour:

> Where he had once looked for passion born of violation and distress he now found inviolability.
>
> She had invested little in this relationship. She had from the start, as it now seemed, held herself back, for this moment of withdrawal. The gesture, of leaving London and coming out to live with him, so soon after meeting him, had appeared to him grand, part of her passionate nature; yet it was contained within this sense of inviolability, her belief that everything could be undone (*G*, pp. 100–1).

Gale Benson wasn't raped before her murder: Naipaul compounds the degradation of Jane's murder with the sexual assault, as if he seeks to punish her for her inviolability by having her good and properly violated. Her murder, however, exposes the illusory basis of the rage against her supposed security, which did not render her invulnerable to attack.

"Violation" is a significant term for Naipaul, used in a variety of unexpected and metaphorical contexts, as a means of delineating the legacy and experience of imperial displacement. Michael Gorra observes that Naipaul finds in the mixing of peoples, in displacement and cultural interfusion, "only a sense of violation, of estrangement from one's origins, and a consequent longing for an idealized home".[30] Indian "mimicry of the West" is described as "the Indian self-violation" (*AD*, p. 226). Personal relations are a trope for political relations; violation serves as a metaphor to describe the process of imperial expansion.

> The dream of the untouched, complete world, the thing for ourselves alone, the dream of Shangri-la, is an enduring fantasy. It fell to the Spaniards to have the unique experience. Generosity and romance, then, to the discoverer; but the Spaniards will never be forgiven. And even in the violated New World the Spaniards themselves remained subject to the fantasy (*OB*, p. 206).

The Mimic Men connects the colonial peoples' sense of violation, of inhabiting a ruptured, fractured, incomplete world, with apocalyptic desires: "We had no force of nationalism even, only the negative frenzy of a deep violation" (*MM*, p. 245). Elsewhere, Naipaul has used violation as a trope for self-betrayal: Ralegh's re-engagement in the world of action after his imprisonment is described as "an act of self-violation" (*LED*, p. 75). Taken loosely, in the sense of a betrayal of one's cultural integrity, violation is something that Jane has done to herself, by betraying Naipaul's ideal of England, and setting in motion a chain of events that culminate in her literal violation:

> The old society was one which was *not artificial.* The links were instinctive *and* have reasons. People do themselves violations when they start overthrowing these. One of the upsetting things about England has been the colonialization of its politics and politicians.[31]

Jane is furthermore endowed with a masochistic streak which implies that, in some measure, she enjoys her treatment. This smacks of the rapist's logic: she deserved and wanted what she got. Naipaul describes an episode from Jane's past which is reminiscent of the sex scene with Jimmy; in the course of having sex with a former partner she casts him aside, and her lover revenges himself on her by means of a physical assault, rendered in an impersonal manner which recalls the description of Benson's murder: "She was slapped, so hard that her jaw jarred, her cigarette fell from her hand; and then she was slapped again" (*G*, p. 48). She discovers that, in spite of herself, she has been sexually excited by the violence. She is shown struggling against and greatly distressed by her rape, but it is prefaced by some nasty foreplay, which Jane appears to relish:

> He held her face between his hands, jammed the heels of his palms on the corners of her mouth, covering her almost vanished period spots, distending her lips. He covered her mouth with his; her lips widened and she made a strangled sound; and then he spat in her mouth. She swallowed and he let her face go. She opened her eyes and said, "That was lovely" (*G*, p. 236).

Inter-racial sexual violence, in which personal relations serve as a metaphor for the political, is a recurring feature of Naipaul's writing. This scene prefigures the way that Salim insults Yvette in *A Bend in the River*: "I held her legs apart. She raised them slightly — smooth concavities of flesh on either side of the inner ridge — and then I spat on her between the legs until I had no more spit".[32]

The narrative strategies of *Guerrillas* are echoed in Jimmy's work of fiction. This is based on material drawn from Malik's life: Malik began a novel which is narrated from the point of view of an upper-class English woman, Lena Boyd-Richardson, who is fascinated by him.

> A well-appointed house, Malik's, is being described: modern furniture imported from England, fitted carpets, radio phono-

graph, records, "a gigantic bookshelf Shakepeare [*sic*] Shaw Marx Lenin Trotsky Confucius Hugo." The narrator takes up "Salammbo that masterpiece of Flaubert's" and finds it dust-free. "I discover that he not only have the books but actually reads and understands them I was absolutly bowld, litteraly. I took a seat, and gazed upon this marvel, Mike" (*REP*, p. 60).

Naipaul follows his source extremely closely, describing:

> A square of English carpet, electric blue with splashes of black and yellow, almost covered the floor. The furniture was also English and had a similar innocent stylishness; it was of a kind seen in the windows of furniture shops on the high streets of English market towns. A three-piece suite, square and chunky, with fat cushions, was covered in a tiger-striped synthetic material, thick and furry. On the fitted bookshelves a number of books in the same magenta binding stood solidly together: The Hundred Best Books of the World (*G*, pp. 23–4).

Jimmy rewrites the passage from the viewpoint of Clarissa, the character in his novel:

> *But Jimmy's house is something else, I can scarcely believe my eyes when I enter, wall to wall, everything of the best and everything neat and clean and nicely put away. And what a collection of books, no skimping there. He's obviously a man of considerable refinement rare for these days.*
>
> *I said "Do you mind" and went to the shelves. He said "By all means, they're not dummies" and I took up Wuthering Heights. "Ah" he said breaking into my thoughts "you are looking at that great work of the Brontës. What a gifted family, it makes you believe in heredity. Would you like some tea?"* (*G*, pp. 39–40.)

Malik's novel, Naipaul contends, expounds a fantasy of power, a desire to strike terror into the heart of his middle-class English audience. Likewise Jimmy's novel demonstrates a desire to impress, a craving for approval, and a thirst for power over the girl. Jimmy's novel is not merely an occasion for ironies at the expense of his absurd aspirations: it also determines the conclusion of the plot of *Guerrillas*, anticipating the rape that comes at the end of the work. Naipaul's narrative gives Jimmy the power he wishes for: Jane is indeed drawn to her attacker, like a mesmerized rabbit. There is a similarity in the method by which both Jimmy and Naipaul go about putting ideas into the girl's head — ideas that may be meant to diminish the crime of the rapist, who was only giving her what she wanted.

Jane is repeatedly seen from Roche's viewpoint. Roche figures her as a kind of man-eating sea anemone, "waving its strands at the bottom of the ocean. Rooted and secure, and indifferent to what it attracted. The dragon-lady, infinitely casual, infinitely unconsciously calculating" (*G*, p. 22). Since his relationship with her is foundering, his perceptions are inevitably tainted with bitterness, but this view of her is not substantially at odds with the portrait constructed by the book as a whole. She is accused of hypocrisy — of professing a desire for revolutionary change, while retaining underlying "certainties, of class and money" (*G*, p. 100). She is charged with being "without consistency or even coherence" (*G*, p. 25). The narrator shares Roche's hostility:

> She was privileged: it was the big idea, the one that overrode all the scattered, unrelated ideas deposited in her soul as she had adventured in life, the debris of a dozen systems she had picked up from a dozen men (*G*, p. 55).

She is accused of pursuing the thrill of revolutionary excitement, and is disappointed that the island does not turn out to be the "centre of world-disturbance" (*G*, p. 49) she had imagined it. She is portrayed as an echo-chamber in which fashionable pieties resound, an amalgam of the attitudes of a class. In this way, she comes to stand for an entire social group.

Jane's rape and murder are horrendous occurrences provoking moral revulsion, part of their bleakness consisting in the moral vacuum in which the terse detail of the narrative unfolds. The revulsion, however, is not so clear to all: some critics have questioned the nature of Naipaul's interest in the sadomasochistic scenes he represents, and argued that the unflinching gaze with which he relates their smallest detail, without reprehending or obviously judging them as undesirable, may be construed as problematic.[33] Discussing the writing of the murder, Naipaul observes:

> The fact that it shocks you is part of its success. But it's the wrong kind of success if you just think, God she was such an unpleasant girl. If she was really all that unpleasant, if you hadn't been made to understand her, you wouldn't have found her death to be so appalling.[34]

A striking feature of the critical reaction to the novel is the number of critics who participate in Naipaul's animosity towards the character, as if by virtue of being white and wealthy Jane had forfeited all right to their sympathies. When not actively hostile, critics tend to be dismissive of her fate, seeing it as an element of Jimmy's psychodrama: Jane is reduced to a projection of Jimmy's psyche.[35]

Guerrillas, like "Michael X", sets the story of its protagonists against the background of a political uprising, loosely modelled on events in Trinidad in 1970. The novel's narrative technique entails a relegation of these events to its periphery, where they lie shrouded in mystery and menace. It derives its narrative energy from the frisson of fear which results from the invocation of the possibility of imminent social conflagration. There is a background of social disaffection, viewed generally from the perspective of "the hysteria of the people who lived on the Ridge, people who felt threatened by what lay below, and moved higher and higher up the hills" (*G*, p. 57). There is a "whole parallel society" (*G*, p. 30) of derelicts, who are perceived through the eyes of those who have something to lose, and reason to fear them. Jane sees "wild disordered men tramping along old paths, across gardens, between houses" (*G*, p. 31). The dismissiveness of Naipaul's prose re-enacts the indifference and neglect of a society: "They were like Bryant, boys spawned by the city, casually conceived, and after the backyard drama and ritual of their birth gradually abandoned" (*G*, p. 34).

The uprising in *Guerrillas* is viewed from the vantage point of the Ridge, where the expatriates and the prosperous seek refuge, and is perceived by the novel's protagonists as something intensely disturbing and threatening. Events unfold in the distance and soundlessly:

> Just after noon she [Jane] saw the first fire in the city below. Not the thin white smoke of bush fires, or the brown-grey spread of the burning rubbish dump; but a small inky eruption of the densest black, erupting and erupting and not becoming less dense or less black, with little spurts and streaks of red that then fell back into the blackness (*G,* p. 181).

This description, for all its careful minuteness, leaves one in the dark about what might be going on. The novel's characters, powerless to intervene, are left waiting on events. The fires of urban destruction parallel the bush fires caused by the drought, as if the riot were an element in nature, part of a cycle of upheaval and cataclysm, in which it would be foolish to attempt to intervene. The silence in *Guerrillas* is broken by the arrival of the American helicopters; order is mysteriously restored, a return to normality marked by a resumption of the sound of radios. The revolt fizzles out; the threatened apocalypse does not occur, and the crisis is acted out in the sphere of personal relations.[36] The revolt turns out to be a huge anti-climax. The novel therefore derives excitement from the evocation of an imminent apocalypse, while renouncing the romantic satisfactions that such an apocalypse might provide.

Comparable images are used to portray political disturbances elsewhere in Naipaul's work. In *The Mimic Men*, as mentioned earlier, he writes:

> We had no force of nationalism even, only the negative frenzy of a deep violation which could lead to further frenzy alone, the vision of the world going up in flames: it was the only expiation (*MM*, p. 245).

Naipaul also employs such imagery in *A Bend in the River*, when he likens the civil war which periodically erupts in the background of the novel to a forest fire (*BR*, p. 75). The fire imagery reappears in Jane's vision of metropolitan decline. Jane's viewpoint echoes that of Santosh, in *In a Free State*, as he watches the Washington race riots from his hermetically-sealed apartment; Santosh, however, feels some sympathy with the forces of destruction, the fires of the riot answering his desire for a ritual of purification, although he fails to recognize the kinship claimed by the designation "*Soul Brother*"(*IFS*, 61), daubed outside his house at a time of later disturbances. This distanced and detached viewpoint serves as in *Guerrillas* to signal a lack of solidarity with the aims of the rioters.

The riot amounts ultimately only to a senseless bacchanal of destruction, as ineffective to promote change as the hollow pretence of Jimmy's commune. *The Enigma of Arrival* perceives the unrest in Trinidad on which the revolt in *Guerrillas* is loosely based as the expression of "a wish to destroy a world judged corrupt and too full of pain, to turn one's back on it, rather than to improve it" (*EA*, p. 147). Ralph Singh in *The Mimic Men* observes that the disenfranchised, however, lack even the power to effect destruction:

> I saw that in our situation the mob, without skills, was unproductive, offered nothing, and was in the end without power. The mob might burn down the city. But the mob is shot down, and the power of money will cause the city to be built again (*MM*, p. 245).

Real power resides with the possessors of the helicopters. The notion is again drawn from *The Mimic Men*:

> In a society like ours, fragmented and inorganic, no link between man and the landscape, a society not held together by common interests, there was no true internal source of power, and ... no power was real which did not come from the outside (*MM*, p. 246).

Lurking on the fringes of the novel is the figure of Stephens, gang member and one-time participant in Jimmy's commune. Enormous significance is attached to him, although the precise nature of his influence and power is never defined, and Godot-like, he never appears in person. His death sparks the revolt; its significance is to be inferred from the controlled hysteria of Roche's response to the news: "Roche didn't believe in the guerrillas the newspapers, the radio and the television spoke about. But he believed in the city gangs" (*G*, p. 104). In respect of the treatment of Stephens and the gangs, the novel appears almost perversely to be withholding necessary information, so as to contrive a thrilling sense of danger, in a manner which recalls something of the tactics of the mystery novel, which conceals information, or engages in narrative deceptions, in order to create the mystery it will ultimately explain away. The novel, however, doesn't illuminate the nature of revolt, preferring to furnish an impressionistic account of the bewildering experience of witnessing such events from the outside. *Guerrillas* offers some of the excitements of vicarious participation in an anxiety reassuringly remote from its readers.

One might wish to argue a case for Naipaul's portrayal of the revolt in *Guerrillas* as merely realistic, miming the uncertainties that are part of the experience of living through confused events as they unfold. *Guerrillas* might be thought to owe something to the conventions of a form of political tourism described by Benedict Anderson — a mode devoted to conveying the difficulties of determining what is going on in foreign trouble-spots.[37] There is a certain amount of irony in the notion that Naipaul should choose to adopt these conventions in order to describe a land modelled on his native Trinidad. It is possible that he had been absent from Trinidad for so long that the outsider's view had become the most accessible to him. As early as 1953 he had written, "I do wish I could see Trinidad more clearly".[38] His notebooks show, moreover, that, in planning the novel, the revolt was never visualized by him in detail.

Both documentary and literary sources act to shape *Guerrillas*, and it is the literary influences on the novel which this discussion will now proceed to consider. Naipaul has testified to the extent of Conrad's influence on him: " ...I found that Conrad — sixty years before, in the time of a great peace — had been everywhere before me".[39] Comparisons are often made between *Guerrillas* and *The Secret Agent*, with reference to their shared subject matter — the senseless revolutionaries, and the privileged woman who befriends revolution. Enigma and mystery are qualities readily ascribed to the alien, the unfamiliar, and the exotic. *Guerrillas'* mood of imprecise menace, based on a failure to understand events, is closely analogous also to the example of *Heart of Darkness*, which employs the technique of epistemological incertitude in a profoundly influential manner. Examples of Marlow's failure to comprehend his surroundings proliferate. Marlow's account repeatedly asserts that the wilderness is a "mystery" (*HD*, 67), and emphasizes that the land is "impenetrable to human thought" (*HD*, p. 94). Its inhabitants are presented as posing an insoluble enigma: "The prehistoric man was cursing us, praying to us, welcoming us — who could tell? We were cut off from the comprehension of our surroundings" (*HD*, p. 68).

At the heart of the tale's pessimism is Kurtz's moral degeneration, which is said to consist, among other things, in presiding "at certain midnight dances ending with unspeakable rites" (*HD*, p. 86). "Unspeakable" is evasive, and it is as if anything more specific would not sound bad enough. The point of Marlow's journey seems to be the process of getting there rather than its end or purpose. The tale occasions a measure of curiosity as to what Kurtz will be like, and Marlow's meeting with him therefore has the effect of a resolution, satisfying our expectations in this respect. But Kurtz's dying insight nevertheless comes as something of an anti-climax: melodramatic, perhaps even banal. The core of the tale's mystery, rather like the "extravagant mystery" (*HD*, p. 71) of the Russian's marginal annotations to the book on seamanship, turns out under investigation to have little substance, but the pleasure of the text lies in its presentation of an enigma rather than its resolution. *Heart of Darkness* very effectively portrays the experience of being a stranger in a foreign land; and in so doing, it may be thought to illuminate European anxieties rather than the African scene which is its setting.

There is a marked contrast between Conrad's style — the profusion of words reaching after a diffuse, symbolic resonance — and Naipaul's clipped, succinct clarity, resolutely exact and literal in its rendering of the minute detail of garbage dumps, the decaying industrial estate, neglected roads, excrement and human dereliction: "He saw the dull, close-set eyes, a pimple on the right eyelid: the mind half eaten away, human debris already, his cause already lost" (*G*, p. 104).

> Diseased pariah dogs wandered about; some lay prostrate on the crowded pavements; and she studied one, dead-eyed, with a growth like raw flesh protruding out of its mangy yellow fur (*G*, p. 75).

The humans are given the same treatment as the dogs. Naipaul's tone of combined distaste and merciless fascination could be thought to collude with as well as to condemn the attitudes which have consigned them to the social rubbish dump. The repeated journeys from the Grange to the Ridge enable Naipaul to deploy his stock of images of desolation:

> After the market, where refrigerated trailers were unloading;

after the rubbish dump burning in the remnant of the mangrove swamp, with black carrion corbeaux squatting hunched on fence-posts or hopping about on the ground; after the built-up hillsides; after the new housing estates, rows of unpainted boxes of concrete and corrugated iron already returning to the shanty towns that had been knocked down for this redevelopment; after the naked children playing in the red dust of the straight new avenues, the clothes hanging like rags from backyard lines; after this, the land cleared a little (*G*, p. 9).

The paratactic structure of this long sentence, which begins the novel, brings to mind the structure of journeys: one thing follows another. The mangrove swamp is the remnant of an older, pastoral landscape, scarcely legible amid the squalor of the human constructions which deface it; while the new developments are consigned to premature decay, as if they had never had a chance. One way in which the island's absence of possibilities is suggested is by means of Naipaul's reversion to the reiteration of this roll-call of images of dereliction and decay. *Heart of Darkness* describes one central journey culminating in a moment of insight; *Guerrillas* a series of journeys going back and forth. *Heart of Darkness*'s culminating insight is presented as a nihilistic anti-epiphany, its abysses romanticized as heroic, in a Faustian way: the bush has beguiled Kurtz's "unlawful soul beyond the bounds of permitted aspirations" (*HD*, p. 107), his degradation is "exalted and incredible" (*HD*, p. 107), his final judgement "had a vibrating note of revolt in its whisper, it had the appalling face of a glimpsed truth" (*HD*, p. 113). The climax of *Guerrillas* is a brutal murder, unilluminated by any such heroic moments of insight.

For all the stylistic contrasts between the works, the landscape of *Guerrillas* is as much a landscape of the mind as is that of *Heart of Darkness*. *Guerrillas*, like *The Mimic Men*, presupposes a meaningful connection between humankind and the land it inhabits as the basis of social order: Ralph asserts that the individual needs to feel "strongly there is some connection between the earth on which he walks and himself" (*MM*, p. 248). *A Way in the World* makes a similar connection, in describing the landscapes of independent Trinidad (the "sacrament of the square" refers to nationalist agitation):

It was as though, with the colonial past, all the colonial landscape was being trampled over and undone; as though, with that past, the very idea of regulation had been rejected; as though, after the sacrament of the square, the energy of revolt had become a thing on its own, eating away at the land (*WW*, 35).

The landscape of *Guerrillas* serves as a symbol of the political condition of the island. The drought, which intermittently causes the hills to ignite into flames, communicates the island's ripeness for conflagration.

The textual genesis of *Guerrillas* provides another context for its interpretation. Naipaul's notebooks show that he originally conceived of the novel in conjunction with what were to become *A Bend in the River* and *The Enigma of Arrival*. The disappointment with England which is an important feature of *The Enigma of Arrival* is preceded by Jane's view that England is in a state of decline. The shared origins of these works also draw attention to the similarities between Naipaul's early experience of England, as he portrays it in *The Enigma of Arrival*, and Meredith's — both are unable to read their social environment. At certain points, Naipaul planned that the novel would be narrated by a character called Krishan, who like him has studied at Oxford. Krishan is having an affair with a woman sometimes called Jane (which could be interpreted as suggesting that Naipaul in some measure identifies with the role of Jimmy in the completed work). Initially, Roche was conceived of as someone perhaps closer to the finished Jane, as "someone whose inner security was, surprisingly, total"[40] — a crueller and more antipathetic figure than he became. In the notebooks, Naipaul more explicitly rationalizes the motivation of his characters. Jane is said to have an affair with Jimmy "out of genuine excitement; and also out of irresponsibility and spite. The attitudes of the secure".[41] The muted threat of Meredith's questioning of Roche in a radio interview is interpreted by the writer as an echo of the time he was threatened by an interviewer in England, a "mock interrogation scene ... This occurs because Roche is giving Jimmy a kind of white 'glamour' " (*ibid*). Meredith, originally called Lee Moore, is a parallel figure to Jimmy: he is "at once resentful of personal slights because of his race and contemptuous of his race"; he "has an account to settle with Jimmy. He settles it through Roche, Jimmy's protector" (*ibid*). The notebook describes Jimmy's motives for the killing: it is

> a proof of manhood and blackness; it is also done out of fear of Bryant and the others. Because they discover that Jimmy is not black. . . . Roche tells them so because he wants to be revenged both on Jimmy and Jane. That is also why he goads Jimmy to the act of murder — taunts him with the vision of the escape of all white people (*ibid*).

"Jimmy revenges himself on her, on England, his wife, the people in England" (*ibid*). The fact that the motivation of the characters in the novel remains obscure enhances the mood of mystery and menace.

In the light of its broad equation between images of an infertile land, crisis in the social, political and moral sphere, and failures in personal relations, *Guerrillas* is reminiscent of *The Waste Land*. Richard Kelly points to an analogy between Naipaul's situation and Eliot's: both are literary expatriates in London with a reverential attitude to European history and culture, qualified by a sense of the sordid paucity of the present.[42] *The Waste Land* likewise invokes imagery of the apocalypse, decaying empires, a hysterical woman, a rape, litter. Naipaul's novel, however, does not entertain the possibility of breakdown and crisis in the same way that the disjunction and fragmentation of Eliot's poetry do; his style remains serenely aloof, unaffected by and in control of the crisis it describes, and looking back to a lost order.[43] *Guerrillas* is not the palimpsest *The Waste Land* is, but its literary allusions attract attention, perhaps because of their apparent incongruity. Both texts employ allusion as a way of introducing the consciousness of a remote cultural order, constructing continuities and emphasizing losses: in the case of *The Waste Land*, the distance is temporal, an index of cultural decline; in that of *Guerrillas*, it is also geographical and cultural. An allusion to *Wuthering Heights* is present both in the name of the commune — Thrushcross Grange — and in Jimmy's novel, where Clarissa picks up a copy of *Wuthering Heights*, and is made to imagine the crowd hailing Jimmy as a leader:

> *"This man was born in the back room of a Chinese grocery, but as Catherine said to Heathcliff 'Your mother was an Indian princess and your father was the Emperor of China'"*
> (G, p. 62).

Roche says that he doesn't think that Jimmy sees himself as Heathcliff, but this would seem the most plausible way of accounting for the allusion, which could be taken to express Jimmy's aspirations. In his novel he portrays himself in terms of the stock figure of romance that descends from Heathcliff: the powerful, dark, violent outsider. Like Heathcliff, he wishes to effect a vengeful destruction of the social order in relation to which he is marginal. The name of Clarissa, the heroine of Jimmy's novel, alludes to the most elaborately staged rape in English literature. It can seem to be another presentiment of Jane's doom, and to take its cue from, and to play upon, Malik's christening of his heroine Lena Boyd-Richardson. "Jane" and "Roche" are a reference to *Jane Eyre*. John Thieme and Helen Tiffin[44] observe the use of fire imagery in both works. The revolutionary fires of *Guerrillas* recall Bertha's destructive rage and Jane's childhood angers. Jane is reading *The Woodlanders*: the significance of this reference would appear to lie in the distance of the novel's agricultural commune from the pastoral community which is the setting for Hardy's novel, the rhythms of its life inextricably interwoven with the forest on which it depends for its livelihood. Johannes Riis[45] sees an analogy between Hardy's fatalism, the workings of the "Unfulfilled Intention," and Naipaul's sense of the corruption of causes — the disjunction between good intentions and achievement — which is illustrated by the career of Roche. Hardy's novel, though, is noteworthy for its renunciation of the morose satisfactions of a melodramatic pessimism: Hardy appears to set up an imminent disaster, steering Grace and Fitzpiers towards the man-trap, only at the last to relent, and miraculously to spare them. Jane is not so lucky: she is trapped in a preordained doom.

Critics have interpreted these allusions as the expression of a position of post-colonial cultural resistance — as pointing to the distance of the culture they originate in from the society *Guerrillas* portrays.[46] Naipaul appears to lend credence to such an interpretation, while seeking to emphasize the poverty of a West Indian society unable to sustain such references, rather than to reject the English literary culture for its inapplicability to other societies. As mentioned in the discussion of *A House for Mr Biswas,* he has asserted that, as he grew up in Trinidad, it seemed to him that "the English language was mine; the tradition was not" (*OB*, p. 26).

> To us, without a mythology, all literatures were foreign. Trinidad was small, remote and unimportant, and we knew we could not hope to read in books of the life we saw about us. Books came from afar; they could offer only fantasy (*OB*, p. 23).

He indicates a dissonance between his material and its treatment:

> All the novels I had read were about settled and organised societies, and I was aware of a slight fraudulence in applying a form created by that type of society to the squalor, disorder and shallowness of my own.[47]

The allusions in *Guerrillas* draw an ironic comparison, which they at the same time undercut, between England's past and the West Indian scene. He appears to intend the allusions to summon up a lost world and an aesthetic that is no longer appropriate:

> We no longer have this assurance of the world going on. Societies everywhere have been fractured by all kinds of change: technological, social, political. We can no longer regard the action of a novel as covering a little crisis, a little curve on the graph which will then revert to the nice, flat, straight, ordered life: and I think this is one reason why, as you say, the traditional novel is just no longer possible. . . . I think there's an element of nostalgia in reading Hardy, and even in

reading Dickens or George Eliot. There is narrative there, the slow development of character, and people are longing for this vanished, ordered world.... . So I think the art of fiction is becoming a curious, shattered thing.[48]

Naipaul shares with other twentieth-century European writers a sense that the techniques of their predecessors are no longer appropriate in a changed world, and a tendency to engage in the practice of allusion to remote civilizations, to favour fragmentary structures, and to cultivate a stance of uncertainty.

Notes

1   (London: Hart-Davis MacGibbon, 1977). They do not make reference to *G* (1975), nor to Naipaul's article, "The Killings in Trinidad", first published in *The Sunday Times Magazine* (May 12 1974 & May 19 1974), and collected in *The Return of Eva Perón*.
2   (London: André Deutsch, 1968).
3   Humphry and Tindall, p. vii.
4   Humphry and Tindall, p. 104.
5   Selwyn D. Ryan, *Race and Nationalism in Trinidad and Tobago: A Study of Decolonization a Multiracial Society* (Toronto and Buffalo: University of Toronto Press, 1972), p. 369.
6   Humphry and Tindall, p. 149.
7   Humphry and Tindall, p. 155.
8   National Joint Action Committee press release (n.d.), in Humphry and Tindall, p. 188.
9   *REP*, p. 8, repeated pp. 3, 12, 40, 67, 89.
10   "A New King for the Congo: Mobutu and the Nihilism of Africa", *REP*, p. 192.
11   "The Brothels Behind the Graveyard", *REP*, p. 112.
12   Interviewed by Aamer Hussein, p. 4.
13   *REP*, pp. 3, 12, 65, 76.
14   "The Documentary Heresy," p. 23.
15   Interviewed by Bharati Mukherjee and Robert Boyers, p. 16.
16   Interviewed by Aamer Hussein, p. 4.
17   Letter from V. S. Naipaul to Diana Athill (March 7 1972), André Deutsch Archive, 96, *OB* folder.
18   Letter from Diana Athill to V. S. Naipaul (July 26 1973), V. S. Naipaul Archive, II, 3:1.
19   *Make Believe* (South Royalton, Vermont: Steerforth Press, 1993).
20   "An Outpost of Progress", *The Complete Short Fiction*. Vol 1, *The Stories*, ed. by Samuel Hynes (London: William Pickering, 1992), p. 42.
21   "An Outpost of Progress", p. 40.
22   "An Outpost of Progress", p. 52.
23   "An Outpost of Progress", p. 54.
24   As Neil ten Kortenaar points out in "Writers and Readers, the Written and the Read: V. S. Naipaul and *Guerrillas*", *Contemporary Literature*, 31, 3 (Fall 1990), p. 333.

25 For instance, Karl Miller, *Authors* (Oxford: Clarendon Press, 1989), p. 63, and John Thieme, "Apparitions of Disaster: Brontëan Parallels in *The Wide Sargasso Sea* and *Guerrillas*", *Journal of Commonwealth Literature*, 14, 1 (August 1979), p. 125.

26 *Guerrillas* (London: André Deutsch, 1975), p. 226.

27 This is observed by Robert Hemenway, "Sex and Politics in V. S. Naipaul", *Studies in the Novel*, 14, 2 (Summer 1982), pp. 189–202, and Anne R. Zahlan, "Literary Murder: V. S. Naipaul's *Guerrillas*", *South Atlantic Review*, 59, 4 (November 1994), pp. 89–106.

28 "Mimics into Puppets: The Fiction of V. S. Naipaul", *London Magazine*, 15, 6 (February — March 1976), p. 117.

29 The case is argued by Elaine Fido in "Psycho-Sexual Aspects of the Woman in V. S. Naipaul's Fiction", *West Indian Literature and its Social Context: Proceedings of the Fourth Annual Conference on West Indian Literature*, ed. by Mark McWatt (Cave Hill, Barbados: Department of English, University of the West Indies, Cave Hill, 1985), pp. 78–95.

30 *After Empire*, p. 78.

31 Interview, "Pooter", *Times* (November 9 1968), p. 23.

32 *A Bend in the River* (London: André Deutsch, 1979), p. 237.

33 E.g. Fido.

34 Interviewed by Bharati Mukherjee and Robert Boyers, p. 16.

35 Helen Tiffin,"Travelling Texts: Intertextuality and Resistance in V. S. Naipaul's *Guerrillas* and Jean Rhys's *Wide Sargasso Sea*", *Journal of West Indian Literature* 6, 1 (July 1993), p. 62; Jeffrey Robinson, "V. S. Naipaul and the Sexuality of Power", in *West Indian Literature and its Social Context*, p. 75; Zahlan, p. 78.

36 This argument is proposed by John Thieme, *The Web of Tradition: Uses of Allusion in V. S. Naipaul's Fiction* (Hertford: Hansib/Dangaroo, 1987), p. 177.

37 Benedict Anderson, "James Fenton's Slideshow", *New Left Review*, 158 (July–August 1986), p. 81.

38 *Letters Between a Father and Son*, p. 291.

39 "Conrad's Darkness", *REP*, p. 216.

40 Typed manuscript, V. S. Naipaul Archive, II, 3:5.

41 Notebook, II, 3:4.

42 *V. S. Naipaul* (New York: Continuum, 1989), p. 91.

43 This argument is made by Michael Gorra, "Naipaul or Rushdie", p. 377.

44 John Thieme, "Apparitions of Disaster", p. 129, and Helen Tiffin, "Travelling Texts", pp. 60–63.

45 "Naipaul's *Woodlanders*", *Journal of Commonwealth Literature*, 14, 1 (August 1979), pp. 109–116.

46 Helen Tiffin,"Travelling Texts", and John Thieme, "Apparitions of Disaster".

47 Interviewed by Francis Wyndham, "Writing is Magic", *Sunday Times* (November 10 1968), p. 57.

48 Interviewed by Ronald Bryden, p. 368.

6 | Images of Africa and Europe in *A Bend in the River*

A Bend in the River is the last of the novels of Naipaul's most pessimistic period. It recreates essentially the same situation as *In a Free State* and *Guerrillas*: all portray expatriates or migrants adrift in states of disorder; a background of civil disturbance is glimpsed obliquely, and the narrative focuses on instances of interracial sex and violence, which refract and reverse political power relations. The works which emerged from Naipaul's travels in Zaire in 1975 — *A Congo Diary* and "A New King for the Congo: Mobutu and the Nihilism of Africa" — also form part of the context of *A Bend in the River*, furnishing the detail of its setting. Another important influence on the novel is the traditional image of Africa in European literature, as the negation of European civilization, the site of a reversion to savagery, where human brutality is exposed in the raw. The novel complicates the dichotomy between Africa and Europe, however, by means of an ambivalence towards Europe, which is treated both as a lost ideal of order and as having given rise to a junk civilization. Europe, seen in the novel as overrun by the human flotsam of global migration, offers little refuge from the prevailing chaos.

A Bend in the River is set in an unnamed African country, modelled on Mobutu's Zaire. The country is bloody, lawless, threatening and unknowable: "The bush muffled the sound of murder, and the muddy rivers and lakes washed the blood away" (*BR*, p. 60). The novel's representation of this country draws extensively on the ideas elaborated in Naipaul's article on Mobutu, in which the bush is presented as a state of mind inimical to development — a form of oblivion: "The bush grows fast over what were once great events or great disturbances".[1] It is a country of ancient tribal conflicts, and of threatening officials who require repeated bribes. It is also a place of aimless violence and "unspeakable rites" (*HD*, p. 86) — as in the senseless murder of Father Huismans, whose head is spiked and exhibited. His fate brings to mind an episode in Conrad's *Heart of Darkness*, a novel which exerts a profound influence on Naipaul's version of Africa. In *Heart of Darkness* it is Kurtz who orders the barbaric display: in *A Bend in the River*, the brutality is ascribed to the uncontrolled rage of Africans. *A Bend in the River* portrays a society liable to collapse at any time into a state of chaos.

172

Salim's friend, Mahesh, may appear to speak for the author, when expressing the view that "stable relationships were not possible here, that there could only be day-to-day contracts between men" (*BR,* p. 227). The novel depicts a world reminiscent of a Hobbesian vision of the state of nature. The social disarray consequent upon colonial interventions in Africa, the effects of which continue to be felt long after decolonization, is mystified by Naipaul, and portrayed as an inherent characteristic of an eternal Africa.

The landscapes of the novel are invested with a quality of menace: "The river and the forest were like presences, and much more powerful than you. You felt unprotected, an intruder" (*BR,* p. 14). The threat of an alien social organization is compounded by the sense of being surrounded by a hostile landscape. The water hyacinth in Naipaul's novel is an emblem of this natural hostility: this vegetation relentlessly clogs the river which serves as an essential means of communication. In the article on Mobutu, the symbolism is made explicit: "It is the Congo hyacinth that may yet imprison the river people in the immemorial ways of the bush" (*REP,* p. 184). The novel can envisage village life only as shrouded in mystery; Salim imagines "being transported to the hidden forest villages, to the protection and secrecy of the huts at night — everything outside shut out, kept beyond some magical protecting line" (*BR,* pp. 86–7). The surrounding countryside remains almost entirely unknown: "No one liked going outside his territory" (*BR,* p. 15).

Naipaul's evocation of the enigma that is village life echoes Conrad:

> You felt the land taking you back to something that was familiar, something you had known at some time but had forgotten or ignored, but which was always there. You felt the land taking you back to what was there a hundred years ago, to what had been there always (*BR,* p. 15).

This recalls the moment when Marlow acknowledges a sense of "remote kinship with this wild and passionate uproar" (*HD,* p. 69). Conrad portrays Kurtz's degeneration into depravity as resulting from a kinship with the primitive; the wilderness is animated, and is seen to exert a force which appeals to him "by the awakening of forgotten and brutal instincts, by the memory of gratified and monstrous passions" (*HD,* p. 107). The landscape of Conrad's Congo is primeval and eternal: "Going up that river was like travelling back to the earliest beginnings of the world, when vegetation rioted on the earth and the big trees were kings" (*HD,* p. 66).

Naipaul's Africa, where "people would be living in villages more or less as they had lived for centuries" (*BR,* p. 269), has, in a like manner, remained unchanged from time immemorial and since Conrad's visit (Naipaul's non-fictional works refer to the country which was then called

Zaire as the Congo, harking back to the past). Ancient beliefs survive: "The bush was full of spirits; in the bush hovered all the protecting presences of a man's ancestors" (*BR*, p. 71). The novel suggests the survival of ancestral African ways by portraying the political power exercised in this modern state as a form of magic: the Big Man, sinister and elusive, is said to have special powers and to wield a fetish in his stick. Traditional beliefs resurface at the time of the second of the three rebellions in the book: the rebels believe that they are protected by spirits, and that bullets are powerless to harm them.

Modernity is therefore represented as shallow and superficial — a mere graft onto "the immemorial life of the forest" (*IFS*, p. 213). The incongruity of imported European notions of progress is suggested by such enterprises as the construction of the Domain, which Salim depicts as a magician's conjuring trick. The Big Man imposes the trappings of a modern state on what is essentially bush, in Naipaul's terms.

> He was creating modern Africa. ... He was bypassing real Africa, the difficult Africa of bush and villages, and creating something that would match anything that existed in other countries (*BR*, p. 110).

The irrelevance of the Domain is suggested by the way in which it remains for a time unused, as if its principal purpose were to serve as an assertion of pride. The alien nature of European systems of production and consumption is suggested by Mahesh's Bigburger enterprise, imported whole. There is a paradox in Naipaul's representation of European civilization, which at times embodies a lost order and at other times is portrayed as imposing a culture of junk on its colonies. He suggests that the President has plundered Europe in search of an unearned modernity, while simultaneously implying that modernity is not worth having, tawdry and gimcrack, an absurd irrelevance, rather than the achievement of a "universal civilization".[2]

The locals are portrayed as campers in the ruins of the civilization of the departed Europeans: When Salim first arrives at the town at the bend in the river, loosely based on Kisangani, it forms a landscape of decay and dereliction. The deserted European suburb has been plundered, in an image of the inexorable tendency of order to revert to chaos.

> The houses had been set alight one by one. They had been stripped — before or afterwards — only of those things that the local people needed — sheets of tin, lengths of pipe, bath tubs and sinks and lavatory bowls (impermeable vessels, useful for soaking cassava in). The big lawns and gardens had returned to bush; the streets had disappeared; vines and creepers had

grown over broken, bleached walls of concrete or hollow clay
brick. . . .

Sun and rain and bush had made the site look old, like the
site of a dead civilization. The ruins, spreading over so many
acres, seemed to speak of a final catastrophe (*BR*, p. 33).

This work supplies an apocalyptic vision of the end of civilization.
Naipaul's post-colonial states are consistently portrayed as operating
according to the "politics of plunder".[3] The image of encroaching bush
is a significant one for Naipaul, suggesting "the breakdown of
institutions, of the contract between man and man". For him, bush
signifies "theft, corruption, racist incitement".[4] The locals squat in these
ruins, and are depicted as unable to master the technologies of the
departed civilization, and as filled with a Luddite rage against it: ". . . the
rage of simple men tearing at metal with their hands" (*BR*, p. 89).

The details of such descriptions are drawn from Naipaul's *A Congo
Diary,* which records his impressions of a visit to Zaire. A motif of the
Diary is its imagery of decay: in Kisangani, "ruin seems quite close"
(*CD*, 22). Naipaul notes a monument on a Kinshasa boulevard which
carries a commemorative tableau, "the inscription defaced" (*CD*, p. 10).
The city has been superimposed on traditional ways of life, which prove
the more durable: "How quickly the city of dirt streets and shoddy
concrete buildings reverts to African bush" (*CD*, p. 24). Disorder is
portrayed as partly the responsibility of the people of Zaire:
"Independence as pillage, laying a claim, stripping the place clean"
(*CD*, p. 25). Near to Kisangani, locals have "camped in the buildings of
the rich garden suburb, pillaged, and left shells of concrete, which were
quickly overgrown" (*CD*, p. 23). A kind of nostalgia attaches to the
ruins, which recall the grandeur that was Belgian rule; and Naipaul's
enigmatic reference to "Rome and Belgium" (*CD*, p. 24) seems to imply
that he thinks there is some basis for a comparison between the two
empires. Naipaul is ambivalent, however: the landscape of ruin also
serves as a reproach to the departed Belgians, and as a criticism of
European civilization. Naipaul writes of "the perishability of the
machine civilization. How quickly things fail" (*CD*, p. 41), noting
elliptically: "The empire of things. Exporters of what civilization? The
perishable" (*CD*, p. 42). He contrasts it with "earlier imperialism: the
source of new *ideas*" (*CD*, p. 15). In *A Congo Diary* Naipaul is more
explicitly critical of nineteenth-century imperialism and its aftermath
than he is in either the essay on Mobutu or *A Bend in the River.*

The action of the novel is punctuated by outbreaks of political unrest.
The first rebellion occurs before the beginning of the novel's action, at
the time of independence:

> I had heard dreadful stories of that time, of casual killings over many months by soldiers and rebels and mercenaries, of people trussed up in disgusting ways and being made to sing certain songs while they were beaten to death in the streets (*BR*, p. 74).

Disorder and destruction may temporarily be held in abeyance, but periodically erupt into the narrative, producing a cyclical recurrence of rebellion and repression. This destructive rage is again unleashed at the end of the novel, which culminates in a vision of impending chaos, outlined by Ferdinand:

> "They're going to kill everybody who can read and write, everybody who ever put on a jacket and tie, everybody who put on a *jacket de boy*. They're going to kill all the masters and all the servants. When they're finished nobody will know there was a place like this here. They're going to kill and kill. They say it is the only way, to go back to the beginning before it's too late" (*BR*, p. 293).

The advent of modern technology serves only to multiply the incidence of violence. Nazruddin reports from Uganda, generalizing the novel's perception of Africa: "The country was now too small for its tribal hatreds. . . . Africa, going back to its old ways with modern tools, was going to be a difficult place for some time" (*BR*, p. 217). The novel's conception of the society portrayed endorses Naipaul's contention that "Africa has no future".[5]

Naipaul nowhere acknowledges that he draws on a historically-constructed myth of an unchanging African reality which has served specific political ends. This discussion does not seek to suggest that the history of post-colonial Africa has not been marked by conflict and disorder, but that these events can be better understood in relation to a historical context, rather than by calling on the notion of an essential African brutality and disorder.

A Bend in the River's depiction of Africa is in conformity with the traditional representation of the continent. The standard image of Africa prior to the twentieth century, according to Dorothy Hammond and Alta Jablow,[6] showed a tendency to portray Africans as irrational, childlike and undisciplined. Africa was perceived as unchanging, untouched by history; an absence of development was ascribed to idleness. Twentieth-century representations have turned Africa into a landscape expressive of the inner being of European man, with Africans on many occasions relegated to the periphery of the visitor's self-exploration. It is depicted as a place where civilized values confront their savage negation, an arena for the regressive display of savage instincts, in which the visiting

Englishman discovers his true identity, normally concealed by social constraints. Its climate and vegetation are depicted as hostile — the intruder's alienation from his environment fosters a feeling of menace — and as the testing-ground of a man's worth. Africa is presented as resistant to the outsider's understanding — which does not prevent the visitor from subjecting it at will to a symbolic re-shaping. Regardless of whether it is treated as a place of raw evil, or whether doubts about Western civilization are expressed by means of a sense of the beauty of the exotic, Africa unerringly serves as a foil to Europe, the image in which Europeans see themselves reflected in negative definition. Africans are commonly shown as capable of acquiring only the trappings of modern civilization, and as subject to retrograde impulses: they therefore find themselves caught between two worlds. Hammond and Jablow point out that the literary representation of Africa reveals an internal coherence which implies the extent of the influence of these writings upon one another.

Christopher Miller's *Blank Darkness*[7] explores a similar theme with reference to French literature. Miller argues that what distinguishes the manner in which Africa has been imagined from Europe's literary treatment of, say, the Orient, is the element of uncertainty: Africa represents the unknown and unexplored, rather than a place which can be mastered, catalogued and classified. *Heart of Darkness* has a profoundly influential place in this colonial tradition. The novella's deployment of a technique of uncertainty as a means of contriving an atmosphere of menace has been discussed here in relation to *Guerrillas*. Like *A Bend in the River*, Conrad's novella was preceded by a visit to the area, and both Naipaul and Conrad have recorded the details of their travels in a *Congo Diary*. Miller points out that Conrad's revisions to *Heart of Darkness* excised references to place-names, as if to confine the narrative to any specific or known place would lessen the mythic quality of the tale. This is comparable to a similar decision in relation to *A Bend in the River*, which identifies neither the country nor the town in which it is set. Like Marlow, Conrad finds himself unable to comprehend his Congolese surroundings: "Name not known to me. Villages quite invisible".[8]

The essential contradiction of *Heart of Darkness* consists in the way that it at once discredits the rhetoric of imperialism while reproducing its attitudes,[9] using degraded images of Africa in order to represent the abuses and lawlessness attributable to the Belgians who colonized the region. *Heart of Darkness* can therefore be read either as an imperialist or an anti-imperialist text. Michael Thorpe argues that Conrad seeks to undermine the dichotomy between Europe and Africa, or civilized and savage, by showing how thoroughly at home the Belgians are in the practice of barbarity.[10] He discusses the divided response that Conrad has elicited: he has been read by post-colonial writers either as a precursor of theirs — by Ngugi wa Thiong'o for one — or as an enemy, by, for instance, Chinua Achebe. Achebe accuses Conrad of "a haze of distortions and cheap mystifications",[11] of reproducing the dominant image of Africa in the Western imagination: of being a "purveyor of comforting myths"[12] who does violence to the image of a despised people. Similar controversies have attached to Naipaul's work: Achebe uses an identical formulation to express his hostility towards Naipaul — "a new purveyor of the old comforting myths" of the white race.[13] The fact that Naipaul, too, has written a *Congo Diary* suggests that Naipaul has aspired to the role of Conrad's successor.

Graham Greene's depiction of Africa in *Journey Without Maps*, based on a visit to Liberia, is also indebted to Conrad. While Greene's values are opposed to Conrad's — savagery functions as a positive term for him — he, too, turns African travel into an exercise in psychological self-exploration:

> I thought for some reason even then of Africa, not as a particular place, but a shape, a strangeness, a wanting to know. The unconscious mind is often sentimental; I have written "a shape", and the shape, of course, is roughly that of the human heart.[14]

The "heart" inevitably suggests darkness: "But what had astonished me about Africa was that it had never been really strange. . . . The 'heart of darkness' was common to us both" (*JWM*, pp. 310–11). To travel in Africa is, according to this familiar motif, to visit the site of the origins of the species. African travel is a form of psychoanalysis, the method of which "is to bring the patient back to the idea which he is repressing: a long journey backwards without maps" (*JWM*, pp. 109–10).

Greene unambiguously values the simplicity and spontaneity of rural Liberians, who conform to the type of the noble savage. Innocent of cerebration, they remain attuned to their instincts. Greene wishfully writes, "If one could get back to this bareness, simplicity, instinctive friendliness, feeling rather than thought, and start again . . ." (*JWM*, p. 234.) Those, in contrast, who "have been touched by civilization, have learned to steal and lie and kill" (*JWM*, p. 278). Greene's Liberians serve as a reproach to European civilization: as a mirror to reflect back the writer's sense of the ills of Europe. One compares the uses of Montaigne's cannibals, for example, or Lawrence's West African carving in *Women in Love*: this evokes a condition of "mindless"[15] knowledge and aspires to inject a form of barbaric energy into Lawrence's text. Greene idealizes where Conrad had denigrated. Noble his savages may be, but savages they remain, rather than the possessors of a civilization in their own right (as in Achebe's novels).

Naipaul has defined his work in contrast to the example of Greene: "My travel is so different from that of Graham Greene and others. They're travellers in a world that's been made safe for them by empire".[16] Nevertheless, both create a landscape of global disorder in which all countries are alike in illustrating the author's perception of the human predicament. Kerry McSweeney observes a comparable focus on the distasteful, the sordid, the ugly; and a shared preoccupation with failure on the part of individuals and societies.[17] Greene gives the impression of being comfortable with failure and seediness, while Naipaul's work registers the threat of disorder more acutely, and exhibits a revulsion from the sordid which fascinates him.

Chinua Achebe's work was a bid to redress the balance, and "to help my society regain belief in itself and put away the complexes of the years of denigration and self-abasement".[18] His essential theme is

> that African peoples did not hear of culture for the first time from Europeans; that their societies were not mindless but frequently had a philosophy of great depth and value and beauty, that they had poetry and, above all, they had dignity.[19]

He refers to Joyce Cary's portrait of a feckless, child-like, happy-go-lucky African clerk in *Mister Jonson* as having provoked him to write. Achebe's antagonism to Conrad is felt in *Arrow of God*, where there is an allusion to *Heart of Darkness*. Achebe ridicules Winterbottom's sleepless imaginings:

> He would lie awake, tossing about until he was caught in the distant throb of drums. He would wonder what unspeakable rites went on in the forests at night, or was it the heart-beat of the African darkness? Then one night he was terrified when it suddenly occurred to him that no matter where he lay awake at night in Nigeria the beating of the drums came with the same constancy and from the same elusive distance. Could it be that the throbbing came from his own heat-stricken brain?[20]

Achebe's novels explore the reverences, rituals and order of Ibo civilization, providing an insight into a form of social organization then little studied in the novel. He portrays a society in which the individual life is defined in relation to the community: behaviour is regulated by ritual, which gives shape to agricultural practice and marks the passing of the seasons. The society Achebe portrays in *Things Fall Apart* draws no rigid distinctions between secular and sacred: "The land of the living was not far removed from the domain of the ancestors".[21] Individualism accommodates itself uneasily to such a society, where it is apt to function as a disruptive force, as in the case of Okonkwo, with his pathological fear of weakness. The strength of will which enabled him to achieve prosperity leads to his alienation and suicide: he fails to carry the village with him in his desire to meet the English with armed resistance. The communal ethos is also enshrined in the novel's narrative voice, as David Carroll has argued: the narrator speaks in the manner of a village elder, sympathetic to the customs of the tribe, whose measured tones are an element of the social order he describes.[22] By expanding the scope and direction of the literary representation of Africa, Achebe's work serves to illustrate by contrast the extent to which Naipaul depends on a conventional discourse of the West.

Achebe shows himself aware of the paradox that writing is a medium alien to this society, a tool of its colonizers: hence the sudden shift in perspective at the end of the novel to the consciousness of the District Commissioner, who will produce an uncomprehending travesty of Okonkwo's life in his book on the *Pacification of the Primitive Tribes of the Lower Niger*. Achebe writes as if he were one of the community, but is caught somewhere between these incompatible worlds. He describes himself as from an upwardly mobile Christian family, living "at the crossroads of cultures",[23] and refers to having felt "a fascination for the ritual and the life on the other arm of the crossroads".[24] *Things Fall Apart* signifies an "act of atonement with my past, the ritual return and homage of a prodigal son":[25] the loving care with which he records Ibo customs is the result of an initial distance from the ancient ways.

Naipaul has identified a fissure between reportage and invention in *Heart of Darkness (REP*, p. 223), and Michael Thorpe applies Naipaul's insight to *A Bend in the River* (Thorpe, p. 50). It is also possible to read Naipaul's *Congo Diary* as disclosing a conflict between empirical observation and recurring fictions about Africa. On the one hand, his observations seem to lead him, falteringly, to a recognition of the existence of a "complex primitive world" (*CD*, p. 33) in rural Zaire: "The life is complex" (*CD*, p. 33). He mentions his surprise that the steamer should not pass through the primeval forests described by Conrad, but, for much of the journey, through peopled and cultivated land. At the end of the journey, on the other hand, he reshapes his experience to suit the Conradian archetype. Alluding to "the heart of darkness" (*CD*, p. 41), he re-casts the life of the river as unchanging: "So repetitive the scenes, the dug-outs, the huts. . . . We who were visitors go on, but that life on the river also goes on, goes on now" (*CD*, p. 41). Here, he contrasts the visitor's mobility with the stability and continuity of the society of rural Zaire. He encourages the impression that Zaire is a country outside narrative progression, where "history has vanished" (*CD*, p. 9).

Naipaul's refashioning of this material in "A New King for the Congo: Mobutu and the Nihilism of Africa", stands at a further remove from his experience, and shows an increased dependence on customary European modes of imagining Africa. At the end of the article, Naipaul appears to derive a pessimistic pleasure from enacting a metaphoric swoon into his conception of the bush — a denial of rationality and European notions of progress:

> To arrive at this sense of a country trapped and static, eternally vulnerable, is to begin to have something of the African sense of the void. It is to begin to fall, in the African way, into a dream of a past — the vacancy of river and forest, the hut in the brown yard, the dugout — when the dead ancestors watched and protected, and the enemies were only men (*REP*, p. 204).

His attempt to imagine African experience brings him up against an imaginative blank: mere vacancy.

The portrait of Mobutu, for all that he is intermittently styled as a modernizer, is in keeping with Naipaul's contention that traditional ways persist: he is seen as a composite of Leopold II and a traditional chief. His grandiose projects function as an assertion of pride, to ease the psychic wounds of colonialism. He is said to embody the country's contradictions: "He is citizen, chief, king, revolutionary; he is an African freedom-fighter; he is supported by the spirits of the ancestors" (*REP*, p. 176). Naipaul unquestioningly assumes Mobutu's popularity among the people of Zaire. Mobutu, however, was a U. S.-sponsored combatant in the war against Communism. Mobutu was given overt diplomatic support by the U. S. in the consolidation of power after his coup in 1965, and there is evidence to suggest that, prior to this date, he was given covert assistance by the C. I. A., in the form of intelligence and logistical support.[26] Mobutu's glorification of traditional ways, and of an African authenticity, is perceived by Naipaul as obstructing progress. The nihilism of the essay's title is elsewhere applied to the forces of destruction Naipaul associates with the Mulele rebellion. (Mulele, former Education Minister under Lumumba, Zaire's first prime minister, organized a Maoist peasant uprising in 1964; his supporters adapted the revolt to traditional beliefs.) The essay can thereby give the impression of conflating Mobutu and Mulele. Naipaul refers to a wish in the populace "to wipe out and undo, an African nihilism, the rage of primitive men coming to themselves and finding that they have been fooled and affronted" (*REP*, p. 195). Naipaul likens Mulele to a black Kurtz, "maddened not by contact with wilderness and primitivism, but with the civilization established by those pioneers who now lie on Mont Ngaliema, above the Kinshasa rapids" (*REP*, p. 196). Basil Davidson describes Mulele in similar terms,[27] but emphasizes, however, that the country's problems (including inter-tribal enmities, and an absence of skilled personnel due to Belgian educational policy) were inherited with independence.

Naipaul here alludes to Conrad initially in order to question the validity of his perceptions, by pointing out that, at the time of Conrad's journey up the Congo, river traffic was frequent, and that he was not "penetrating to the untouched heart of darkness" (*REP*, p. 181). However, the notion of a black Kurtz serves to validate Conrad's prescience; and Naipaul refers to "An Outpost of Progress" (also mentioned in "The Killings in Trinidad") in order to express his view that, when unredeemed by a sense of the civilizing mission, colonial civilization was philistine and ephemeral. This much survives of the *Diary*'s critical attitude towards Europe; but, for the most part, the article mutes such criticisms. The article presents Belgium as having bequeathed those traces of organization and modernity which the locals are now destroying. "The plundering of the inherited Belgian state has been so easy" (*REP*, p. 202).

> The nationalizations are petty and bogus; they have often turned out to be a form of pillage and are part of no creative plan; they are as short-sighted, self-wounding and nihilistic as they appear, a dismantling of what remains of the Belgian-created state (*REP*, p. 200).

Comparisons between Belgium and Rome serve to indicate the seeming antiquity of the relics of Belgian rule: all that remains of the monument to King Albert in Kinshasa "are two tall brick pillars, like the pillars at the end of some abandoned Congolese Appian Way" (*REP*, pp. 187–8). "A New King for the Congo" holds the people of Zaire responsible for the problems faced by the country; in the grip of the "lunacy, despair" (*REP*, p. 199) of the idea of authenticity, the nation has, like Mulele, been maddened by its contact with European civilization:

> So the borrowed ideas — about colonialism and alienation, the consumer society and the decline of the West — are made to serve the African cult of authenticity; and the dream of an ancestral past restored is allied to a dream of a future of magical power (*REP*, pp. 198–9).

A Bend in the River is more divided in its attitude towards Europe. The motto inscribed on the monument in Kinshasa is "To Open the Land to the Nations" (*REP*, p. 187); in the novel, the inscription on the steamship monument is a misquotation of Virgil, which reads, " 'He approves of the mingling of the peoples and their bonds of union' " (*BR*, p. 69). In *The Aeneid*, Venus, who is attempting to prevent a union between Dido and Aeneas, declares to Juno that she is uncertain "whether Jupiter . . .

approves the blending of peoples and the league of union".[28] Salim reflects on the temerity and hubris of the departed power:

> I was staggered. Twisting two-thousand-year-old words to celebrate sixty years of the steamer service from the capital! Rome was Rome. What was this place? To carve the words on a monument beside this African river was surely to invite the destruction of the town. Wasn't there some little anxiety, as in the original line in the poem? (*BR*, p. 69.)

Naipaul's oeuvre as a whole testifies to the inadvisability of this mingling of peoples, in dissecting its disastrous legacy. The classical allusions,[29] and the image of Africans vandalizing the ruins of a departed civilization, cast the Belgians in the role of representatives of a lost order, to be elegiacally mourned. They also raise the question of whether Belgian rule in the Congo can sustain comparison with the Roman Empire, or whether the comparison serves instead to flatter the empty vanity of the conquerors. When Conrad refers to the Roman Empire, it is to remind us that England was once one of the dark places of the earth. Naipaul's relation to the idea of European civilization is ambivalent. "I feel no nostalgia for the miserable security of the old ways",[30] he declares, but the novel cannot be thought entirely to discredit the classical analogy.

Michael Gorra points to another aspect of this ambivalence in his observation that, in Naipaul's work, "the opposition between civilization and bush is never so absolute as it seems".[31] Europe is represented in the novel by means of the junk which has survived it: catalogues of junk are a recurring feature of the work. Salim describes the stock of his shop as a "sea of junk" (*BR*, p. 46).

> It was antiquated junk, specially made for shops like mine; and I doubt whether the workmen who made the stuff — in Europe and the United States and perhaps nowadays Japan — had any idea of what their products were used for (*BR*, p. 47).

This implies that the West is the repository of technological expertise, while simultaneously disdaining its products. Salim itemizes the unlikely uses to which his products are put, including the storage of grubs and soaking of cassava. This confirms the distance between the two civilizations, and suggests that the Africans misappropriate the imported products they depend on. "Junk" is also a word which Salim applies to the artistic endeavours of the departed Belgian woman whose flat he inhabits; her paintings lie scattered around the flat, and are evocative of the detritus of colonial civilization: "It was as if the lady had lost faith in her own junk and, when the independence crisis came, had been glad to go" (*BR*, p. 48). "Junk" is also a word which Salim uses to describe the contents of Ferdinand's mind: "His mind wasn't empty, as I had begun to think. It was a jumble, full of all kinds of junk" (*BR*, p. 61). The novel suggests that Europe has bequeathed a legacy of ideological confusion:

> If it was Europe that gave us on the coast some idea of our history, its was Europe, I feel, that also introduced us to the lie. . . . [T]he Europeans could do one thing and say something quite different. . . . The Europeans wanted gold and slaves, like everybody else; but at the same time they wanted statues put up to themselves as people who had done good things for the slaves (*BR*, p. 23).

Salim here distinguishes between word and deed, ideal and practice — a distinction which may help to account for the author's ambivalence towards European civilization: Naipaul generally values its ideals, while at times recognizing a failure to put them into practice. Father Huismans' ambivalence towards people of his own nationality suggests itself for application to the attitudes of the author himself: "He had his own idea of Europe, his own idea of his civilization" (*BR*, p. 70).

Europe is variously construed as serving as an ideal of reason and order, and as having sown the seeds of the disorder which now prevails: "There had been order once, but that order had had its own dishonesties and cruelties — that was why the town had been wrecked" (*BR*, p. 64). Elsewhere, Salim is not so critical. An emotional attachment to the legacy of the Europeans is implied by the pathos associated with images of its destruction:

> The steamer monument had been knocked down. With all the other colonial statues and monuments. . . . The wish had only been to get rid of the old, to wipe out the memory of the intruder. It was unnerving, the depth of that African rage, the wish to destroy, regardless of the consequences (*BR*, p. 33).

Europe also bestows the gift of historical assessment:

> All that I know of our history and the history of the Indian Ocean I have got from books written by Europeans. . . . Without Europeans, I feel, all our past would have been washed away, like the scuff-marks of fishermen on the beach outside our town (*BR*, p. 18).

Naipaul may here be intimating an excessive dependence, on Salim's part, on the European viewpoint. Elsewhere, Salim unctuously refers to colonial rule in terms of "the miraculous peace of the colonial time" (*BR*, p. 41). Michael Gorra interprets this statement as ironically indicative of Salim's naivety, while, at a deeper level, possessing some truth: it exemplifies the complexity underlying the apparent simplicity of the work's narrative tone. "Simple words . . . seem immediately clear in their referents but . . . also carry the weight of the arguments developed at length in Naipaul's other work".[32]

The novel's narrative technique communicates further uncertainty regarding the authorial attitude towards Europe and Africa: it is not clear how far its assertions should be read ironically, as the attitudes of the narrator rather than the author. As in the case of *The Mimic Men,* Naipaul creates in Salim a narrator whose opinions are close enough to his own, as known to us from discursive contexts, to cause some difficulty in distinguishing between their views. Like Naipaul, Salim describes himself as coming from a static, decaying, displaced Indian community which lacks a sense of history, and leads an enclosed and blinkered life in its adopted country, in thrall to its own traditions. His community is fatalistic and helpless: "We couldn't protect ourselves; we could only in various ways hide from the truth" (*BR*, p. 26). Salim, like his author, feels that he belongs nowhere: "We could no longer say we were Arabians or Indians or Persians; when we compared ourselves with these people, we felt like people of Africa" (*BR*, p. 17). He proceeds to cut himself off from this displaced community by adopting a new country. Salim feels himself adrift in an "unfriendly world. . . . I was homesick, had been homesick for months. But home was hardly a place I could return to. Home was something in my head. It was something I had lost" (*BR*, p. 117). Another way in which Salim resembles his creator is that he values a capacity for objective self-assessment: "So from an early age I developed the habit of looking, detaching myself from a familiar scene and trying to consider it as from a distance" (*BR*, p. 22).

The novel's opening sentence seemingly issues from Salim's clear-sightedness: "The world is what it is; men who are nothing, who allow themselves to become nothing, have no place in it" (*BR*, p. 9). This statement is a call for self-assertion, but in weary tones. Salim is an elusive character, and the novel leads one to wonder whether he is to be seen as fatalistic or as active, aloof or worldly, traditional or modern in his allegiances. It is open to question whether he has mastered the ways of the world, or is one of those who have no place in it. He asserts, "With me the fatalism was bogus; I cared very much about the world and wished to renounce nothing" (*BR*, p. 25). "I could be master of my fate only if I stood alone" (*BR*, p. 26). But by the end of the novel, he has fulfilled a prophecy made by Nazruddin concerning his fidelity: he remains faithful to his community, by becoming engaged to Nazruddin's daughter.

Salim is akin to Biswas, in feeling the allure of the remote, and the desolation of his present environment. He has migrated to the town at the bend in the river in pursuit of a European glamour which he fails to find there: "It seemed without further human promise. . . . I was waiting for some illumination to come to me, to guide me to the good place and the 'life' I was still waiting for" (*BR*, p. 105). He temporarily imagines that his life has been transfigured by this glamour, as he listens in the Domain to Joan Baez songs. His dealings with the Domain suggest a tendency on his part to idealize Europe, and a distance between the author's and the character's views. Naipaul also distinguishes himself from the opinions of his narrator by creating in Salim a figure less educated than himself, which has the effect of making his narration less than plausible: it is as if Naipaul has invented a distinct, not to say inferior, character, and then proceeded to ventriloquize through him, regardless.

The sources of *A Bend in the River* are not exclusively to be found in Naipaul's non-fiction: the novel can also be understood in relation to his other works of fiction. It is this context which this discussion will now proceed to examine. The ambivalence towards European civilization of *A Bend in the River* suggests itself for comparison with Naipaul's attitude towards England in *The Enigma of Arrival*. England is variously portrayed in this novel as representing a youthful dream of culture and possibilities of fulfilment; as dilapidated and a disappointment; and, in Wiltshire, as having gone down in the world, as littered with ruins, yet, for all that, as bearing traces of a resemblance to the timeless pastoral enshrined in English literature. In both works, a distinction is made between idea and reality, past and present, expectation and disappointment. Both works draw classical comparisons, and depict the effects of post-colonial migration on the metropolis. Salim visits England, only to find it "shrunken and mean and forbidding" (*BR*, p. 247). London is described as aimlessly busy. It is awash with the human detritus of global displacement: Salim sees other African-Asians who trade, in the self-imposed imprisonment of their kiosks and grocery shops, as if they were still in Africa: "They were cut off from the life of the great city where they had come to live" (*BR*, p. 247) — with London restored to grandeur for the purpose of establishing this contrast.

An account of disillusionment with England forms a significant part of *A Bend in the River*. The earliest elements of its composition are fragments which Naipaul produced at the time he began to plan *Guerrillas*, and the contiguity of the origins of the two novels reinforces a recognition of the proximity of their themes. The prototype of Indar's experience is sketched out in the fragments of a narrative which is clearly based on autobiographical experience, but was ascribed to a character called Anil. This character has gone to Oxford to study, "expecting to be washed clean of his shabby past".[33] The narrative describes his panic at the necessity and embarrassments of job hunting, related in a tone at once comic and self-pitying. The experiences are elsewhere recorded in the first person, or are ascribed to a character called Krishan, a narrator Naipaul experimented with for *Guerrillas*. The fragments, like *A Bend in the River*, represent England as shrunken and mean. The notebooks for *A Bend in the River* contain a lengthy account of these experiences, given to an unnamed character who appears to have been an incipient writer: "If I have to define the glamour I looked for in my life I could define it like this: the organization and recording of experience, the constant engagement of the mind".[34] This character describes himself as "at sea, adrift" (*ibid*) in England. The experiences are eventually ascribed to Indar, who has gone to Oxford expecting a " 'wonderful life' " (*BR*, p. 153), and spent his time there " 'understanding nothing, accepting everything, getting nothing' " (*BR*, p. 154): cut off from the comprehension of his surroundings, he was " 'hardly aware of the passing of the seasons' " (*BR*, p. 154). Indar has also undergone the anxieties and humiliations of job hunting. The fact that the germ of the novel, predating even the visit to Zaire in 1975, consisted in this autobiographical material, and in the evocation of a mood of disillusionment with a world which seems to have exhausted its possibilities, might be thought to suggest that the novel's African setting is not Naipaul's foremost concern. This setting might be interpreted as serving to express a sense of decline and crisis which is as much attributable to Naipaul's response to Europe.

At the heart of *A Bend in the River* is an evocation of the terrors and dereliction of displacement. The mood is established by Salim's historical vignette regarding the slaves:

> The further away they got from the centre and their tribal area, the less liable they were to cut loose from the caravans and run back home, the more nervous they became of the strange Africans they saw about them, until at the end, on the coast, they were no trouble at all, and were positively anxious to step into the boats and be taken to safe homes across the sea (*BR*, p. 10).

This notion underlies the dynamics of Salim's relations with Metty: Salim as master aspires to provide security and protection. Salim's displacement is echoed by that of the Indian couple with whom he dines — the couple "didn't seem to know where they were" (*BR*, p. 34); Shoba and Mahesh "were empty in Africa, and unprotected, with nothing to fall back on" (*BR*, p. 245). Ferdinand, Indar and Yvette: the novel is peopled by transients and migrants, and the locals, too, are said to be displaced in their own country. The overriding mood of *A Bend in the River* is one of nervousness:

> I once again had to think of myself as exposed, with nothing to
> hold on to. . . . If there had been a safe house waiting for me in
> some far city which would have allowed me in, I believe I
> might have left during this time. . . . But there was no such
> house now (*BR*, p. 230).

Salim accounts for his condition in terms of his isolation from his
community and its traditions: "I had stripped myself of the support the
rules gave. To think of it like that was to feel myself floating and lost"
(*BR*, p. 207). The condition of displacement has a variety of
manifestations, however, and Salim portrays his community as itself
collectively isolated and vulnerable. Salim's vulnerability is apparent in
the expropriation of his business, and his harassment by the police.

The novel offers a perception of a " 'world . . . in movement' " (*BR*,
p. 153): Indar's and Nazruddin's narratives do much of the work of
broadening this perception. Nazruddin's accounts of his business
enterprises in Canada and England flesh out a global vision of plunder,
migration and disorder. He affirms,

> "All over the world money is in flight. People have scraped the
> world clean, as clean as an African scrapes his yard, and now
> they want to run from the dreadful places where they've made
> their money and find some nice safe country" (*BR*, p. 251).

He has invested in property in London, and found himself giving shelter
to a " 'whole tentful of poor Arabs' " (*BR*, p. 255), about whom he
muses: " 'What were they doing in London? . . . What place is there in
the world for people like that?' " (*BR*, p. 255) The ponderous gloom of
his narrative is relieved, though, by his daughter's contention that he is a
" 'happy man' " (*BR*, p. 257), and Salim's that he is "all right" (*BR*,
p. 257).

Naipaul has described himself as the interpreter of a "disordered and
fast-changing world":[35] a perception of global disorder and displacement is also integral to *In a Free State*. This theme connects the disparate
components — journal entries, short stories and novella — which make
up the work. *In a Free State* is akin to *A Bend in the River* in its dispersed
geographical distribution: the main substance of the work is located in
Africa, and is complemented and generalized by means of short stories
set in Washington and London. *In a Free State* is populated by
"casualties of . . . freedom" (*IFS*, p. 10); the conversational platitudes of
the tramp who is set upon in the first section ironically state the work's
internationalist theme: " 'But what's nationality these days? I myself, I
think of myself as a citizen of the world' " (*IFS*, p. 11). The two short
stories focus on the experience of protagonists from Southern countries

adrift in the metropolitan centre. They portray an anxiety to arrive mingled with a fear of arrival; the threat which attaches to the unfamiliar place; agoraphobia and the dereliction of displacement. Santosh thinks, "I wanted the journey to end but I couldn't say I wanted to arrive at Washington" (*IFS*, p. 29); the unnamed narrator of "Tell Me Who to Kill", on the way from the West Indies to England, tells himself that "you will never be a free man again.... I don't want the ship to stop. I don't want to touch land again" (*IFS*, p. 85). The menace of the adopted country is suggested by the narrator's nostalgia for the ship, once he is on land: "It is white and big and safe, it is saying goodbye, it is in a hurry to get away and to leave you behind" (*IFS*, p. 85). This urge to get back on the ship is one which Naipaul describes having experienced himself on first arriving in England; and he has acknowledged that much of *In a Free State* is autobiographical: "It distils my own experience of coming to England, in a way it is my own life".[36]

If the journey is a form of imprisonment, so, too, is the life of the emigrant, as symbolized by Santosh's cupboard. The threat of his new environment results in a kind of agoraphobia: "I was glad I had a place to hide. I had thought of myself as a prisoner. Now I was glad I had so little of Washington to cope with" (*IFS*, p. 39). Santosh is seen as restricted by his own culturally-conditioned perceptions. The tale explores

> the immigrant's view of the capital of the world, the view of a man from another, enclosed culture. Rather like my own of London, twenty years ago.... Since I went to India I've become interested in the way different cultures have different ways of seeing.... Gandhi coming to England and leaving not a word of description, remembering only that when he arrived at Southampton, he was dressed in white.[37]

The dissociation of the narrator of "Tell Me Who to Kill" from the life around him imparts a claustrophobic quality to the story: from the moment of arrival "you are like a man in blinkers" (*IFS*, p. 85). He subsequently imprisons himself, effectively, in work, then in his roti-and-curry shop. Naipaul's representation of the limitations of the emigrant's perceptions raises the question of why it should be that he so often chooses to write from this point of view. Here the outsider's perspective functions as a defamiliarizing device. We see Washington afresh through Santosh's eyes, and his view is worked for the comedy which results from a discrepancy between his and the author's values and understanding. Santosh's wise naivety engenders, for example, the notion that the Americans are not quite real — people temporarily absent from their television-cleaning duties. The joke is partly on him, but more on the Americans. "Tell Me Who to Kill" possesses an element of modernist impenetrability as a result of the incompleteness and confusion of the narration (inconsistently maintained, since the narrator is sometimes capable of great penetration and insight), which leaves the reader responsible for piecing together the character's story. Naipaul's use of his narrative persona in these stories recalls the device of the child narrator of *Miguel Street*, who mingles moments of sagacity with a tendency to naive approval, which the reader interprets as ironic.

Both Santosh and the narrator of "Tell Me Who to Kill" have displaced their sense of self onto another: respectively, the Bombay employer, the narrator's brother. Like Metty in *A Bend in the River*, Santosh realizes his selfhood through the process of displacement, associated in the tale with self-recognition in the mirror. The bleak, negative epiphany with which the tale concludes implies that, at the last, Santosh again loses his sense of self, having pared it away to a recognition of what is common to all, the needs of the organism:

> I was once part of the flow, never thinking of myself as a
> presence. Then I looked in the mirror and decided to be free.
> All that my freedom has brought me is the knowledge that I
> have a face and have a body, that I must feed this body and
> clothe this body for a certain number of years. Then it will be
> over (*IFS,* p. 61).

These short stories share certain themes with the novella: *In a Free State* is "about journeys, unhappy journeys, by people switching countries, switching cultures",[38] and all of its component parts represent casual cruelties and shifting power relations. A recurring mood of menace is promoted by a distance between the perceiving consciousness and an unfamiliar environment. The various narratives note a disparity between the empty symbolism of advertisements and the squalor and anguish of people's lives; there are repeated cinematic references; a similar character reappears in Bobby and Frank: both appear to derive strength, parasitically, from those they assist.

In a Free State, Guerrillas and *A Bend in the River* all set the themes of liberal delusion, and sexual and racially-motivated violence among expatriates, against a backdrop of imperfectly apprehended political upheaval, and a landscape of neglect and ruin, in order to express a conception of post-colonial disorder. There are elements of misogyny in all these works. Naipaul's imagination seems drawn to the representation of violent or insulting behaviour towards women. Sexual violence generally serves to elaborate the pervasive nature of power relations: a male representative of a former subject people seeks a substitute for the power he lacks in an act of violence against a female representative of Europe. Personal relations reflect and are shaped by politics. *In a Free*

State is an exception in that there is no racial dimension to the sexual politics, although there is a sense in which Bobby, by virtue of his sexual predilections, is placed in the position customarily assumed by the woman in Naipaul's novels when he takes a beating from the soldiers. The sexual overtones of the attack are suggested by the way in which it recalls the opening scenes of the novel, when Bobby is insulted in a bar by a man he is trying to pick up (he spits in Bobby's face — an action reminiscent of Salim's treatment of Yvette). There is an echo: "Black skin on pink" (*IFS*, p. 237) remembers "Bobby's fingers edged along the cap until they were next to the Zulu's. Then he looked down at the fingers, pink beside black" (*IFS*, p. 115).

In all the novels, political delusions parallel those operative in private relations. In his jacket copy for *Guerrillas*, Naipaul wrote: "No one really believes what he says or does. No one absolutely understands the other, everyone appears bogus to everybody else. All relationships are fraudulent".[39] Jane has expected to find a hero in Roche; Roche has imagined Jane to be something she is not; Jimmy's writings provide access to a private world of fantasy. Salim's initial impression of Yvette is part of his glamourized misapprehensions as to the Domain; Yvette, Salim comes to think, has also been misled by a spurious idea of Raymond's importance. These delusions correspond to the misleading notions that are in circulation about Jimmy's status as a revolutionary leader, or the fantasies about Africa that are common currency at the Domain.

These novels dwell on the dynamics of shifting power relations. Naipaul defines *In a Free State* as "a book perhaps about power and powerlessness. One of those things that one is hoping that people who read this will get is that the roles are so easily switched".[40] "Exploiter, exploited: the roles ceaselessly shift".[41] The prologue describes the persecution of an English tramp by those who have shared a cabin with him. The tramp appears to attract this treatment by virtue of his oddity, solitude and weakness. The narrator, like the rest of the passengers, "feared to be involved with him" (*IFS*, p. 14). In the novella itself, the persecution is conducted at a political level: the president, who is stronger, and is supported by the white men, sends his army against the king's tribe. Bobby, possibly to be counted among the weak in his own society, finds acceptance in Africa and the opportunity to victimize others. This occurs in spite of his supposed liberalism and love of Africa, which is implicated in the possibilities for sexual gratification which result from his economic advantage there. In the epilogue, the narrator intervenes to halt the degrading treatment of some Egyptian children, but directs his anger, not at the Italian tourists who have provoked the situation, by throwing food for the children, but at an Egyptian official, who is the easier target.

Bobby may take issue with Linda's assumption of superiority over Africans, whom she dismisses as "savages" (*IFS*, p. 221), but he voices prejudices against Asians — who are resented locally for their economic influence — as a way of finding common ground with Linda. In the final section of *A Way in the World*, based on Naipaul's experiences in Uganda in 1966, foreigners show their commitment to the country by trading in anti-Indian sentiment (*WW*, p. 349). The harassment and expropriation of Indians in certain African countries are connected by Naipaul to the politics of independent Trinidad:

> In Trinidad that [the nationalist movement] meant anti-Indian politics and constant anti-Indian agitation; it was how the vote of the African majority was to be secured. Though I was no longer living in Trinidad, I was affected (*WW*, p. 355).

This threat makes itself felt in his literary renderings of Africa. Of *In A Free State*, he asserts:

> The Africa of my imagination was not only the source countries — Kenya, Uganda, the Congo, Rwanda; it was also Trinidad, to which I had gone back with a vision of romance and had seen black men with threatening hair (*EA*, p. 156).

Naipaul's sense of the vulnerability to persecution of Asian immigrant communities helps account for the intensity with which his work registers the menace of post-colonial disorder.[42] The harassment directed against Salim is synecdochal, symbolizing the expropriation of foreigners in Zaire. It also distils Naipaul's own experience of unco-operative and obstructive officials in Zaire. The *Diary* records the reactions elicited by a run-in with one such official:

> The sense of nightmare.... The nervousness, the sense of danger, comes later. The game need never have been called off. Where there is no law there is no illegality or legality. No logic (*CD*, p. 40).

Théotime functions as a case study in the readiness with which the exploited become exploiters, and grow increasingly bold, as a consequence of the exercise of power.

> Théotime was soon looking for new ways of asserting himself .... He was like a man enraged by his own helplessness. He made constant scenes. He was drunken, aggrieved and threatening, and as deliberately irrational as an official who had decided to be *malin* (*BR*, p. 281).

Part of the responsibility for victimization is attributed to the victim:

weakness attracts exploitation. The novel is impatient and critical of Salim's East African community, portraying it as complicitous with its own victimization, as having cultivated a wilful blindness towards impending disaster — "We continued to live as we had always done, blindly" (*BR*, p. 23) — and as incapable of defending itself. Reflecting on his father's life, in a statement reminiscent of the opening of *A Bend in the River,* Naipaul had written, "I have little sympathy with people who ... do not protect themselves".[43] This recalls Shiva Naipaul's attitude towards recently-arrived Ugandan Asian refugees in Britain, whom he criticizes for their apathy and dependence, and for having allowed disaster to overtake them.[44] A character in *A Bend in the River* makes the mistake of displaying his vulnerability:

> By that fall, that momentary appearance of helplessness, he had invited the first blow with one of the concrete blocks; and the sight of blood then had encouraged a sudden, frenzied act of murder by dozens of small hands (*BR*, p. 223).

Bobby's gratuitous beating results from a similarly fatal display of subservience.

Many of the features of *A Bend in the River*'s Africa are prefigured by *In a Free State*. *In a Free State* is like *A Bend in the River* in its depiction of Africa as unreformable — a landscape of interior darkness. It is a place of bloody tribal conflict. European ways and modern cities, as elsewhere, are perceived as an unearned gift and as a fragile façade, in a state of premature decay, imposed upon an unchanging bush. The "African" in the capital city is described as

> the man flushed out from the bush, to whom, in the city, with independence, civilization appeared to have been granted complete. It was still a colonial city, with a colonial glamour. Everyone in it was far from home (*IFS*, p. 112).

Linda's formulaic observation — " 'I feel that sort of forest life has been going on forever' " (*IFS*, p. 169) — is recalled in the narrator's contention that "it was the immemorial life of the forest. The paths were simple forest paths, leading to nothing else" (*IFS*, p. 213). These paths contrast with the road which Bobby and Linda follow, which leads to the security and constriction of the compound: " 'All you know is that you want to be safe in the compound' " (*IFS*, p. 225). The insulated life of the compound is analogous to the fantasy world of the Domain, and also to the limited viewpoint of Santosh and the narrator of "Tell Me Who to Kill". The vantage point of Bobby and Linda, as they travel through the country by car, is characterized by a lack of engagement: the land outside is reduced to a passing spectacle for them.

In a Free State reworks the traditional motif of the unknowability of Africa. The action of the novella, and its background of political disturbance, are glimpsed through the eyes of expatriates, cut off from the life of the country. As in *Guerrillas*, their perceptions and understanding are incomplete, and the effect of uncertainty which results from a reliance on their viewpoint fosters an atmosphere of menace. The narrative dwells on the impassivity of the faces of African characters — "His face held a half-smile and then went African-blank" (*IFS*, p. 188) — as if to be African were to be resistant to comprehension.

> Sitting up in bed, looking at the inflamed African face coming nearer to his, he saw it invaded by such blank and mindless rage that his own anger vanished in terror, terror at something he sensed to be beyond his control, beyond his reason (*IFS*, p. 204).

Michael Gorra contends that failures of understanding on Bobby's and Linda's part serve as an aspect of the work's political analysis, indicating their unsuitability to play a part in the running of the country. He interprets the story both as an example of "Africanist discourse"[45] — which exploits Africa as the site of whatever fantasy one cares to propose — and as a comment on it.

The locals excite either repugnance or fear; the narrative attaches to their behaviour, however innocuous, an implied threat, from which the novella derives much of its impulsion. The work shows affinities with a novel of suspense: sections often end with intimations of danger. The jacket copy promises, "Simply as an 'adventure' it is masterly in its mounting menace". An ominous and sinister mood is promoted by Linda's harking back to archaic stereotypes of the bloodthirsty cannibal indulging in unspeakable rites:

> "They are going to swear their oaths of hate. You know what that means, don't you? You know the filthy things they are going to do? The filth they are going to eat? The blood, the excrement, the dirt?" (*IFS*, p. 130.)

The narrative introduces the excitement of danger without needing to lend credence to Linda's view. The value of her opinions is called into question by Bobby's reproach, " 'You've been reading too much Conrad' " (*IFS*, p. 170); but, for the most part, there is a lack of sympathy between Bobby's and the author's views. Linda's opinions read as a parody of the position of the settler. She declares,

> "Every night in the compound you hear them raising the hue

and cry, and you know they're beating someone to death
outside.... You should either stay away, or you should go
among them with the whip in your hand. Anything in between
is ridiculous'' (*IFS*, p. 226).

However grotesque Linda's opinions may appear, they are ultimately
invested with a measure of prescience. The gratuitous beating inflicted on
Bobby implies that these fears were not misplaced. The colonel's view of
the country — '' 'There's no good and bad here. They're just Africans.
They do what they have to do' '' (*IFS*, p. 193) — may seem to be borne
out by the action of the narrative.

A Bend in the River employs a similar narrative viewpoint. The
cyclical eruptions of rebellion and civil war are obliquely viewed, located
at the limit of the novel's range of vision. Salim, the outsider, represents a
recurrent type of narrator in Naipaul's works: "I was neutral. I was
frightened of both sides" (*BR*, p. 76). The second rebellion is indirectly
portrayed by means of the sound of distant gunfire and the rumours
passed on by Metty: we, as much as Salim, are left guessing about what is
going on. Salim invokes images of natural disaster, which recall the
analogies between fire and revolt in *Guerrillas:*

> Such rage! Like a forest fire that goes underground and burns
> unseen along the roots of trees it has already destroyed and
> then erupts in scorched land where it has little to feed on, so in
> the middle of destruction and want the wish to destroy flared
> up again (*BR*, p. 75).

Salim registers the thrill associated with the unleashing of destructive
urges: "I couldn't say things were better, yet the violence came as a relief
and for a while, to me as well as to the people I saw in the streets and
squares, was even exhilarating" (*BR*, p. 228). This is consistent with the
way in which, throughout his work, Naipaul presents popular revolt as
the expression of an inarticulate and destructive rage, as satisfying the
emotional need for a spectacle, and as an outburst of despair and
powerlessness, amounting only to "simple rejection" (*BR*, p. 74).

Naipaul's employment of an outsider's viewpoint in *A Bend in the
River* may serve to disguise a lack of understanding of the country in
which it is set. The novel's success in evoking the narrator's alienation is
in inverse relation to its failure to imagine the country. Ferdinand is the
only African character who is located in its foreground. The work draws
attention to Salim's inability to understand him, and turns Ferdinand's
inconsistency to advantage. His character is seen as elusive and hard to
define.

Now I felt that his affectations were more than affectations, that his personality had become fluid. I began to feel that there was nothing there, and the thought of a lycée full of Ferdinands made me nervous (*BR*, p. 55).

As elsewhere, that which cannot be interpreted is readily ascribed a menacing quality. A failure to comprehend him is implied by a reliance on the traditional image of the mask to describe his physiognomy, with its suggestions of impassivity and concealment: "I saw the whites of his eyes, and I thought I saw the corners of his mouth pulling back in a smile. That face, that reminder of frightening masks!" (*BR*, p. 64.) When Ferdinand is not impassive, he seems prone to hysteria: "His face had been like a mask at the beginning. Now he was showing his frenzy" (*BR*, p. 291).

The doubts and mystery which surround the details of the novel's political action may form an element of its political analysis. The novel is concerned with the workings of tyranny; and, like *Midnight's Children*, it implies that there is a symbiotic relation in a dictatorship between a disregard for the truth and violations of law and rights. Things are put to improper uses; officials are seen as failing to perform their functions; and newspapers don't report the news: they either misrepresent and elide the facts or peddle propaganda, aggrandizing the Big Man.

The Big Man is at first mentioned casually by Salim, but becomes an increasingly pervasive presence. The President is depicted as a remote "guiding intelligence" (*BR*, p. 84) behind the apparent chaos of events, who brings an ambiguous and sinister kind of order, which involves copious bloodshed. His imagery is based on Mobutu's style of leadership — the blend of African and European dress, the accoutrements of the chief — and he reproduces the contradictions Naipaul ascribes to Mobutu in "A New King for the Congo": "He is the modernizer and he is also the African who has rediscovered his African soul. He's conservative, revolutionary, everything" (*BR*, p. 149). Like Mobutu, he seeks to conjure up a modern country out of the void, as an assertion of pride and as a cure for the wounds of the colonial period. Eventually it comes to seem to Salim that "we all were serving him" (*BR*, p. 200). His voice is heard directly only late on in the novel, and shocks by virtue of its crude populism (*BR*, p. 224). The Big Man is due to visit the town at the bend in the river; Ferdinand anticipates that his presence will amount to a loosing of "mere anarchy".[46] The depiction of the increasing influence of the Big Man is compatible with Irving Howe's definition of the workings of the political novel — his sense that its drama unfolds in the tension it sets up between the personal and the political: in the conflict it creates between the abstract forces of ideology and private experience.[47] The conclusion of *A Bend in the River* comes as something of an anti-climax, with Salim resolving this tension by fleeing the country for the security of his community in exile. The possibility of escape belies his sense that he has no refuge or home; the Big Man is diminished by Salim's ability to flee.

A Bend in the River seeks to consider the basis of its own viewpoint, and to meditate on the validity of the outsider's perspective. Salim is a different kind of outsider to the protagonists of *Guerrillas* and *In a Free State*; he is less of a transient, and he has made more of an investment in his adopted society. Nevertheless, he remains an outsider, and mixes with other outsiders.

While Salim feels that it is only thanks to Europeans that he is able to understand the history of his community, the novel gives rise to a contrasting recognition of the limitations of an external perspective. Like Naipaul in *The Enigma of Arrival*, and Meredith in *Guerrillas*, Indar explains that he was initially unable to interpret his social milieu in England, or even to perceive the passing of the seasons. Salim is able to piece together only an unsatisfactory and fragmented idea of London from his forays up from the Underground. Their restricted view of English life recalls the viewpoint of Santosh, or of the narrator of ''Tell Me Who to Kill'': the ironic effect of the writings in question presupposes that the reader will see beyond the limitations of the narrator's view. Such ironies are made less easy to detect — in so far as they are detectable at all — in the representation of Africa and the Caribbean in *Guerrillas, A Bend in the River* and ''In a Free State'' by the difficulty there is in determining how far the author's viewpoint transcends the limitations of his characters' perceptions in these three works. Naipaul seems at times to imply that it is only migrants from the South in metropolitan countries who cannot read their adopted environment.

A Bend in the River is ambivalent towards Father Huismans' anthropological eye for the wonder and richness of African carving. Contradictions are associated with his position: he appears to treasure the products of traditional African civilization just as much as he does those of the colonial presence, which has disrupted and proved inimical to traditional ways of life. He sees himself as ''part of an immense flow of history'' (*BR*, p. 70), and it appears that it is his confident belief in progress which allows him to indulge in an affection for traditional societies. His story is similar to Naipaul's conception of Gale Benson's: security brings him into contact with danger. His viewpoint is portrayed as incomplete and irresponsible as well as enviable:

> And yet, though Father Huismans knew so much about African religion and went to such trouble to collect his pieces, I never

> felt that he was concerned about Africans in any other way; he
> seemed indifferent to the state of the country. . . . His Africa, of
> bush and river, was different from mine. His Africa was a
> wonderful place, full of new things (*BR*, p. 68).

This last sentence recalls an allusion to Pliny made earlier in the novel
(*"Semper Aliquid Novi"*; *BR*, p. 42). After his death, Salim both pays
tribute to Father Huisman's view — "a little bit of the world was lost
with him" (*BR*, p. 89) — and questions its basis: "His idea of his
civilization was also like his vanity" (*BR*, p. 90).

Salim is not without ambivalence in his assessment of the point of
view entertained by the foreigners on the Domain. In so far as it is critical
of African society, it is treated as perspicacious. The outsider's
perspective causes him to reassess his life in the town: "And really,
looking at the place with his [Indar's] eyes, I was amazed at the little I
had been living with. And I had stopped seeing so much" (*BR*, p. 126).
Salim participates in the view held by the people on the Domain, which
offers a new idea of the possibilities of human association, transcending
the meanly mundane considerations of economic survival which engross
the inhabitants of the town. The Domain initially seems to satisfy Salim's
longings for a wider world. In the light of day, however, his notion of the
glamour of the Domain is observed by him to be fraudulent; the
shabbiness, cracks and dilapidation of its buildings suggest deeper flaws:
"What fantasies I had built around this room!" (*BR*, p. 184.) The
Domain is thereafter seen as a place where unrealistic and romantic
notions of Africa's future are nurtured. It is a "hoax", though an
appealing one. The fantasies of the Domain are presented as reliant on the
security of its inhabitants. The treatment of the Domain is in keeping with
the way in which Naipaul elsewhere portrays what he refers to as liberal
delusion, by which he means a tendency to sentimentalize and
romanticize post-colonial societies.

It is a charge which has been made against Naipaul that, secure in the
possession of a return air ticket, he is able to indulge in despair about the
prospects of the post-colonial countries he visits and writes about. In *A
Bend in the River*, unusually, Naipaul thinks himself into the position of
those who are left behind: "Satire like this from people who were just
passing through, . . . people who were safe it their own countries, satire
like this was sometimes wounding" (*BR*, p. 210). The novel shows an
awareness of the limitations both of a critical and of an unduly approving
view: of the different forms of blindness produced by an insufficient
knowledge of, and by an excessive familiarity with, a given society.
There is some sense in the novel of a play of various viewpoints: Salim
wonders, "Was there a truth outside men? Didn't men make the truth for

themselves?'' (*BR*, p. 135.) Ultimately, however, although the novel can be found to question its own assumptions, the scruples that are associated with such questioning give the impression of amounting only to cosmetic gestures. Salim is presented as a narrator who combines the virtues both of insider and outsider, his clear-sightedness set off by the delusions of the Domain. A range of opinions regarding the place is made to appear possible in the novel, but it is the voice of disenchantment which carries the greatest weight; the events it describes justify nothing other than pessimism. No other viewpoint can begin to challenge the authority of Salim's narration, and the action of the novel bears out his judgements.

A Bend in the River is deeply ambivalent in its account of European society. Europe represents a lost ideal of peace and order, but has also given rise to a junk civilization. The novel suggests that its deeds fall short of its ideals; Europe itself has succumbed to the pull of disorder, and it exports naive ideologues to the rest of the world. In setting out to discredit what Naipaul sees as their sentimental delusions about Africa, the novel draws on an older set of myths. Africa remains what it has always been to Europeans — a threateningly chaotic place where destructive forces are unleashed without restraint. The novel employs traditional images of Africa to give symbolic form to a confusion and disruption not confined to Africa; it recalls Naipaul's portrayal of the chaos which afflicts other post-colonial societies, and gives expression to his perception of a crisis in metropolitan civilization. The African setting of the novel supplies Naipaul with a familiar stock of images of social breakdown in which to clothe his pessimism and fear of disorder.

Notes

1 ''A New King for the Congo: Mobutu and the Nihilism of Africa'', *REP*, p. 190, first published in the *New York Review of Books*, 22 (June 26 1975), pp. 19–25.
2 The phrase is taken from Naipaul's article ''Our Universal Civilization'', *New York Review of Books*, 38 (January 31 1991), pp. 22–25.
3 Interviewed by Raoul Pantin, p. 18.
4 Interviewed by Elizabeth Hardwick, p. 36.
5 Interviewed by Elizabeth Hardwick, p. 36.
6 *The Africa That Never Was: Four Centuries of British Writing About Africa* (New York: Twayne, 1970).
7 *Blank Darkness: Africanist Discourse in French* (Chicago: University of Chicago Press, 1985).
8 *Congo Diary and Other Uncollected Pieces*, ed. by Zdzislaw Najder (New York: Doubleday, 1978), p. 8.
9 As argued by Edward Said, *Culture and Imperialism*, p. 34.
10 ''Echoes of Empire: Conrad and Caliban'', *Encounter*, 66, 3 (March 1986), pp. 43–51.
11 *Hopes and Impediments*, p. 12.

12 *Hopes and Impediments*, p. 3.
13 *Hopes and Impediments*, p. 19.
14 *Journey Without Maps* (London: Heinemann, 1950), p. 32.
15 *Women in Love* (Penguin: Harmondsworth, 1960), p. 285.
16 Interviewed by Charles Michener, "The Dark Visions of V. S. Naipaul", *Newsweek* (November 16 1981), p. 109.
17 "V. S. Naipaul: Sensibility and Schemata", *Critical Quarterly*, 18, 3 (1976), p. 77.
18 *Hopes and Impediments*, p. 30.
19 "The Writer in a New Nation", *Nigeria Magazine*, 81 (June 1964), p. 157.
20 *Arrow of God* (London: Heinemann, 1964), pp. 35–6. The allusion is noted by Michael Thorpe, p. 46.
21 *Things Fall Apart* (London: Heinemann, 1958), p. 109.
22 *Chinua Achebe: Novelist, Poet, Critic* (Basingstoke: Macmillan, 1980), p. 35.
23 *Hopes and Impediments*, p. 22.
24 *Hopes and Impediments*, p. 23.
25 *Hopes and Impediments* p. 25.
26 Stephen Weissman, "The C. I. A. and U. S. Policy in Zaire and Angola", in *Dirty Work 2: The C. I. A. in Africa*, ed. by Ellen Ray, William Schaap, Karl van Meter and Louis Wolf (London: Zed Press, 1980), pp. 183–207.
27 *Africa in Modern History: The Search for a New Society* (Harmondsworth: Penguin, 1978), pp. 338–9.
28 *Aeneid*, Book 4, 110–12, in *Eclogues, Georgics and Aeneid, 1–VI*, tr. by H. Rushton Fairclough (Cambridge, Massachusetts: Harvard University Press, 1935; London: Heinemann, 1935), p. 402. The Latin motto on the dock gates reads, "*Miscerique probat populos et foedera jungi*".
29 The novel also alludes to Pliny: "*Semper Aliquid Novi*" (*BR*, p. 42).
30 Interviewed by Elizabeth Hardwick, p. 36.
31 *After Empire*, p. 104.
32 *After Empire*, p. 108.
33 Notebook, 1972–4, containing plans for *G*, V. S. Naipaul Archive, II, 3:4.
34 Notebook, 1977, containing the first draft of *BR*, V. S. Naipaul Archive, II, 6:3.
35 Interviewed by Adrian Rowe-Evans, p. 55.
36 Interviewed by Margaret Drabble, *Bookcase*, BBC World Service (November 26 1971), André Deutsch Archive, 96, *IFS* folder.
37 Interviewed by Ian Hamilton, Hamner, p. 45.
38 Interviewed by Jim Douglas Henry, "Unfurnished Entrails – The Novelist V. S. Naipaul in Conversation with Jim Douglas Henry", *Listener*, 86 (November 25 1971), p. 721.
39 V. S. Naipaul Archive, II, 4:2.
40 Interviewed by Margaret Drabble, *Bookcase*, BBC World Service (November 26 1971), André Deutsch Archive, 96, *IFS* folder.
41 Naipaul's blurb for *IFS*, André Deutsch Archive, 96, *IFS* folder.
42 This argument is suggested by Bruce King, *V. S. Naipaul* (Basingstoke: Macmillan, 1993), pp. 156–7.
43 Notebook containing plans for "Prologue to an Autobiography", 1973, V. S. Naipaul Archive, I 1:3.
44 "Passports to Dependence", *Beyond the Dragon's Mouth*, pp. 221–9.
45 *After Empire*, p. 103.
46 W. B. Yeats, "The Second Coming", which provides the title and the epigraph to Achebe's *Things Fall Apart*.
47 Irving Howe, *Politics and the Novel* (New York: Horizon, 1957), pp. 20–22.

Conclusion

This book has sought to provide a variety of historical, literary and biographical contexts in which to understand Naipaul's writing. It has argued that his early work forms part of a familial literary dialogue. His allusions and debt of influence to his father's work might be seen to originate in, and to belie, his sense that he lacked literary models for the treatment of Trinidadian society. *A House for Mr Biswas*'s attitude of mingled acceptance and rebellion towards the society it portrays, and its combination of an insider's and outsider's view, are ascribed by Naipaul to Seepersad's influence. This complex perspective, compounded of sympathy and irony, is a recurring feature of Naipaul's writing.

Most of his works incorporate an important element of autobiographical material, more or less overt: this book has contended that the repeated rewriting of his life might suggest both a consistency of theme and instability of identity; it implies that the self is open to variable interpretations. *The Enigma of Arrival* is more overtly autobiographical than other works, although it also blurs the boundaries between autobiography and fiction. Like a more conventional work of autobiography, it is shaped by a dialogue between past and present selves, and by an unfolding drama of revised opinion. It elaborates a complex portrait of England as at once a disappointment and the fulfilment of an ideal. Other records of migration from the colonies or former colonies tend more unambiguously to portray the experience as a disillusionment. The work can be interpreted as laying claim to Naipaul's new home and to a place in its literary tradition, and it prominently invokes the figure of Wordsworth, as if to suggest a continuity.

Naipaul often reworks the material of earlier books in later ones: the relation between *The Loss of El Dorado* and *A Way in the World* is particularly close. In both, history shows a tendency to repeat itself. Recurrences, this discussion has contended, characterize the relations between Naipaul's various works, as well as the structure of individual books. *A Way in the World* makes of recurrence a stylistic principle, and its syntax mirrors its overall shape. Its view of history is the product of a dialogue between present and past — a hostility towards radicalism and revolutionaries is evident in its treatment of historical material as well as in the autobiographical sections. The work dramatizes a reluctance to conform to the pressures of audience expectation as Naipaul sees them, but their influence is nevertheless felt indirectly in a readiness to dispute such beliefs.

Naipaul's writing on India, I have argued, is shaped by a dialogue with certain Indian writers, as well as being indebted to some of the conventions according to which English writers have traditionally represented India. Naipaul is influenced by Chaudhuri, but perhaps misreads Narayan in order that his novels conform to Naipaul's thesis that Indian civilization is doomed. The Indian travel books are animated by the tensions consequent on his uncomfortable personal relation to the country, and are distinguished by the irony that his thought often reproduces features of Indian civilization of which he is critical: his analysis of the society can also be read as self-analysis. An examination of the manner in which he reworks earlier writings indicates the extent to which his observations are driven by personal preoccupations, and in some measure contradictory. His Indian books also demonstrate the sense in which concern may tend to present itself as akin to contempt in the literary treatment of victims.

This discussion has endeavoured to demonstrate that *Guerrillas* is the product of the interaction of documentary sources and literary influences. The article on the killings provided an opportunity to develop a literary technique subsequently employed in places in the novel: this technique of uncertainty can also be traced in part to the powerful influence of Conrad. Perhaps Naipaul no longer understands Trinidadian society: the novel, this book argues, does not illuminate the nature of revolt. Naipaul's antipathy towards the political radicalism of the 1960s leads him to assume, in his hostile portraits of Gale Benson and Jane, a position not dissimilar to the one he condemns: Malik's animosity towards his London supporters is akin to Naipaul's, and, despite their conflicting political positions, Naipaul shows sympathy for the figure of Jimmy, with his sense of betrayal and affront. The novel's allusions suggest the inapplicability of English literature to Trinidad, but Naipaul uses literary techniques which resemble those of his modernist predecessors.

This book has shown that the sources of Naipaul's representation of Africa can be found in his journalism and travel writing, and in the traditional European conception of the continent, particularly Conrad's: these two elements are in places in conflict. Naipaul's Africa can also be seen as a landscape of the mind: it is akin to post-colonial states portrayed elsewhere in his works — and *Guerrillas, In a Free State* and *A Bend in the River* closely resemble one another in terms of the situations they portray and their outlook. The perception of disorder he associates with post-colonial nations is based on an opposition between metropolis and periphery that sometimes breaks down, producing some ambivalence in his attitude; much of *A Bend in the River*'s complexity derives from the elusive tone that results from this ambivalence. Naipaul's use of the outsider's perspective might be thought to disguise a failure to understand African societies.

Naipaul tends to present himself as largely self-originating, but his work can be located in a network of literary allusion. His work can also be seen to be shaped in contradistinction to the work of writers and beliefs towards which he is hostile. This book has undertaken to show that his tendency to dwell on an absence of affiliations may better be understood in relation to the circumstances of his development and education — in the context of the cultural displacement that was one of the consequences of colonialism. He describes himself as having emerged from and writing in a vacuum — as lacking a settled culture such as other writers feed on, as unsupported and betrayed by his native society. He nevertheless returns repeatedly to his origins, to tell the story of his life over and over again in a variety of forms. This belies his sense that his origins provide unsuitable material for literary treatment; while he often writes dismissively of the unimportance of Trinidad, it has not been unimportant to his literary output.

Bibliography

Works by Naipaul

The Mystic Masseur. London, André Deutsch, 1957.
The Suffrage of Elvira. London, André Deutsch, 1958.
Miguel Street. London, André Deutsch, 1959.
A House for Mr Biswas. London, André Deutsch, 1961.
The Middle Passage: The Caribbean Revisited. Impressions of Five Societies — British, French and Dutch — in the West Indies and South America. London, André Deutsch, 1962.
Mr Stone and the Knights Companion. London, André Deutsch, 1963.
An Area of Darkness: An Experience of India. London, André Deutsch, 1964.
A Flag on the Island. London, André Deutsch, 1967.
The Mimic Men. London, André Deutsch, 1967.
The Loss of El Dorado: A History. London, André Deutsch, 1969.
In a Free State. London, André Deutsch, 1971.
The Overcrowded Barracoon and Other Articles. London, André Deutsch, 1972.
Guerrillas. London, André Deutsch, 1975.
India: A Wounded Civilization. London, André Deutsch, 1977.
A Bend in the River. London, André Deutsch, 1979.
A Congo Diary. Los Angeles, Sylvester and Orphanos, 1980.
The Return of Eva Perón: With the Killings in Trinidad. London, André Deutsch, 1980.
Among the Believers: An Islamic Journey. London, André Deutsch, 1981.
Finding the Centre: Two Narratives. London, André Deutsch, 1984.
The Enigma of Arrival: A Novel in Five Sections. Harmondsworth, Viking, 1987.
A Turn in the South. New York, Alfred A. Knopf, 1989.
India: A Million Mutinies Now. London, Heinemann, 1990.
A Way in the World: A Sequence. London, Heinemann, 1994.
Beyond Belief: Islamic Excursions Among the Converted Peoples. London, Little, Brown and Company, 1998.
Reading and Writing: A Personal Account. New York, New York Review of Books, 2000.
Letters Between a Father and Son. London, Abacus, 2000.

Articles

"Honesty Needed in West Indian Writing," *Trinidad Guardian,* October 28, 1956, p. 29.
"A Letter to Maria," *New Statesman,* 56, July 5, 1958, p. 14.
"The Little More," *Times,* July 13, 1961, in *Critical Perspectives on V. S. Naipaul,* ed. by Robert D. Hamner. Washington, Three Continents Press, 1977, pp. 13–15.
"Trollope in the West Indies," *Listener,* 67, March 15, 1962, p. 461.

"Newsletters: London: A Return to England," *Illustrated Weekly of India*, 84, April 14, 1963, p. 21.

"Newsletters: London: The New Developments," *Illustrated Weekly of India*, 84, May 12, 1963, pp. 14–15.

"Newsletters: London: A Case for Future Historians," *Illustrated Weekly of India*, 84, July 28, 1963, pp. 14–15.

"Newsletters: London: Of Goats and Monkeys," *Illustrated Weekly of India*, 84, August 25, 1963, pp. 22–3.

"London Letter: All About Cricket," *Illustrated Weekly of India*, 84, September 29, 1963, p. 15.

"Newsletters: London: The Householder," *Illustrated Weekly of India*, 84, October 20, 1963, p. 18.

"London Letter: Society of the Mini-Mice," *Illustrated Weekly of India*, 84, November 24, 1963, p. 23.

"London Letter: The Christmas Spirit," *Illustrated Weekly of India*, 84, December 22, 1963, p. 25.

"London Letter: The Race Problem," *Illustrated Weekly of India*, 85, January 19, 1964, p. 15.

"London Letter: Current Linguistic Trends," *Illustrated Weekly of India*, 85, February 16, 1964, p. 19.

"London Letter: The Publicity Machine," *Illustrated Weekly of India*, 85, March 22, 1964, p. 17.

"London Letter: The Old Houses Go," *Illustrated Weekly of India*, 85, April 26, 1964, p. 21.

"Newsletters: London: Talk About Violence," *Illustrated Weekly of India*, 85, May 31, 1964, p. 22.

"London Letter: The Book World," *Illustrated Weekly of India*, 85, June 28, 1964, p. 15.

"London Letter: Radio and Television," *Illustrated Weekly of India*, 85, July 19, 1964, p. 15.

"Critics and Criticism," *Bim*, 10(38), 1964, pp. 74–7.

"The Documentary Heresy," *Twentieth Century*, 173, Winter 1964–5, pp. 107–8, in *Critical Perspectives on V. S. Naipaul*, pp. 23–4.

"A West Indian Culture?" *Illustrated Weekly of India*, 86, May 30, 1965, p. 23.

"What's Wrong with Being a Snob?" *Saturday Evening Post*, June 3, 1967, in *Critical Perspectives on V. S. Naipaul*, pp. 34–8.

"Biafra's Rights," *Times*, November 13, 1968, p. 11.

"Et in America Ego!" *Listener*, 82, September 4, 1969, pp. 302–4.

"Books of the Year: A Personal Choice," *Observer*, December 21, 1969, p. 17.

"New Year Predictions," *Listener*, 83, January 1, 1970, p. 17.

Foreword, *The Adventures of Gurudeva and Other Stories*. London, Deutsch, 1976, pp. 7–25.

"Indian Art and its Illusions," *New York Review of Books*, 26, March 22, 1979, pp. 6, 8–10, 12, 14.

"Flight from the Fire", *New York Review of Books*, 26, May 3, 1979, pp. 28–30.

Introduction, *East Indians in the Caribbean: Colonialism and the Struggle for Identity. Papers Presented to a Symposium on East Indians in the Caribbean, The University of the West Indies, St Augustine, Trinidad, June 1975*, [ed. by Bridget Brereton and Winston Dookeran]. Millwood, New York: Kraus International Publications, 1982, pp. 1–9.

"A Note on a Borrowing by Conrad," *New York Review of Books*, 29, December 16, 1982, pp. 37–8.

"Writing *A House for Mr Biswas*," *New York Review of Books*, 30, November 24, 1983, pp. 22–3.
"Among the Republicans," *New York Review of Books*, 31, October 25, 1984, pp. 5, 8, 10, 12, 14–17.
"India After Indira Gandhi," *New York Times*, November 3, 1984, p. 24.
"Reflections of a Reluctant Gardener," *House and Garden*, 158, January 1986, pp. 118–9.
"My Brother's Tragic Sense," *Spectator*, 258, January 24, 1987, pp. 22–3.
"Some Thoughts on Being a Writer," *Chronicles: A Magazine of American Culture*, 11 (5), May 1987, pp. 13–15.
"Our Universal Civilization," *New York Review of Books*, 38, January 31, 1991, pp. 22–5.
"A Handful of Dust: Return to Guiana," *New York Review of Books*, 38, April 11, 1991, pp. 15–20.
"Argentina: Living with Cruelty," *New York Review of Books*, 39, January 30, 1992, pp. 13–18.
"The End of Peronism?" *New York Review of Books*, 39, February 13, 1992, pp. 47–53.
"Acceptance Speech of the First David Cohen British Literature Prize," *Wasafiri*, 21, Spring 1995, pp. 7–8.
"Letters to a Young Writer," *New Yorker*, June 26 — July 3, 1995, pp. 144–53.

Reviews

"Wonne With a Nut," *New Statesman*, 54, November 23, 1957, pp. 703–4.
"Insider Out," *New Statesman*, 54, December 21, 1957, p. 859.
"Where the Rum Comes From," *New Statesman*, 54, January 4, 1958, pp. 20–1.
"Letter from Little Rock," *New Statesman*, 55, January 25, 1958, p. 112.
"New Fiction," *New Statesman*, 55, April 5, 1958, pp. 444–5.
"Autobiographies," *New Statesman*, 55, April 19, 1958, p. 507.
"New Novels," *New Statesman*, 55, May 3, 1958, pp. 572–3.
"Flowers for the Frau," *New Statesman*, 55, May 17, 1958, p. 645.
"New Novels," *New Statesman*, 55, May 31, 1958, p. 705.
"New Novels," *New Statesman*, 55, June 28, 1958, pp. 844–5.
"New Novels," *New Statesman*, 56, July 12, 1958, pp. 54–5.
"Three Boyhoods," *New Statesman*, 56, July 26, 1958, pp. 123–4.
"New Novels," *New Statesman*, 56, August 9, 1958, pp. 174–5.
"New Novels," *New Statesman*, 56, August 30, 1958, pp. 252–3.
"New Novels," *New Statesman*, 56, October 4, 1958, p. 471.
"New Novels," *New Statesman*, 56, November 1, 1958, pp. 608, 610.
"New Novels," *New Statesman*, 56, December 6, 1958, pp. 826–7.
"New Novels," *New Statesman*, 57, January 17, 1959, p. 79.
"Other New Novels," *New Statesman*, 57, February 14, 1959, pp. 229–30.
"New Novels," *New Statesman*, 57, March 14, 1959, p. 376.
"Death on the Telephone," *New Statesman*, 57, March 28, 1959, p. 452.
"Other New Novels," *New Statesman*, 57, April 18, 1959, pp. 551–2.
"New Fiction," *New Statesman*, 57, May 16, 1959, p. 700.
"New Novels," *New Statesman*, 57, June 20, 1959, p. 871.
"New Novels," *New Statesman*, 58, July 18, 1959, pp. 89–90.
"New Fiction," *New Statesman*, 58, August 15, 1959, pp. 200–1.

"Shorter Reviews," *New Statesman*, 58, September 5, 1959, pp. 286–7.
"New Novels," *New Statesman*, 58, September 26, 1959, pp. 401–2.
"New Novels," *New Statesman*, 58, October 17, 1959, pp. 516–7.
"New Novels," *New Statesman*, 58, November 7, 1959, pp. 637–8.
"New Novels," *New Statesman*, 58, November 28, 1959, pp. 770–1.
"New Novels," *New Statesman*, 59, January 9, 1960, p. 49.
"New Novels," *New Statesman*, 59, February 6, 1960, pp. 95–6.
"New Novels," *New Statesman*, 59, February 27, 1960, pp. 306–7.
"New Novels," *New Statesman*, 59, March 26, 1960, pp. 461–2.
"New Novels," *New Statesman*, 59, April 23, 1960, p. 602.
"New Novels," *New Statesman*, 59, May 21, 1960, pp. 764–5.
"New Novels," *New Statesman*, 59, June 18, 1960, pp. 914–5.
"New Novels," *New Statesman*, 60, July 16, 1960, pp. 97–8.
"New Novels," *New Statesman*, 60, August 20, 1960, pp. 251–2.
"On St George's Hill," *New Statesman*, 61, May 12, 1961, p. 758.
"Reliques," *New Statesman,* 61, June 9, 1961, p. 924.
"Taluqdars," *New Statesman*, 62, July 7, 1961, pp. 22–3.
"Tricks and Secrets," *New Statesman*, 62, July 28, 1961, pp. 126–7.
"Dark Places," *New Statesman*, 62, August 18, 1961, pp. 221–2.
"Red Rat-Traps," *New Statesman*, 62, August 25, 1961, pp. 248–9.
"England, Half-English," *Listener*, 66, September 7, 1961, p. 358.
"Vacancies," *New Statesman*, 62, September 22, 1961, pp. 394–5.
"When I Was a Kid," *New Statesman,* 62, December 22, 1961, pp. 963–4.
"Castles of Fear," *Spectator*, 211, July 5, 1963, p. 16.
"Black Man's Burden, *New York Review of Books*, 1, October 31, 1963, pp. 19–20.
"Sebastian Rides Again," *Spectator,* 212, April 24, 1964, p. 559.
"Australia Deserta," *Spectator*, 213, October 16, 1964, p. 513.
"Images," *New Statesman*, 70, September 24, 1965, in *Critical Perspectives on V. S. Naipaul*, pp. 26–9.
"Rome After Hannibal," *Manchester Guardian*, December 24, 1965, p. 5.
"The Writer," *New Statesman,* 71, March 18, 1966, in *Critical Perspectives on V. S. Naipaul*, pp. 30–3.
"A Rolls-Royce Job," *New Statesman*, 72, October 28, 1966, pp. 628, 630.
"Theatrical Natives," *New Statesman*, 72, December 2, 1966, p. 844.
"In Black Ink," *Listener*, 79, May 23, 1968, p. 666.
"Without a Dog's Chance," *New York Review of Books*, 19, May 18, 1972, pp. 29–31.

Radio Broadcasts

BBC Written Archives Centre, Caversham Park
(Arranged according to date of transmission, or, when not available, date of recording.)
"This is Home," *Caribbean Voices*, June 24, 1951.
"Potatoes," *Caribbean Voices*, April 27, 1952.
"Old Man," *Caribbean Voices*, April 26, 1953.
"Epicurean Service," *Caribbean Voices*, October 19, 1953.
Caribbean Voices, May 1, 1955, Review of Selvon's *An Island is a World*.
Caribbean Voices, November 13, 1955, Review of Mittelholzer's *My Bones and My Flute*.
Caribbean Voices, January 22, 1956.
Caribbean Voices, February 12, 1956.

Caribbean Voices, February 19, 1956.
Caribbean Voices, March 4, 1956.
Caribbean Voices, September 16, 1956, Review of Mittelholzer's *Of Trees and the Sea.*
The Third Programme, April 21, 1958, Discussion of British Caribbean writers.
Caribbean Voices, August 31, 1958.
The World of Books, October 24, 1961, Interviewed by Walter Allen.
The Masters, April 10, 1962.
The World of Books, June 7, 1963, Interviewed by Francis Wyndham.
The World of Books, October 5, 1964, Interviewed by John Morris.
The World of Books, July 15, 1965, Discussion with Anthony Burgess of the Literature of Empire.
The Arts This Week, October 29, 1969, Interviewed by Julian Mitchell.

Unpublished materials

V. S. Naipaul Archive
Special Collections, McFarlin Library, University of Tulsa

André Deutsch Archive
Special Collections, McFarlin Library, University of Tulsa

Interviews

"An Area of Brilliance," *Observer,* November 28, 1971, p. 8.
Bates, David. "Portrait Gallery: V. S. Naipaul," *Sunday Times Supplement,* May 26, 1963, pp. 12–13.
Bingham, Nigel. "The Novelist V. S. Naipaul Talks to Nigel Bingham about his Childhood in Trinidad," *Listener,* 88, September 7, 1972, pp. 306–7.
Blandford, Linda. "Man in a Glass Box," *Sunday Telegraph Magazine,* September 23, 1979, pp. 77, 81, 86, 90.
Bryden, Ronald. "The Novelist V. S. Naipaul Talks About his Work to Ronald Bryden," *Listener,* 89, March 22, 1973, pp. 367–70.
"Children of a Greater God," *Guardian,* August 20, 1993, p. 18.
Cowley, Jason. "The Long Road to Happiness," *Times,* May 11, 1998, p. 17.
Cunningham, John. "Floating up to a Point," *Guardian,* April 20, 1984, p. 9.
Fraser, Fitzroy. "A Talk with Vidia Naipaul," *Sunday Gleaner* (Jamaica), December 25, 1960, pp. 14, 19.
Geniès, Bernard and Nicole Zand. "Un Observateur Féroce du Tiers-Monde," *Le Monde,* June 26, 1981, pp. 15, 20.
Gussow, Mel. "It is Out of this Violence I've Always Written," *New York Times Book Review,* September 16, 1984, pp. 45–6.
———. "V. S. Naipaul in Search of Himself: A Conversation," *New Yorks Times Book Review,* April 24 , 1994, pp. 3, 29, 30.
———. "Writer Without Roots," *New York Times Magazine,* December 26, 1976, pp. 8–9.
Hamilton, Alex. "Living Life on Approval," *Manchester Guardian,* October 4, 1971, p. 8.
———. "Without a Place," *Sacavou,* 9–10, 1974, in *Critical Perspectives on V. S. Naipaul,* pp. 39–47.

Hardwick, Elizabeth. "Meeting V. S. Naipaul," *New York Times Book Review*, May 13, 1979, pp. 1, 36.

Henry, Jim Douglas. "Unfurnished Entrails — The Novelist V. S. Naipaul in Conversation with Jim Douglas Henry," *Listener*, 86, November 25, 1971, p. 721.

Hussein, Aamer. "Delivering the Truth," *Times Literary Supplement*, September 2, 1994, pp. 3–4.

Kakutani, Michinko. "Naipaul Reviews his Past from Afar," *New York Times*, December 1, 1980, 3, p. 15.

Kazin, Alfred. "V. S. Naipaul: Novelist as Thinker," *New York Times Book Review*, May 1, 1977, pp. 7, 20, 22.

Levin, Bernard. "A Perpetual Voyager," *Listener*, 109, June 23, 1983, pp. 16–17.

Michener, Charles. "The Dark Visions of V. S. Naipaul," *Newsweek*, November 16, 1981, pp. 104–5, 108–110, 112, 114–5.

Mukherjee, Bharati, and Robert Boyers. "A Conversation with V. S. Naipaul," *Salmagundi*, 54, Fall 1981, pp. 4–22.

Niven, Alastair. "V. S. Naipaul Talks to Alastair Niven," *Wasafiri*, 21, Spring 1995, pp. 5–6.

Pantin, Raoul. "Portrait of an Artist," *Caribbean Contact*, 1, May 1973, pp. 15, 18–19.

"Pooter," *Times*, November 9, 1968, p. 23.

Pryce-Jones, David. *Radio Times*, March 24–30, 1979, pp. 9, 11.

Rashid, Ahmed. "Death of the Novel," *Observer*, February 25, 1996, p. 16.

Roach, Eric. "Fame a Short-Lived Cycle, says Vidia," *Trinidad Guardian*, January 4, 1972, pp. 1–2.

Robinson, Andrew. "Going Back for a Turn in the East," *Sunday Times*, September 16, 1990, 8, p. 14.

_____. "Andrew Robinson meets V. S. Naipaul," *Literary Review*, 148, October 1990, pp. 21–4.

_____. "Stranger in Fiction," *Independent on Sunday*, August 16, 1992, p. 23.

Rouse, Ewart. "Naipaul: An Interview with Ewart Rouse," *Trinidad Guardian*, November 28, 1968, pp. 9, 13.

Rowe-Evans, Adrian. "An Interview with V. S. Naipaul," *Quest*, 78, September — October, 1972, pp. 47–56.

Schiff, Stephen. "The Ultimate Exile," *New Yorker*, May 23, 1994, pp. 60–71.

Shenker, Israel. "V. S. Naipaul: Man Without a Society," *New York Times,* 1971, in *Critical Perspectives on V. S. Naipaul*, pp. 48–53.

Sheppard, R. Z. "Wanderer of Endless Curiosity," *Time*, July 10, 1989, pp. 58–60.

Singh, Rahul. "A Miraculous Achievement," *Newsweek*, July 3, 1989, p. 48.

"Speaking of Writing: V. S. Naipaul," *Times*, January 2, 1964, p. 11.

Streitfeld, David. "Caustic V. S. Naipaul Gentle on U.S. South," *International Herald Tribune*, April 13, 1989, p. 18.

Suplee, Curt. "Voyager With the Dark and Comic Vision," *Washington Post*, November 19, 1981, pp. C1, C17.

"V. S. Naipaul Tells How Writing Changes a Writer," *Tapia*, December 2, 1973, p. 11.

Weatherby, W. J. "Naipaul's Prize?" *Sunday Times*, September 21, 1980, p. 32.

Wheeler, Charles. "It's Every Man for Himself — V. S. Naipaul on India," *Listener*, 98, October 27, 1977, pp. 535–7.

Winokur, Scott. "The Unsparing Vision of V. S. Naipaul," *Image: The San Francisco Chronicle Magazine*, May 5, 1991, pp. 8–12, 14–15.

Wood, James. "The Mystic Martyr," *Guardian*, May 16, 1994, p. 8.

Wyndham, Francis. "Writing is Magic," *Sunday Times*, November 10, 1968, p. 57.

Critical works

Articles

Achebe, Chinua. "Viewpoint," *Times Literary Supplement*, February 1, 1980, p. 113.

_____. "The Writer in a New Nation," *Nigeria Magazine*, 81, June 1964, pp. 157–60.

Anderson, Benedict. "James Fenton's Slideshow," *New Left Review*, 158, July — August 1986, pp. 81–90.

Appiah, Kwame Anthony. "Is the Post- in Postmodernism the Post- in Postcolonial?" *Critical Inquiry,* 17, Winter 1991, pp. 336–386.

_____. "Out of Africa: Topologies of Nativism," *Yale Journal of Criticism*, 2(1), Fall 1988, pp. 153–78.

Athill, Diana. "Editing Vidia," *Granta,* 69, Spring 2000, pp. 179–205.

Bardolph, Jacqueline. "Son, Father and Writing: A Commentary," *Commonwealth: Essays and Studies*, 9(1), Autumn 1986, pp. 82–90.

Belitt, Ben. "The Heraldry of Accommodation: A House for Mr Naipaul," *Salmagundi*, 54, Fall 1981, pp. 23–42.

Bhabha, Homi. "Representation and the Colonial Text," in *The Theory of Reading*, ed. by Frank Gloversmith. Sussex, Harvester, 1984, pp. 93–122.

Boxhill, Anthony. "Mr Biswas, Mr Polly and the Problem of V. S. Naipaul's Sources," *Ariel*, 8(3), July 1977, pp. 129–41.

_____. "V. S. Naipaul's Starting Point," *Journal of Commonwealth Literature*, 10(1), August 1975, pp. 1–9.

Casmier, Stephen. "Black Narcissus: Representation, Reproduction, Repetition and Seeing Yourself in V. S. Naipaul's *A House for Mr Biswas* and *The Enigma of Arrival*," *Commonwealth: Essays and Studies*, 18(1), Autumn 1995, pp. 92–105.

Clemens, Walter C. Jr. "The Third World in V. S. Naipaul," *Worldview,* 25, September 1982, pp. 12–14.

Cooke, Michael. "Rational Despair and the Fatality of Revolution in West Indian Literature," *Yale Review*, 71(1), Autumn 1981, pp. 28–38.

Cronin, Richard. "Quite Quiet India: The Despair of R. K. Narayan," *Encounter,* 64(3), March 1985, pp. 52–59.

Dayan, Joan. "Gothic Naipaul," *Transition*, 59, 1993, pp. 158–70.

Duyck, Rudy. "V. S. Naipaul and John Donne: The Morning After," *Journal of Commonwealth Literature,* 24(1), 1989, pp. 155–62.

Fersch, Annabelle. "V. S. Naipaul's *A Bend in the River* and the Art of Re-reading," *Commonwealth Novel in English*, 5(2), Fall 1992, pp. 1–8.

Goodheart, Eugene. "Naipaul and the Voices of Negation," *Salmagundi*, 54, Fall 1981, pp. 44–58.

Gorra, Michael. "Naipaul or Rushdie," *Southwest Review*, 76(3), Summer 1991, pp. 374–89.

Gurnah, Abdulrazak. "Fantasies of Trinidad: V. S. Naipaul and the Nihilism of Primitive Peoples," *Times Literary Supplement*, May 20, 1994, p. 12.

Gurr, Andrew. "The Freedom of Exile in Naipaul and Doris Lessing," *Ariel*, 13(4), October 1982, pp. 7–18.

Hassan, Dolly. "The Messianic Leader in V. S. Naipaul's West Indian Works," *Commonwealth Novel in English*, 4(2), Fall 1991, pp. 55–67.

Hearne, John. "Unsentimental Journey with V. S. Naipaul," *Sunday Guardian* (Trinidad), February 3, 1963, pp. 3–4.

Hemenway, Robert. "Sex and Politics in V. S. Naipaul," *Studies in the Novel*, 14(2), Summer 1982, pp. 189–202.

Howe, Irving. "A Dark Vision," *New York Times Book Review*, May 13, 1979, pp. 1, 37.

Huggan, Graham. "Anxieties of Influence: Conrad in the Caribbean," *Commonwealth: Essays and Studies,* 11(1), Autumn 1988, pp. 1–12.

Ismond, Patricia. "*Another Life:* Autobiography as Alternative History," *Journal of West Indian Literature*, 4(1), January 1990, pp. 41–49.

Jacobson, Dan. "After Notting Hill," *Encounter*, 11(6), December 1958, pp. 3–10.

James, C. L. R. "A History of Negro Revolt," *Fact*, September 1938, pp. 5–86.

_____. "The Disorder of Vidia Naipaul," *Sunday Guardian Magazine* (Trinidad), February 21, 1965, pp. 6–7.

Johnstone, Richard. "Politics and V. S. Naipaul," *Journal of Commonwealth Literature*, 14(1), August 1979, pp. 100–9.

Kanga, Firdaus. "Seeing and Looking Away," *Times Literary Supplement*, October 5–11, 1990, p. 1059.

Kermode, Frank. "Novel, History and Type," *Novel*, 1, Spring 1968, pp. 231–8.

_____. "Memory and Autobiography," *Raritan*, 15(1), Summer 1995, pp. 36–50.

Kortenaar, Neil ten. "Writers and Readers, the Written and the Read: V. S. Naipaul and *Guerrillas*," *Contemporary Literature*, 31(3), Fall 1990, pp. 324–34.

Kramer, Jane. "From the Third World," *New York Times Book Review*, April 13, 1980, pp. 1, 30–2.

Kreiger, Murray. "Fiction and Historical Reality," in *Literature and History: Papers Read at a Clark Library Seminar, March 3, 1973*, ed. by Ralph Cohen and Murray Kreiger. Los Angeles: University of California, 1974, pp. 47–71.

Krikler, Bernard. "V. S. Naipaul's *A House for Mr Biswas*," *Listener*, 71, February 13, 1964, pp. 270–1.

Lamming, George. "A Trinidad Experience," *Time and Tide*, 42(40), October 5, 1961, p. 1657.

Leitch, Thomas. "To What is Fiction Committed?" *Prose Studies*, 6(2), September 1983, pp. 159–75.

Lewis, Peter. "The Ficts of Life: Biography, Autobiography, Faction, Fiction," *Stand*, Spring 1985, pp. 43–9.

Lolla, Maria Grazia. "V. S. Naipaul's Poetics of Reality: 'The Killings in Trinidad' and *Guerrillas*," *Caribana*, 1, 1990, pp. 41–50.

MacDonald, Bruce F. "The Birth of Mr Biswas," *Journal of Commonwealth Literature*, 11(3), April 1977, pp. 50–4.

Madhusudan Rao, K. I. "V. S. Naipaul's *Guerrillas*: A Fable of Political Innocence and Experience," *Journal of Commonwealth Literature*, 14(1), August 1979, pp. 90–100.

McCarthy, Mary. "The Fact in Fiction," in *On the Contrary*, London, Heinemann, 1962, pp. 249–70.

McSweeney, Kerry. "V. S. Naipaul: Sensibility and Schemata," *Critical Quarterly,* 18 (3), 1976, pp. 73–9.

McWatt, Mark. "The West Indian Writer and the Self: Recent 'Fictional Autobiography' by Naipaul and Harris," *Journal of West Indian Literature*, 3(1), January 1989, pp. 16–27.

Miller, Karl. "Elephant Head," *London Review of Books*, 12, September 27, 1990, pp. 11–13.

_____. Introduction, *A House for Mr Biswas*, by V. S. Naipaul. London, Everyman, 1995, pp. vii–xxii.

Mellors, John. "Mimics into Puppets: The Fiction of V. S. Naipaul," *London Magazine*, 15(6), February — March 1976, pp. 117–21.

"Naipaul and the Blacks," *The New Voices*, 3, 7&8, 1976, pp. 19–23, 62–4 & 87.

Neill, Michael. "Guerrillas and Gangs: Frantz Fanon and V. S. Naipaul," *Ariel,* 13(4), October 1982, pp. 21–62.

212 The Enigma of V. S. Naipaul

Niven, Alastair. "Crossing the Black Waters: Nirad C. Chaudhuri's *A Passage to England* and V. S. Naipaul's *An Area of Darkness,*" *Ariel,* 9(3), July 1978, pp. 21–36.

Nixon, Rob. "Caribbean and African Appropriations of *The Tempest,*" *Critical Inquiry,* 13(3), Spring 1987, pp. 557–78.

Oberbeck, Stephen. "Angry Young Indian," *Newsweek,* April 19, 1965, pp. 64–6.

Parekh, Bhikhu. "From India With Hope," *New Statesman and Society,* 3(3), October 5, 1990, pp. 33–4.

Patterson, John. "Challenging C. L. R. and the Naipauls," *Sunday Guardian* (Trinidad), October 18, 1970, pp. 7, 10.

Prescott, Lynda. "Past and Present Darkness: Sources for V. S. Naipaul's *A Bend in the River,*" *Modern Fiction Studies,* 30(3), Autumn 1984, pp. 547–59.

Putnam, Hilary. "Is There a Fact of the Matter about Fiction?" *Poetics Today,* 4(1), 1983, pp. 77–81.

Rattansi, Afshin. "Lamentation in Raj-Time," *Guardian,* September 27, 1990, p. 23.

Richmond, Angus. "V. S. Naipaul: The Mimic Man," *Race and Class,* 24(2), 1982, pp. 125–37.

Ricks, Christopher. "Version of Pastoral," *London Review of Books,* 9, April 2, 1987, pp. 16–18.

Riis, Johannes. "Naipaul's *Woodlanders,*" *Journal of Commonwealth Literature,* 14(1), August 1979, pp. 109–16.

Rohlehr, F. G. "Predestination, Frustration and Symbolic Darkness in Naipaul's *A House for Mr Biswas,*" *Caribbean Quarterly,* 10(1), March 1964, pp. 3–11.

_____. Interviewed by Selwyn Cudjoe, "Talking about Naipaul," *Carib,* 2, 1981, pp. 39–63.

Said, Edward. "Bitter Dispatches from the Third World," *Nation,* 230, May 3, 1980, pp. 522–25.

_____. Introduction to *Kim.* Harmondsworth, Penguin, 1987, pp. 7–46.

_____. "Third World Intellectuals and Metropolitan Culture," *Raritan,* 9(3), Winter 1990, pp. 27–51.

Salgado, Gamini. "V. S. Naipaul and the Politics of Fiction," in *The New Pelican Guide to English Literature,* ed. by Boris Ford. Vol. 8, *The Present.* Harmondsworth, Penguin, 1983, pp. 314–28.

Sandall, Roger. "Two Naipauls: Father and Son: Journey through Darkness", *Quadrant,* 31(6), June 1987, pp. 62–5.

Searle, Chris. "Naipaulicity: A Form of Cultural Imperialism?" *Race and Class,* 26(2), Autumn 1984, pp. 45–63.

Searle, John R. "The Logical Status of Fictional Discourse," *New Literary History,* 6, 1975, pp. 319–32.

Sheppard, R. Z. "Notes from the Fourth World," *Time,* May 21, 1979, pp. 89–90.

Spice, Nicholas. "Inspector of the Sad Parade," *London Review of Books,* 16(15), August 4, 1994, pp. 10–11.

Stevenson, Robert Louis. "A Humble Remonstrance," in *Memories and Portraits,* London, Chatto and Windus, 1888, pp. 275–298.

Thorpe, Michael. "Echoes of Empire: Conrad and Caliban," *Encounter,* 66(3), March 1986, pp. 43–51.

Thieme, John. "Apparitions of Disaster: Brontëan Parallels in *The Wide Sargasso Sea* and *Guerrillas,*" *Journal of Commonwealth Literature,* 14(1), August 1979, pp. 116–132.

_____."A Hindu Castaway: Ralph Singh's Journey in *The Mimic Men,*" *Modern Fiction Studies,* 30(3), Autumn 1984, pp. 505–18.

Tiffin, Helen. "Rites of Resistance: Counter-Discourse and West Indian Biography," *Journal of West Indian Literature,* 3(1), January 1989, pp. 28–46.

_____.''Travelling Texts: Intertextuality and Resistance in V. S. Naipaul's *Guerillas* and Jean Rhys's *Wide Sargasso Sea*,'' *Journal of West Indian Literature*, 6(1), July 1993, pp. 58–70.

Tinkler-Villani, Valeria. ''Fact and Fiction in V. S. Naipaul's 'The Killings in Trinidad' and *Guerrillas*,'' in *Shades of Empire in Colonial and Post-Colonial Literatures*, ed. by C. C. Barfoot and Theo D'haen. Amsterdam and Atlanta, Rodopi, 1993, pp. 235–249.

Tsomondo, Thorell. ''Metaphor, Metonymy and Houses: Figures of Construction in *A House for Mr Biswas*,'' *World Literature Written in English*, 29(2), August 1989, pp. 83–94.

Walcott, Derek. ''The Achievement of V. S. Naipaul,'' *Trinidad Guardian*, April 12, 1964, p. 15.

_____. ''Is V. S. Naipaul an Angry Young Man?'' *Sunday Guardian* (Trinidad), August 6, 1967, p. 9.

_____. ''The Garden Path,'' *New Republic*, 196(15), April 13, 1987, pp. 27–31.

Weissman, Stephen. ''The C. I. A. and U. S. Policy in Zaire and Angola,'' in *Dirty Work 2: The C. I. A. in Africa*, ed. by Ellen Ray, William Schaap, Karl van Meter and Louis Wolf. London, Zed Press, 1980, pp. 183–207.

Woodcock, George. ''Two Great Commonwealth Novelists: R. K. Narayan and V. S. Naipaul,'' *Sewanee Review*, 87, 1979, pp. 1–28.

Wyndham, Francis. ''V. S. Naipaul,'' *Listener*, 86, October 7, 1971, pp. 461–2.

Zahlan, Anne R. ''Literary Murder: V. S. Naipaul's *Guerrillas*,'' *South Atlantic Review* 59 (4), November 1994, pp. 89–106.

Books

Achebe, Chinua. *Arrow of God*. London, Heinemann, 1964.

_____. *Hopes and Impediments: Selected Essays 1965–87*. London, Heinemann, 1988.

_____. *A Man of the People*. London, Heinemann, 1966.

_____. *Things Fall Apart*. London, Heinemann, 1958.

Anand, Mulk Raj. *Untouchable: A Novel*. 1935. London, Hutchinson, 1947.

Anderson, Benedict. *Imagined Communities: Reflections on the Origin and Spread of Nationalism*, (rev. ed.). London and New York, Verso, 1991.

Anniah Gowda, H. H., ed. *The Colonial and the Neo-Colonial Encounters in Commonwealth Literature*. Mysore, University of Mysore Press, 1983.

Archivo del General Miranda. 24 vols. Caracas and Havana, Editorial Sur-América and Lex, 1929–50. [Vols 1–14 ed. by Vincente Dávila; Vol. 15 ed. by a commission of the Academia Nacional de la Historia; Vols. 16–24 ed. by José Nucete Sardi, Antonio Alamo, Jacinto Fombona Pachano and Edurado Arroyo Lamela.]

Ashcroft, Bill, Gareth Griffiths and Helen Tiffin. *The Empire Writes Back: Theory and Practice in Postcolonial Literatures*. London and New York, Routledge, 1989.

Athill, Diana. *Make Believe*. South Royalton, Vermont, Steerforth Press, 1993.

Bethell, Leslie, ed. *The Cambridge History of Latin America*. Vol. 3, *From Independence to c. 1870*. Cambridge, Cambridge University Press, 1985.

Bhabha, Homi K., ed. *Nation and Narration*. London and New York, Routledge, 1990.

Boyers, Robert. *Atrocity and Amnesia: The Political Novel Since 1945*. New York and Oxford, Oxford University Press, 1985.

Buhle, Paul, ed. *C. L. R. James: His Life and Work*. London, Allison and Busby, 1986.

_____. *C. L. R. James: The Artist as Revolutionary*. London and New York, Verso, 1988.

Canary, Robert H., and Henry Kozicki, eds. *The Writing of History: Literary Form and Historical Understanding*. Madison and London, University of Wisconsin Press, 1978.

Carr, E. H. *What is History?* 1961. Harmondsworth, Penguin, 1964.

Carroll, David. *Chinua Achebe: Novelist, Poet, Critic*. Basingstoke, Macmillan, 1980.

Cary, Joyce. *Mister Jonson*. London, Michael Joseph, 1952.

Céline, Louis-Ferdinand. *Journey to the End of the Night*, tr. by Ralph Manheim. London, Calder, 1988. First published 1932.

Chaudhuri, Nirad C. *The Autobiography of an Unknown Indian*. 1951. Berkeley and Los Angeles, University of California Press, 1968.

_____. *A Passage to England*. London, Macmillan, 1959.

Clifford, James. *The Predicament of Culture: Twentieth Century Ethnography, Literature and Art*. Cambridge, Massachusetts and London, Harvard University Press, 1988.

Coleridge, Samuel Taylor. *The Collected Works of Samuel Taylor Coleridge*. Vol. 7, *Biographia Literaria: Or Biographical Sketches of My Literary Life and Opinions*. Vol. 2, ed. by James Engell and W. Jackson Bate. London, Routledge and Kegan Paul, 1983; Princeton, Princeton University Press, 1983.

Conrad, Joseph. *Congo Diary and Other Uncollected Pieces*, ed. by Zdzislaw Najder. New York, Doubleday, 1978.

_____. *The Complete Short Fiction*. Vol. 1, *The Stories*, ed. by Samuel Hynes. London, William Pickering, 1992.

_____. *Heart of Darkness*. 1902. Harmondsworth, Penguin English Library, 1983.

_____. *Nostromo*. 1904. London, Dent, 1957.

_____. *The Secret Agent: A Simple Tale* (The Cambridge edition of the works of Joseph Conrad), ed. by Bruce Harkness and S. W. Reid. 1907. Cambridge, Cambridge University Press, 1990.

_____. *Under Western Eyes*. 1911. London, Everyman's Library, 1991.

Coote, Stephen. *A Play of Passion: The Life of Sir Walter Ralegh*. London, Macmillan, 1993.

Crowder, Michael, ed. *The Cambridge History of Africa*. Vol. 8, *From c.1940 to c.1975*. Cambridge, Cambridge University Press, 1984.

Cudjoe, Selwyn R. *V. S. Naipaul: A Materialist Reading*. Amherst, University of Massachusetts Press, 1988.

Davidson, Basil. *Africa in Modern History: The Search for a New Society*. Harmondsworth, Penguin, 1978.

Eagleton, Terry, Frederic Jameson and Edward Said. *Nationalism, Colonialism and Literature*. Minneapolis, Minnesota, University of Minnesota Press, 1990. A Field Day Company Book.

Eliot, T. S. *Collected Poems 1909–62*. London, Faber and Faber, 1963.

Ellison, Ralph. *Invisible Man*. 1952. Harmondsworth, Penguin, 1965.

The English Institute. *The Literature of Fact: Selected Papers for the English Institute*. Introduction by Angus Fletcher. New York: Columbia University Press, 1976.

Ezekiel, Nissim. *Selected Prose*. Delhi, Oxford University Press, 1992.

Fanon, Frantz. *The Wretched of the Earth*, tr. by Constance Farrington. Harmondsworth, Penguin, 1967. First published 1961.

Fitzgerald, F. Scott. *The Great Gatsby*, 1925. London, Everyman, 1991.

Forster, E. M. *A Passage to India*, 1924. London, Dent, 1942.

Gandhi, M. K. *An Autobiography, or the Story of My Experiments With Truth*, (2nd ed.), tr. by Mahadev Desai. Ahmedabad, Navajivan Press, 1940. First published 1927.

Giddings, Robert. *Literature and Imperialism*. London, Macmillan, 1990.

Gorra, Michael. *After Empire: Scott, Naipaul, Rushdie*. Chicago and London, University of Chicago Press, 1997.

Gould, Tony. *Inside Outsider: The Life and Times of Colin MacInnes*. London, Chatto and Windus, The Hogarth Press, 1983.

Green, Martin. *Dreams of Adventure, Deeds of Empire*. London, Routledge and Kegan Paul, 1980.

Greene, Graham. *The Comedians*. 1966. London, Bodley Head and Heinemann, 1976.

_____. *The Heart of the Matter*. 1948. London, Heinemann and Bodley Head, 1971.

_____. *Journey Without Maps*. 1936. London, Heinemann, 1950.

Gurr, Andrew. *Writers in Exile: The Identity of Home in Modern Literature*. Brighton, Harvester, 1981.

Hammond, Dorothy, and Alta Jablow. *The Africa That Never Was: Four Centuries of British Writing About Africa*. New York, Twayne, 1970.

Hamner, Robert D., ed. *Critical Perspectives on V. S. Naipaul*. Washington, Three Continents Press, 1977.

Harlow, V. T. *Ralegh's Last Voyage*. London, The Argonaut Press, 1932.

Hassan, Dolly. *V. S. Naipaul and the West Indies*. New York, Peter Lang, 1989.

Hazlitt, William. *Lectures on the English Poets*, (3rd ed.). New York, Russell and Russell, 1841.

Hennessy, Alaistair, ed. *Intellectuals in the Twentieth Century Caribbean*. London and Basingstoke, Macmillan, 1992.

Henry, Paget, and Paul Buhle, eds. *C. L. R. James's Caribbean*. Durham, Duke University Press, 1992.

Herbert, George. *The English Poems of George Herbert*, ed. by C. A. Patrides. London, Dent, 1974.

Hobsbawm, Eric, and Terence Ranger, eds. *The Invention of Tradition*. Cambridge, Cambridge University Press, 1983.

Horne, Philip. *Henry James and Revision*. Oxford, Clarendon Press, 1990.

Howe, Irving. *Politics and the Novel*. New York, Horizon, 1957.

Hughes, Peter. *V. S. Naipaul*. London, Routledge, 1988.

Hulme, Peter. *Colonial Encounters: Europe and the Native Caribbean 1492–1797*. London, Routledge, 1992.

Humphry, Derek, and David Tindall. *False Messiah: The Story of Michael X*. London, Hart-Davis MacGibbon, 1977.

Innes, C. L., and Bernth Lindfors. *Critical Perspectives on Chinua Achebe*. 1978. London, Heinemann Educational, 1979.

Jacobs, Naomi. *The Character of Truth: Historical Figures in Contemporary Fiction*. Southern Illinois University Press, Carbondale and Edwardsville, 1990.

Jacobson, Dan. *Time of Arrival and Other Essays*. London, Weidenfeld and Nicolson, 1953.

Jagan, Cheddi. *The West on Trial: My Fight for Guyana's Freedom*. London, Michael Joseph, 1966.

James, C. L. R. *Beyond a Boundary*. London, Hutchinson, 1963.

_____. *The Black Jacobins: Toussaint L'Ouverture and the San Domingo Revolution*, (rev. ed.). New York, Random House, 1963.

_____. *Minty Alley*. 1936. London, New Beacon Books, 1971.

_____. *The Future in the Present: Selected Writings*. London, Allison and Busby, 1977.

_____. *Nkrumah and the Ghana Revolution*. London, Allison and Busby, 1977.

_____. *Spheres of Existence: Selected Writings*. London, Allison and Busby, 1980.

_____. *At the Rendezvous of Victory: Selected Writings*. London, Allison and Busby, 1984.

Jhabvala, Ruth Prawer. *Heat and Dust*. London, John Murray, 1975.

Joyau, Isabelle. *Investigating Powell's Dance to the Music Time*. New York, St Martin's Press, 1994.

Kamra, Shashi. *The Novels of V. S. Naipaul: A Study in Theme and Form.* New Delhi, Prestige, 1990.

Kelly, Richard. *V. S. Naipaul.* New York, Continuum, 1989.

Kermode, Frank. *The Sense of an Ending: Studies in the Theory of Fiction.* 1967. London, Oxford University Press, 1968.

King, Bruce. *V. S. Naipaul.* Basingstoke, Macmillan, 1993.

Kipling, Rudyard. *Kim.* 1901. London, Macmillan, 1949.

Kortenaar, Neil Ten. *History in the Fiction of V. S. Naipaul.* Ph.D. Dissertation, University of Toronto, 1988.

Lamming, George. *The Emigrants.* London, Michael Joseph, 1954.

_____. *The Pleasures of Exile.* 1960. London, Allison and Busby, 1984.

Lawrence, D. H. *Women in Love.* 1921. Harmondsworth, Penguin, 1960.

Levy, Judith. *V. S. Naipaul: Displacement and Autobiography.* New York and London, Garland Publishing, 1995.

Lukács, Georg. *The Historical Novel,* tr. by Hannah and Stanley Mitchell. Merlin Press, London, 1962. First published 1920.

Lynch, John. *The Spanish American Revolutions 1808–1826.* London, Weidenfeld and Nicolson, 1973.

MacInnes, Colin. *City of Spades.* London, MacGibbon & Kee, 1957.

Madariaga, Salvador de. *Bolívar.* London, Hollis and Carter, 1952.

Malik, Abdul Michael. *From Michael de Freitas to Michael X.* London, André Deutsch, 1968.

Malik, Yogendra K. *East Indians in Trinidad: A Study in Minority Politics.* London, Oxford University Press, 1971.

Marable, Manning. *Race, Reform and Rebellion: The Second Reconstruction in Black America, 1945–1990.* Basingstoke, Macmillan Educational, 1991.

Marquez, Gabriel García. *The General in His Labyrinth,* tr. by Edith Grossman. London, Jonathan Cape, 1991. First published 1989.

Marshall, Arthur Calder. *Glory Dead: Impressions of Trinidad.* London, Michael Joseph, 1939.

Mason, Nondita. *The Fiction of V. S. Naipaul.* Calcutta, The World Press, 1986.

McWatt, Mark, ed. *West Indian Literature and its Social Context: Proceedings of the Fourth Annual Conference on West Indian Literature.* Cave Hill, Barbados, Department of English, University of the West Indies, Cave Hill, 1985.

Miller, Christopher. *Blank Darkness: Africanist Discourse in French.* Chicago, Chicago University Press, 1985.

Miller, Karl. *Authors.* Oxford, Clarendon Press, 1989.

Montaigne, Michel de. *Essays,* tr. by J. M. Cohen. Harmondsworth, Penguin, 1958.

Mudimbe, V. Y. *The Invention of Africa: Gnosis, Philosophy and the Order of Knowledge.* Bloomington and Indianapolis, Indiana University Press, 1988.

Mustafa, Fawzia. *V. S. Naipaul.* Cambridge, Cambridge University Press, 1995.

Nabokov, Vladimir. *Speak, Memory: An Autobiography Revisited,* (rev. ed.). London, Weidenfeld and Nicolson, 1967.

Naipaul, Seepersad. *The Adventures of Gurudeva and Other Stories.* London, André Deutsch, 1976.

Naipaul, Shiva. *Beyond the Dragon's Mouth: Stories and Pieces.* London, Hamish Hamilton, 1984.

_____. *The Chip-Chip Gatherers.* London, André Deutsch, 1973.

_____. *Fireflies.* London, André Deutsch, 1970.

_____. *A Hot Country.* London, Hamish Hamilton, 1983.

_____. *An Unfinished Journey.* London, Hamish Hamilton, 1986.

Nandan, Satendra, ed. *Language and Literature in Multicultural Contexts.* Suva, University of the South Pacific and the Association for Commonwealth Language and Literature Studies, 1983.

Narasimhaiah, C. D., ed. *Awakened Conscience: Studies in Commonwealth Literature.* New Delhi, Stirling, 1978.

Narayan, R. K. *The English Teacher.* 1945. London, Mandarin Paperback, 1991.

_____. *The Man-Eater of Malgudi.* London, Heinemann, 1962.

_____. *Mr Sampath — The Printer of Malgudi.* 1949. London, Mandarin Paperback, 1990.

_____. *The Painter of Signs.* 1976. Harmondsworth, Penguin, 1982.

_____. *The Vendor of Sweets.* 1967. London, Heinemann, 1980.

_____. *Waiting for the Mahatma.* 1955. London, Mandarin Paperback, 1990.

Nightingale, Peggy. *Journey Through Darkness: The Writings of V. S. Naipaul.* St Lucia, University of Queensland Press, 1987.

Nixon, Rob. *London Calling: V. S. Naipaul, Post-Colonial Mandarin.* New York, Oxford University Press, 1992.

Orwell, George. *Collected Essays,* (2nd ed.). London, Secker and Warburg, 1962.

Oxaal, Ivar. *Black Intellectuals Come to Power: The Rise of Creole Nationalism in Trinidad and Tobago.* Cambridge, Massachusetts, Schenkman Publishing, 1968.

_____. *Race and Revolutionary Consciousness: A Documentary Interpretation of the 1970 Black Power Revolt in Trinidad.* Cambridge, Massachusetts, Schenkman Publishing, 1971.

Padmanabham Nair, Dr. K. N. *Irony in the Novels of V. S. Naipaul and R. K. Narayan.* Trivandrum, C. B. H. Publications, 1993.

Parry, Benita. *Delusions and Discoveries: Studies on India in the British Imagination 1880–1930.* London, Allen Lane, The Penguin Press, 1972.

Picon-Sala, Mariano. *Miranda.* Caracas, Coleccion Vigilia, 1966.

Pilkington, Edward. *Beyond the Mother Country: West Indians and the Notting Hill White Riots.* London, I. B. Taurus, 1988.

Powell, Anthony. *A Dance to the Music of Time: A Question of Upbringing, A Buyer's Market, The Acceptance World.* London, Heinemann, 1962.

_____. *To Keep the Ball Rolling: The Memoirs of Anthony Powell.* London, Heinemann, 1976–82.

_____. *Miscellaneous Verdicts: Writing on Writers, 1946–1989.* London, Heinemann, 1990.

Prescott, Lynda. *Reading V. S. Naipaul: Fiction and History, 1967–87.* Ph.D. Dissertation, Open University, 1990.

Ralegh, Sir Walter. *The Discoverie of the Large and Bewtiful Empire of Guiana,* ed. by V. T. Harlow. London, The Argonaut Press, 1928.

_____. *The Discovery of the Large, Rich and Beautiful Empire of Guiana,* ed. by Robert H. Schomburgk. London, The Hakluyt Society, 1848.

_____. *Sir Walter Ralegh: Selected Writings,* ed. by Gerald Hammond. Manchester, Carcanet, 1984.

Rhys, Jean. *After Leaving Mr Mackenzie.* London, André Deutsch, 1969.

_____. *Smile Please: An Unfinished Autobiography.* London, André Deutsch, 1979.

Ricks, Christopher. *T. S. Eliot and Prejudice.* London, Faber and Faber, 1988.

Robertson, William Spence. *The Life of Miranda.* 2 Vols. Chapel Hill, University of North Carolina Press, 1929.

_____. *Miranda and the Revolutionizing of Spanish America.* Washington, Annual Report of the American Historical Association, 1908.

Rodney, Walter. *How Europe Underdeveloped Africa,* (rev. ed.). Washington, Howard University Press, 1982.

Rushdie, Salman. *Imaginary Homelands: Essays and Criticism 1981–1991*. London, Granta Books in association with Penguin, 1991.

_____. *Midnight's Children*. London, Jonathan Cape, 1981.

Ryan, Selwyn D. *Race and Nationalism in Trinidad and Tobago: A Study of Decolonization in a Multiracial Society*. Toronto and Buffalo, University of Toronto Press, 1972.

Ryan, William. *Blaming the Victim*, (rev. ed.). New York, Vintage, 1976.

Said, Edward. *Culture and Imperialism*. 1993. London, Vintage, 1994.

_____. *Orientalism*. 1978. Harmondsworth, Penguin, 1985.

Schulze, Leonard and Walter Wetzels, eds. *Literature and History*. Lanham and London, University Press of America, 1983.

Scott, Sir Walter. *Kenilworth*. 1821. Edinburgh, Adam and Charles Black, 1870.

Selvon, Samuel. *A Brighter Sun*. 1952. Port of Spain and Harlow, Longman, 1971.

Soyinka, Wole. *Myth, Literature and the African World*. Cambridge, Cambridge University Press, 1976.

Sprinker, Michael, ed. *Edward Said: A Critical Reader*. Oxford and Cambridge, Massachusetts, Blackwell, 1992.

Sturrock, John. *The Language of Autobiography: Studies in the First Person Singular*. Cambridge and New York, Cambridge University Press, 1993.

Swinden, Patrick. *The English Novel of History and Society, 1940–1980: Richard Hughes, Henry Green, Anthony Powell, Angus Wilson, Kingsley Amis, V. S. Naipaul*. London and Basingstoke, Macmillan, 1984.

Tennyson, Alfred Lord. *Tennyson: A Selected Edition* (Longman Annotated English Poets), ed. by Christopher Ricks. Harlow, Longman, 1989.

Theroux, Paul. *Sir Vidia's Shadow: A Friendship Across Five Continents*. London, Hamish Hamilton, 1998.

_____. *V. S. Naipaul: An Introduction to his Work*. London, André Deutsch, 1972.

Thieme, John. *The Web of Tradition: Uses of Allusion in V. S. Naipaul's Fiction*. Hertford, Hansib/Dangaroo, 1987.

Trilling, Lionel. *Sincerity and Authenticity*. London, Oxford University Press, 1972.

Vertovec, Steven. *Hindu Trinidad: Religion, Ethnicity and Socio-Economic Change*. London and Basingstoke, Macmillan Education, 1992.

Virgil. *Eclogues, Georgics and Aeneid I-VI*, (rev. ed.), tr. by H. Rushton Fairclough. London, Heinemann, and Cambridge, Massachusetts, Harvard University Press, 1935.

Wallace, Willard M. *Sir Walter Raleigh*. Princeton, Princeton University Press, 1959.

Walsh, William. *A Manifold Voice: Studies in Commonwealth Literature*. London, Chatto and Windus, 1970.

_____. ed. *Readings in Commonwealth Literature*. Oxford, Clarendon Press, 1973.

_____. *V. S. Naipaul*. Edinburgh, Oliver and Boyd, 1973.

Watt, Ian. *The Rise of the Novel*. London, Chatto and Windus, 1957.

Wells, H. G. *The History of Mr Polly and the War in the Air*. London, The Literary Press, 1940.

White, Landeg. *V. S. Naipaul: A Critical Introduction*. London, Macmillan, 1975.

Williams, Eric. *History of the People of Trinidad and Tobago*. London, André Deutsch, 1964.

Wordsworth, William. *The Prelude*, ed. by Jonathan Wordsworth, M. H. Abrams and Stephen Gill. London, Norton, 1979.

_____. *William Wordsworth* (The Oxford English Authors), ed. by Stephen Gill. Oxford, Oxford University Press, 1984.

Index